DATE DUE			

Phillips Library
Bethany College
Bethany, W. Va. 26032
DISCARD

BETHANY
DISCARD

BRITISH GOVERNMENT

1966 TO 1975

British Government 1966 to 1975

YEARS OF REFORM

BY

FRANK STACEY

FRANCIS HILL PROFESSOR OF LOCAL GOVERNMENT
UNIVERSITY OF NOTTINGHAM

OXFORD UNIVERSITY PRESS

1975

Oxford University Press, Ely House, London W.1
GLASGOW NEW YORK TORONTO MELBOURNE WELLINGTON
CAPE TOWN IBADAN NAIROBI DAR ES SALAAM LUSAKA ADDIS ABABA
DELHI BOMBAY CALCUTTA MADRAS KARACHI LAHORE DACCA
KUALA LUMPUR SINGAPORE HONG KONG TOKYO

CASEBOUND ISBN 0 19 876035 3
PAPERBACK ISBN 0 19 876036 1

PRINTED IN GREAT BRITAIN
BY RICHARD CLAY (THE CHAUCER PRESS) LTD
BUNGAY, SUFFOLK

PREFACE

THIS is a study of the main changes which have taken place in British government in the last nine years. During this period, there have been major innovations in the Civil Service, in local government and the Health Service, and in the machinery through which an individual can seek redress of grievances against a public service. In other fields, as in Parliament and at the centre of government, there have also been important changes. Even in the area of elections, and electoral legislation, although the changes brought about by law have been relatively minor, there have been interesting developments.

My principal object in writing the book has been to help those who study, and teach, British government and politics to keep track of some of these changes, and to assess their impact on our political system. This book is, in a sense, a sequel to my earlier book *The Government of Modern Britain* (Clarendon Press, 1968) which was mainly concerned with developments in the twenty-one years which followed the Second World War. I have referred in notes, at a number of points, to the earlier book. But I hope that this book will also stand in its own right as a study of developments in the most recent period.

I have benefited a great deal in preparing this study from interviews with public servants. A number of them have read and commented on sections of the book. Although they prefer me not to mention them here by name, my thanks for the care and consideration they gave in advising me are none the less real. I also want to thank my colleagues and students in the Departments of Politics at Swansea and Nottingham who have discussed with me many of the ideas in the book and have been an invaluable stimulus and encouragement.

University of Nottingham FRANK STACEY
July 1975

CONTENTS

LIST OF ABBREVIATIONS

Cmnd.	Command Paper.
H.C.	House of Commons Paper.
H.L.	House of Lords Paper.
H.C.Deb.	House of Commons Debates.
H.L.Deb.	House of Lords Debates.

CHAPTER I

Introduction

THE nine and a half years from the beginning of 1966 to July 1975 were years of rapid change in British government. Many were planned changes which took place as part of an almost unprecedented quickening of activity in the re-shaping of our political institutions, at both central and local level. Other changes were largely, or wholly, unplanned and resulted from the pressure of events. It is the aim of this book to try and assess the nature of these changes, both planned and unplanned, and to consider their impact on our system of government.

During this period, the Labour Party was in office for five years and ten months: from the beginning of 1966, which is our starting-point, until the general election of June 1970, and from the general election of February 1974 until July 1975, when this study ends. The Conservatives were in office for three years and eight months, from June 1970 until February 1974. But it would not be true to say, as regards reform in government, that a 'party of movement' was in office at the outset and close of our period, while a 'party of order' was in power in the intervening years. Both governing parties in this period have been much concerned with reform. How far the principles behind their reforms have differed and how far there have been underlying continuities is one of the questions with which we shall be concerned.

Many of the reforms carried through in this period had their origins in earlier years. For example, reform of Civil Service recruitment and training had been recommended by the Estimates Committee of the House of Commons in 1965. Successive ministers had been trying, with only limited success, to reform the structure of local government since 1946. But it was not until 1972 that legislation providing for a major reorganization of local government in England and Wales reached the statute book.

One may ask how do we account for the quickening of the pace of reform in the years from 1966 to 1974? The answer may partly be that the preceding period, from the late 1950s to the early 1960s, was one in which there were relatively few reforms and in which there was an increasing demand for change. There was, at that time, a spate of 'What is Wrong?' books. A. Hill and A. Whichelow, for example, asked in 1964 'What's Wrong with Parliament?'[1] Bernard Crick in 1959 advocated in a Fabian pamphlet *Reform of the Commons*, and in a book, first published in 1964, *The Reform of Parliament*.[2]

A collection of essays edited by Hugh Thomas in 1959, under the title *The Establishment*, had many caustic things to say about the inappropriateness of Civil Service organization and personnel for the tasks which faced modern government.[3] Brian Chapman in his little book *British Government Observed*, published in 1963, was just as critical, and in 1964 a group of Fabians, while on the whole less sweeping in their judgements, presented a well-reasoned programme for Civil Service reform.[4]

Harold Macmillan, as Conservative Premier from 1957 to 1963, seemed to be largely unconvinced of the need for reform. It is true that some major changes were put through in those years. In 1963 the London Government Act set up a wholly new structure for the government of Greater London. The Treasury was reorganized in 1962 and in the same year the National Economic Development Council was set up. The Tribunals and Inquiries Act of 1958 brought about some useful detailed reforms and set up the Council on Tribunals. But these were isolated instances. More typical, it seemed to many, was the Macmillan Government's reaction to the 1961 Justice Committee report which advocated the establishment of a Parliamentary Commissioner, or Ombudsman, for Britain and a major extension of the Council on Tribunals. The Government delayed for a year after publication of the report and then announced, in November 1962, that it did not propose to implement any of the Justice Committee's recommendations.

As is often the way when people advocate reforms, some of the authors we have mentioned tended to overstate their criticisms. Thus Bernard Crick wrote, in *The Reform of Parliament*:[5] 'The Point and Presumption of this book is that most Members of Parliament have not yet realized how deep a morass of ineffectuality they have fallen into, and that only strong outside criticism, ultimately public opinion, will make them move.' He gave the impression that the House of Commons was not interested in reforming its procedures.

This was certainly an unfair impression since the Commons had greatly speeded up its legislative procedures between 1945 and 1964 by deciding to take virtually all important bills at Committee Stage in an improved system of Standing Committees.[6] In the same period, the Estimates Committee of the Commons immensely improved its methods of scrutinizing administration in the departments.[7] It was true that in 1964 most M.P.s were not particularly interested in, or were sceptical about, the reform which Bernard Crick himself advocated most strongly: the setting-up of specialist committees. It was part of his achievement to help to heighten interest in this kind of reform.

What have been the main themes of reform in the years from 1966 to 1974? This is not easy to answer since each reform has its special complexities and problems. One theme has been the desire to secure greater efficiency. Here there has been a spin-off from the general anxiety about the state of the British economy. Just as, in the late 1960s, it seemed urgent to find better methods of economic management which would end the process of 'stop–go' in the British economy, so, it was argued, there was a need for more efficient management in central and local government. Another theme has been the desire to make government more responsive. As the ramifications of government have become even greater, so the feeling that democratic control needed to be enhanced has grown stronger. If democratic control was to be enhanced, administration needed to be brought more into the open and made less secretive. The demand for 'open government' therefore became steadily more clamant.

Some of these themes, as we shall see, appear at times to be in conflict. The desire for greater managerial efficiency may seem to conflict with the desire for greater responsiveness and more open government. Whether it in fact does so is a matter for consideration. There does seem to be a conflict at times between an essentially 'managerial' ideology of reform and an essentially 'participatory' model. But the picture is a complex one since, as we have noted, many planned changes are intermingled with changes which are not a product of conscious reform but are the result of reaction to the pressure of events. The observer of political change can feel at times like Alice when her croquet mallet turned out to be a flamingo. But part of the fascination of the study of politics is not only that things are not always what they seem, but that they may turn out to work quite differently from the way in which it had been anticipated they would work.

One question which we need to tackle at the outset is whether an important distinction should be made between 'reform' and 'reorganization'. Undeniably, during this period, there were occasions when proposed changes in political arrangements were referred to as reorganization rather than reform. The opponents of change, in particular, were prone to characterize new proposals as 'reorganization' rather than 'reform'. In the author's view the two words are broadly interchangeable. *The Concise Oxford Dictionary* defines a reform as 'a removal of abuses' or 'an improvement made or suggested'. It also defines the verb 'organize' as 'to give an orderly structure to'. Therefore, to reorganize is to rearrange in an orderly structure. The practical difference, in the political context, between a reform and a reorganization cannot, then, be great.

NOTES

1 A. Hill and A. Wichelow, *What's Wrong with Parliament?* (Penguin, 1964).
2 Bernard Crick, *Reform of the Commons* (Fabian Society, 1959), and *The Reform of Parliament* (Weidenfeld and Nicolson, 1964).
3 Hugh Thomas (ed.), *The Establishment* (Anthony Blond, 1959).
4 B. Chapman, *British Government Observed* (Allen and Unwin, 1963); Fabian Society, *The Administrators. The Reform of the Civil Service* (Fabian Tract No. 355, 1964).
5 p. 147.
6 See F. Stacey, *The Government of Modern Britain* (Clarendon Press, 1968), pp. 94–101.
7 Ibid., pp. 135–45.

CHAPTER II

Electoral Reform

WE look first at an area in which there have been only very partial reforms since 1966. The Representation of the People Act, 1969, brought some changes of detail of which easily the most important was the lowering of the voting age to 18. The two larger parties in this period made no concession to the continued Liberal demand that proportional representation should replace the single-member relative majority system in Britain. The problem of redrawing constituency boundaries, in a way which would seem fair-minded and appropriate, was as far from solution as ever. But we shall examine some of the controversies which have continued to surround this question. Finally, in this chapter, we shall look at the failure of all except one of the opinion polls to forecast which of the parties would win the general election of 1970, and the record of the polls in the two 1974 general elections.

The Representation of the People Act, 1969

The general election of 1970 was the first general election at which eighteen-year-olds voted. It seems they did not make as big a numerical impact in the election as had been anticipated. Butler and Pinto-Duschinsky noted that sample surveys in 1970 suggested that only 70 per cent of young people between the ages of 18 and 21 were in fact on the register of electors.[1] Presumably, many heads of household had not realized that young people under 18 should be included on the returns from which the register was compiled, because they would become eligible for a vote during the lifetime of the register. The lowering of the voting age had after all only become law the previous year. The majority of Conservative Members in the Commons had, on a free vote, voted against lowering the qualification age to 18. There was no question, however, of the Conservatives raising the qualification age when they gained office in 1970. Eighteen is now the age of legal majority for most purposes, and there is a world-wide trend to move towards qualification for voting at 18 rather than at 21. For example, the Constitution of the

United States was amended in 1971 to provide for voting at 18. The 1972 election was the first presidential election in the United States at which eighteen-year-olds voted. Then, in January 1973, the newly elected Labour Government in Australia announced that it would be introducing legislation to lower the voting age to 18.

Another historic change in electoral law brought by the United Kingdom Representation of the People Act, 1969, was the introduction of party labels on ballot papers. Previously, party organization, legally speaking, had been unknown to British elections. The absence of party description could cause considerable confusion, particularly in Wales, where it was not uncommon for more than one Jones, Davies, Williams, or Thomas to be on the same ballot paper. The 1969 Representation of the People Act allows each candidate to add a slogan of up to six words after his name. Thus at the 1970 election the Labour Party recommended each of its candidates to describe himself or herself as 'The Labour Party candidate'. The new provision has worked smoothly and, as with many simple reforms, one is left to wonder why it was not adopted long before.

Another minor but necessary change brought about by the 1969 Act was an upward revision of the limit of expenditure permitted for each candidate during a parliamentary election. The limit was increased by a flat £300 for candidates, both in borough and county constituencies. This was a necessary reform because the limit of £450 plus 2*d*. per elector in counties, and 1½*d*. per elector in boroughs, had remained unchanged since 1948. With the fall in the value of money since then, the limit could have severely restricted electioneering activities if it had not been revised.

Another change provided for in the 1969 Act was the extension of polling hours in parliamentary elections, by an extra hour, so that polling booths in 1970 were open from 7 a.m. to 10 p.m. This long period of polling did not, however, succeed in increasing the percentage of the electorate who voted. In fact, the percentage poll, at 72·0 per cent, was the lowest poll since the Second World War. This demonstrated that although it is desirable to make it as easy as possible for people to vote, it is even more important to arouse the interest of the electorate in the election campaign. The 1970 election was a somewhat low-key election. Moreover, it took place in midsummer when many people were on holiday.

The percentage poll at the February 1974 general election was, at

78·1 per cent, much higher, and indeed was the highest percentage poll in the United Kingdom since the 1959 general election. But the February election was fought on a new electoral register, therefore loss of votes through death or removal was minimized. At the October 1974 general election, the poll was again on the low side. Even so, at 72·8 per cent it was 0·8 per cent above the poll in 1970, while the 1970 general election was fought in July when the register was not as out of date as in an October election.

Proportional Representation still a Non-starter

Whereas the 1969 Act introduced some minor but significant reforms, it did not alter the electoral system under which M.P.s are elected by relative majority in single-member constituencies. This was not for lack of prompting by the Liberal Party which, as the third largest party, has long suffered from serious under-representation in Parliament. Did the results of the 1974 general elections strengthen the case for the introduction of some form of proportional representation in British parliamentary elections?

One of the stock arguments against the introduction of P.R. is that the relative majority system in Britain normally provides a majority for one of the two main parties. The party forming a government therefore has a clear and undivided responsibility for the conduct of affairs, and governments are relatively long-lasting and stable. The February general election in 1974 did not produce a majority for any one party. The Conservatives secured a slightly larger share of the poll (37·8 per cent for the United Kingdom as a whole) than did Labour (37·1 per cent). But Labour won five more seats than the Conservatives: 301 seats to the Conservatives' 296 seats. They did not, however, have an over-all majority since the Liberals won 14 seats, the Scottish Nationalists 7, the Welsh Nationalists (Plaid Cymru) 2, and the Ulster Unionists 11. These smaller parties together formed a 'third force' since none of them was allied to either of the two main parties. The Ulster Unionists who were returned in the election belonged to an alliance of groups strongly opposed to the Sunningdale Agreement negotiated by the Conservatives, and therefore were unwilling to give general support to a Conservative government.[2]

Neither the Conservatives nor Labour could then be sure of a majority in the Commons. Either party would have to depend on winning sufficient *ad hoc* support from the minority groups in order to carry its legislative programme and maintain itself in office. Since there had been more sympathy during the election campaign from the third-force group for items in the Labour programme, such as repeal of the Industrial Relations Act and of the Housing Finance Act, than there had been for the Conservatives, Labour was able to form a minority government, which lasted until the second general election of 1974, in October. Edward Heath, before handing his resignation to the Queen after the February general election, sought to come to an agreement with the Liberals which would allow him to continue in office. But the Liberals were not willing to ally themselves with the Conservatives as a coalition partner, nor were they prepared to undertake to give general support to the Conservatives in exchange for legislation of which they would approve.

The minority Labour Government was to some extent successful, as we shall see in Chapter IV, in getting support for its immediate legislative programme but, during the summer months, some important amendments were carried to its Trade Union and Labour Relations Bill and to the Finance Bill, when the Liberals and Nationalists joined the Conservatives in outvoting the Government.[3] It was clear, therefore, that Harold Wilson would choose the first promising opportunity to go to the country. This presented itself in October 1974, and gave him an over-all majority in the Commons, although only of four votes. Labour won 319 seats, the Conservatives 276, the Liberals 13, the Scottish Nationalists 11, Plaid Cymru 3, and the Ulster Unionists 10. But, for a variety of reasons, the new government's majority was reasonably secure. Firstly, it was likely to continue to have the support of the one Social Democratic and Labour Party Member returned in Northern Ireland; while an Independent Republican, returned for Fermanagh, would certainly not give his support to the Conservatives. Secondly, the Liberals would not be able to make common cause with the Nationalists on all issues, since they held diametrically opposing views on the question of the Common Market. On the issue of devolution of power to Scotland and Wales, by contrast, the Liberals were in substantial agreement with the Nationalists. But if the Wilson Government could maintain a reasonable momentum, in preparing schemes for Scottish and Welsh elected assemblies, it would not altogether alienate this section of parliamentary opinion.[4]

The 1974 elections therefore left British politics in a multi-party situation. Although the two main parties still predominated, they had to reckon with a third force of Nationalist parties and re-invigorated Liberals. The case for going over to a more proportional system of election remained as strong as ever from the Liberal point of view. Indeed it was stronger than ever, since the Liberals increased their poll from more than 2 million at the 1970 general election to just over 6 million at the February 1974 general election. They only won 8 more seats, however, returning 14 Members in February 1974 as against 6 in 1970.

In the October 1974 general election, the Liberal poll declined to just over 5,300,000, even though they fought many more constituencies than in February. They still secured more than 18 per cent of the total poll in the United Kingdom, but this won them only thirteen seats in the Commons. Under any form of proportional representation, the Liberals would do much better. For example, Michael Steed estimated that, under the West German combination of a party list system with single-member constituencies, they would have won more than 120 seats in February 1974.[5] They would then have held the balance of power in the House of Commons and every government would have to be a coalition or minority government. The case against proportional representation therefore remains much as it always has been, that it would make coalition or minority governments the rule rather than the exception. From the point of view of the Conservative and Labour parties too, proportional representation would be an unwelcome development since it would minimize the chances of either party forming a government, on its own, with an over-all majority.

While the case for proportional representation in elections to the United Kingdom Parliament made little progress, it was accepted first for local elections in Northern Ireland and then for elections to the Northern Ireland Assembly. In June 1972 when William Whitelaw, then Secretary of State for Northern Ireland, told the Commons that the Heath Government had decided that local elections in Northern Ireland would be held under proportional representation, by the single transferable vote system, this announcement was welcomed by Merlyn Rees, the Labour spokesman for Northern Ireland affairs. Rees said that, given the social and religious barriers in Northern Ireland, P.R. was the only way of giving moderation a chance of expression. He added that, in the Labour Party's view, P.R. would be equally vital in forming a representative assembly for

Northern Ireland. This opinion was taken into account by the Heath Government, as were the submissions from the political parties in Northern Ireland which also showed a good deal of support for the use of the single transferable vote system of P.R.[6] In March 1973, the Heath Government announced that the new Northern Ireland Assembly would consist of about 80 members elected by the single transferable vote.

Elections to the Assembly took place in June 1973. Use of the single transferable vote resulted in a sizeable representation for the Catholic minority, mainly through the Social Democratic and Labour Party (S.D.L.P.). After prolonged negotiations, a 'power-sharing' Executive was formed under the Northern Ireland (Constitution) Act, 1973. The Executive included moderate Unionists as well as members of the S.D.L.P. and the Alliance Party. The other Unionists groups were implacably opposed to this Executive. After the agreement at Sunningdale, between the Executive, the United Kingdom Government, and the Government of the Irish Republic, to set up a Council for Ireland, Protestant workers called a strike which threatened to paralyse food and electricity supplies in Northern Ireland. To end the strike the United Kingdom Government found it necessary to suspend the Constitution and resume direct rule in the Province.

The United Kingdom Government then decided that the people of Northern Ireland should elect a Convention to recommend what kind of constitution should be adopted for Northern Ireland. Elections to this Convention were held in May 1975, under the single transferable vote system of proportional representation. They resulted in the return of 47 'loyalist' Unionist members and 31 members of other groups. If proportional representation is appropriate for Northern Ireland, would it not also be a better method of choosing M.P.s in elections to the United Kingdom Parliament? The argument against this position is that, in the deeply sectarian atmosphere of Northern Ireland, P.R. is desirable since the relative majority system, used until 1972, enhanced the dominant position of the protestant Unionist Party while consistently under-representing the Catholic minority. In Britain, the parties are not organized on religious lines, and neither the Conservative nor the Labour Party predominates. The alleged advantages of maintaining the relative majority system, already discussed, can therefore be realized. This argument, of course, is not acceptable to the Liberal Party. The debate will continue, but the use of the single transferable vote in Northern Ireland elections must, to some extent, give encouragement to the Liberals and other advocates of P.R.

The Controversy over Constituency Boundaries

After the Second World War, a new system for redrawing the boundaries of parliamentary constituencies was introduced. The system, which was brought in by Acts of 1944, 1946, and 1948, and consolidated by the House of Commons (Redistribution of Seats) Act of 1949, was basically sound. Four permanent boundary commissions were set up, one each for England, Wales, Scotland, and Northern Ireland. Each commission was given the task of reviewing constituency boundaries, and of suggesting revisions to Parliament in cases where population changes had produced disparities in the size of electorates.

Two sets of difficulties, however, had arisen over the operation of the system. The first difficulty lay in reconciling the terms of reference of the commissions since they were instructed to attempt to secure equal electoral districts within each of the four countries, and to respect local government boundaries wherever possible, but to depart from these principles if 'special geographical conditions, including in particular the size, shape, and accessibility of a constituency', appeared to justify it. Apart from the difficulty of reconciling the principle of equal electoral districts with respect for local government boundaries, the rule concerning special geographical conditions has never been defined by statute. No one, to this day, knows whether it means that a few very sparsely populated constituencies should have below average electorates, or whether rural constituencies should, in general, have a lower electoral quota than urban constituencies. The boundary commissioners for England seemed to adopt this second interpretation in their first set of recommendations, presented in 1948. These recommendations were modified by Parliament to give a lower weighting to the rural areas, but in the second review completed in 1954 and implemented by Parliament the original recommendations were re-inserted on the whole.

The second difficulty arose from the reshaping of constituencies, which caused upset to local party organization and local pride. Originally, legislation had provided that reviews should take place at intervals of between five and seven years. There was, however, so much opposition to the changes recommended for England in 1954 that Parliament decided to provide for longer intervals of from ten to fifteen years between reviews. The author argued in 1968 that this was a mistake.[7] It is appropriate to consider whether subsequent events led to a modification or reinforcement of this view.

The boundary commissioners completed their next review in 1969. By this time, large disparities had developed in the size of constituencies, and the changes proposed, particularly for England, were extensive. It was generally thought that, if implemented, they would cost the Labour Party a considerable number of seats, since many of the constituencies which had shown a spectacular decline in population were in working-class areas in the large cities, whereas many of the large constituencies, in terms of population, which were scheduled for subdivision, were situated outside cities in the commuter belts, where the Conservative Party normally polls well.

When it became clear in 1969 that the Labour Party only intended to implement a small number of the English commission's recommendations, accusations of bias and gerrymandering were loud on the Conservative side. In reply to these accusations, the Government argued that, since a full-scale revision of local government boundaries was about to take place following the publication of the Redcliffe-Maud Commission's Report on Local Government, it would be undersirable to carry through the wholesale revision proposed by the English boundary commission as further major changes would soon have to take place, in order to make the constituencies conform broadly to the drastically revised local government map which would result from the implementation of the Redcliffe-Maud Report.[8]

On 2 July 1969, the Home Secretary, James Callaghan, introduced the House of Commons (Redistribution of Seats) (No. 2) Bill which proposed to defer major changes in parliamentary boundaries until the reorganization of local government had been completed. Clause 2 of the Bill, however, proposed to implement the boundary commission's proposals for the Greater London Area, since the Labour Government conceded that this was an urgent case for reform. Clause 3 proposed that a number of pairs of adjacent constituencies outside London with over 90,000 electors should be divided into three and that one very large constituency, Cheadle, with over 100,000 electors, should be divided into two.

Quintin Hogg, leading for the Conservatives on Second Reading in the Commons, described the Bill as 'a constitutional enormity'. He accused the Home Secretary of being 'caught with his hand in the parliamentary till'.[9] Upon reaching the Lords the Bill was emasculated, as Conservative peers turned up to vote in very large numbers on 21 July and carried wrecking amendments by a majority of 270 votes to 96. The Commons voted the original Bill again, but on 16 October 1969 the Lords voted to persist in their amendments.

The Labour Government could have used the Parliament Act to pass the Bill, without the assent of the Lords, after a year's delay. They chose instead to abandon both the Bill and the recommendations of the boundary commissions. The Government tabled Draft Orders embodying the recommendations of the boundary commissions and used its majority to defeat these Orders on 12 November 1969. The 1970 general election was then fought in the unrevised constituencies whose shape had been determined as long ago as 1954, thus resulting in some major disparities in the size of electorates. Wokingham, for example, had an electorate of more than 108,000, while Manchester Exchange had barely more than 21,000 electors.

After the Conservatives had won power at the 1970 election they used their majority, in November 1970, to approve the recommendations of the 1969 boundary commission which the Labour majority had previously rejected. The 1974 elections were therefore fought within these boundaries, although the local government map of England and Wales was reorganized in April 1974 following the passage of the Local Government Act, 1972.[10] A local government boundary commission, chaired by Sir Edmund Compton, was set up in 1973 to make proposals for new local government districts within the county areas defined by the Act. Only a small minority of the districts which were formed at that time coincided with the parliamentary constituencies established in November 1970.

The whole matter of constituency boundaries remains unsatisfactory, and the machinery for redrawing boundaries has made no advance since 1949. Indeed, this country may be said to have slipped back in relation, for example, to the United States. Since the decision by the Supreme Court in 1962 that constituency boundaries must be drawn in such a way that the political strength of all voters becomes equal, a great deal has been done throughout the United

States to reduce disparities between electorates. It is possible that equal apportionment is now given greater attention in the United States than in Britain. This does not mean, however, that gerrymandering has been eliminated in the United States. The word gerrymandering, in accurate usage, describes the manipulation of constituency boundaries in order to maximize support for one party and minimize the electoral effect of the other party's voters. Gerrymandering can take place, and to great effect, even in states which have equal electoral districts. In its strict sense gerrymandering has not been practised in Britain, whereas it has been rife in many parts of the United States. Malapportionment, however, has become endemic in Britain so that even when boundaries have just been revised there are considerable disparities between electorates because of the commissioners' deference to local government boundaries and to 'the geographical conditions rule'. By the end of the statutory fifteen-year period between reviews, these disparities may have become really serious in many instances.

What, then, needs to be done to improve the system for revising constituency boundaries? In the first place, the author holds to his view that the intervals between revisions of boundaries should be quite short, and that the extension in 1958 of the period between reviews was a major mistake. One has, of course, to balance the advantages and disadvantages. If revisions are frequent and constituency boundaries are constantly changing, some party workers may find themselves in one constituency at one election, in a different constituency at the next election, and then back in the original constituency, or in another constituency yet again. On the other hand, if there are long intervals between reviews, some constituencies become very large and, almost inevitably, one party becomes resistant to change, since it is likely to be seriously disadvantaged electorally by redistribution. There would seem to be more advantage, then, in having frequent reviews. The boundary commissioners should, in the author's view, be instructed to make recommendations for revision of boundaries every six years, with authority to report more frequently in cases where sudden population changes have led to the appearance of very large constituencies.

Second, there should be several boundary commissions for England; it does not make sense to have one boundary commission for England with a population of more than 43 million, one for Scotland with a population of just over 5 million, and one for Wales with a population of 2,600,000. It is significant that most of the controversy has centred on the work of the English commission, and, clearly, this commission has a far harder task than have the commissions of the other countries. If there were several English commissions, each one would be able to give more time to consideration of local interests, and would be in a better position to find solutions to the boundary problem which would be acceptable to local opinion.

Third, it is probably not necessary to give as much attention to local government boundaries as in the past; but more attention should be given to securing equal electoral districts. This does not mean that local government boundaries should be ignored. Clearly, they should always be adhered to wherever possible, but where there has to be a choice between respecting local government boundaries and providing for broadly equal electoral districts, the latter should have priority. Finally there should be a clear definition of the rule concerning special geographical conditions. A decision should be made whether the rule applies to only a small number of constituencies in areas of very sparse population, or whether it means that rural areas in general, should have greater representation.

The Opinion Polls since the 1970 General Election

Perhaps the most surprising development of the 1970 general election was the defeat, not to say rout, of the opinion polls. The polls had had a consistently good record since the Second World War in predicting which party would win a general election.[11] People who were well informed on the subject knew that American opinion polls had suffered a major setback in 1948 when they had wrongly forecast an easy victory for Dewey, and Harry Truman won the presidential election. But it was thought that there were special conditions which helped to explain this failure: in particular the lower percentage poll in American elections, compared with Britain, and the fact that the last poll in 1948 had been taken more than two weeks before the actual election. In 1970 British experts had to eat humble pie because four out of five opinion polls in this country forecast a Labour victory.

There are two questions of interest here. First, why did most of the polls go wrong? Second, does the failure of the polls at this election mean that they now play a less important role in the political process? That they had come to play a large part in the calculations of political leaders is beyond doubt. Since the 1950s, the polls had seemed to provide such a reliable index of the relative popularity of the parties that Prime Ministers had come to use them as a reliable guide to deciding when to have a general election. The author argued in 1968 that this new power had strenghtened the position of incumbent Prime Ministers and made it harder to turn out the government. This was not to be true in 1970 for Harold Wilson.

The Labour Government had been trailing in the opinion polls over a long period and in May 1968 Labour was 20 per cent behind the Conservatives. The Conservative lead remained at about this level in 1969. It was not until April 1970 that opinion seemed to veer back strongly towards Labour, and in May 1970 all the polls showed Labour ahead. The local elections also showed a trend to Labour, and Harold Wilson decided to go to the country, although he could have continued in office until October 1971.

When the 1970 general election campaign began, the polls all put Labour in the lead; one poll, however, taken by the Opinion Research Centre and published in the *Sunday Times* on 31 October, gave the Conservatives a 2 per cent lead. The polls continued to predict a Labour victory right up to the day of the election. Only one poll, published on the day of the election, predicted a Conservative victory, and that by the narrow margin of 1 per cent. This was the Opinion Research Centre poll, published in the *Evening Standard*.

Harold Wilson was confident of victory during the campaign, while the Conservatives for their part were largely despondent. Marcia Williams, Harold Wilson's Personal and Private Secretary, has described the shock the result of the general election gave to the Labour Leader and his political staff. Whereas she had told the Labour Party staff at 10 Downing Street to be prepared to move out at once after the 1966 general election, there had been no contingency plans for a Labour defeat in 1970.[12] Among the Conservative leaders, only the Leader of the Party himself, Edward Heath, had seemed to show any real confidence in a Conservative victory. Yet the Conservatives won convincingly, polling 3·4 per cent more votes than Labour, taking voting for the United Kingdom as a whole (2·4 per cent more votes taking only Great Britain), and winning a majority of 30 seats over all other parties in the Commons.

The predictions of the five opinion polls published on election day were as follows: the Gallup Poll, published in the *Daily Tele-*

graph, predicted a 7 per cent lead for Labour. The National Opinion Poll, published in the *Daily Mail*, predicted a Labour victory by a 4·1 per cent margin. Marplan, who published in *The Times*, predicted, on the day before the election, an 8·7 per cent lead for Labour. The Harris Poll, published in the *Daily Express*, predicted a Labour lead of 2·0 per cent. Only the Opinion Research Centre poll, published in the *Evening Standard*, predicted, as we have seen, a win for Conservatives by the small margin of 1 per cent.

Even the Opinion Research Centre poll had originally yielded a result which favoured Labour. But the Centre had reinterviewed a sub-sample of 257 electors after its final full poll had been taken. These reinterviews had shown a late swing, during the last phase of the campaign, to the Conservatives. The Centre therefore adjusted its poll findings to show a slight majority for the Conservatives. It also took into account the indication given in some of the poll results that more of those who said they intended to vote Conservative, than of those who intended to vote Labour, had shown a determination to record their votes on the day.

Does the phenomenon of 'late swing' explain the failure of most of the polls at this election? We may first consider some of the other possible explanations of this failure. The different sampling methods used by the polls do not seem to have been decisive. The National Opinion Poll, Marplan, and the Harris Poll used random sampling. The Gallup Poll and the Opinion Research Centre used quota sampling.[13] Random sampling is theoretically more reliable, but the Opinion Research Centre came nearest to the actual result.

Another possible explanation is that the margin of error in predicting the result of a general election from a sample of between 1,000 and 2,500 people is very wide anyway. Although there is considerable truth in this statement, we must explain why, for example, the Gallup Poll and the National Opinion Poll had accurately predicted which party would win at every general election from 1959 to 1966. Even more difficult to explain on this basis is the fact that all five polls predicted a Labour victory in 1970 (note the O.R.C. poll predicted a Labour victory until adjusted). Professor Hugh Berrington has pointed out that for all the polls in 1970 to err in the same direction was statistically very improbable, if the explanation of their failure was merely sampling error.[14]

A further explanation is that the polls consistently overestimate the Labour vote. It can be shown that this was true at the 1966 general election. Although the polls accurately forecast a Labour victory at that election, they did, in general, overestimate the Labour lead. The polling organizations are very conscious of the need to avoid a bias to one party in selecting their sample, in the case of stratified random samples, or in selecting respondents, in the case of quota sampling. It does not seem likely that there is a consistent bias towards selecting Labour-minded respondents in the polling process. Professor Berrington has argued that it is more likely that the apparent Labour bias in the polls can be explained by the fact that the Conservative constituency party organization is more effective than Labour's organization in getting out its potential vote. In particular, it has long been recognized that the Conservatives have been better organized in identifying their supporters among potential postal voters and in seeing that they receive a postal vote.

It has been suggested that the explanation for the failure of the polls in 1970 lies in greater abstention by Labour voters than by Conservative voters: the so-called 'differential abstention'. Richard Rose has quoted the view of the National Opinion Poll that differential absention was 'a small but contributory factor in the final result [which] explains part of the discrepancy between the poll predictions and the result'.[15] Michael Steed's close examination of the results in 1970 led him to the view that the Conservative victory could not be explained on grounds of differential abstention alone. For example, he shows that if the turn-out in each constituency had been as high as it was in 1950 (this was the high-water mark, at 84 per cent of participation in post-1945 elections), the Conservatives would still have won the 1970 election, although by a margin of 2·6 per cent instead of the actual margin, taking the United Kingdom as a whole, of 3·4 per cent.[16]

It seems likely, therefore, that the most important factor which caused the polls to go wrong in 1970 was a swing, late in the campaign, towards the Conservatives. It is impossible to say what caused this late swing, although several hypotheses have been advanced. The announcement of unfavourable trade figures during the latter part of the campaign could have weakened support for Labour, since a principal plank in the Labour programme was the claim to have tackled the balance of payments problem effectively. Other hypotheses are that Enoch Powell's speeches in the campaign had had an increasing effect and that Edward Heath's concentration on the cost of living, and his promise to reduce prices, had influenced opinion among housewives. None of these hypotheses can be proved, but the phenomenon of a late swing in 1970, whatever its cause, seems to be clear enough.[17]

The record of the opinion polls at the two general elections in 1974 did something to restore their tarnished reputation. At first sight, they did not do well in February 1974 since on the day of the election they all forecast a lead for the Conservatives. In fact, although the Conservatives gained five fewer seats than Labour, they did lead in terms of votes, since in Great Britain they received 38·8 per cent of the total votes to Labour's 38·0 per cent. The Conservative lead of 0·8 per cent, in terms of votes, was therefore not far from the Gallup Poll prediction that the Conservatives would have a lead of 2·0 per cent over Labour. The Gallup Poll, which was nearest to the actual result in its eve-of-poll predictions, also wisely refrained from predicting what kind of results, in terms of seats gained, would emerge from the election. Of the other polls which went on interviewing as near as possible to polling day, Opinion Research Centre forecast a 3·8 per cent lead for the Conservatives, the National Opinion Poll a 4·0 per cent lead, and the Louis Harris Poll a 5·0 per cent lead. One poll, which completed interviewing a week before the election, predicted a lead for Labour of 1·5 per cent. This was Business Decisions, published in the *Observer*.

The opinion polls fared somewhat better in predicting the result of the October general election in 1974. They all overestimated the Labour lead in terms of votes cast. Of the polls appearing on election day the Gallup Poll, which was once more closest in its prediction, forecast that Labour would have a lead of 5·5 per cent over the Conservatives, in terms of votes. Again, Business Decisions came nearest to the actual result, predicting, in a poll completed a week before polling day, that the Labour lead would be 4·5 per cent. The actual Labour lead, in terms of votes cast in Great Britain, was 3·7 per cent. All the polls forecast a substantial vote for the Liberals, ranging only from the 20·0 per cent forecast by Business Decisions to the Gallup prediction of 19·0 per cent. The actual Liberal share of votes cast in Great Britain was 18·8 per cent.

The failure of the opinion polls in 1970 has been partially recouped. They continue to play an important role in the political process. Political leaders must view them now with a greater degree of scepticism than they did before 1970. But the polls remain one of the best indicators of the state of opinion in the country, and are still a useful guide to a Prime Minister in deciding when to have a general election.

NOTES

1 David Butler and Michael Pinto-Duschinsky, *The British General Election of 1970* (Macmillan, 1971), p. 263.
2 See pp. 145–6 for discussion of the situation in Northern Ireland at this time.
3 See pp. 51–2.
4 See also pp. 152–4.
5 D. Butler and D. Kavanagh, *The British General Election of February 1974* (Macmillan 1974), p. 329.
6 See Northern Ireland Office, The Future of Northern Ireland, a paper for discussion (H.M.S.O., 1972), para. 53, p. 25.
7 F. Stacey, *The Government of Modern Britain*, pp. 23–4.
8 See pp. 121–3 for discussion of the Redcliffe-Maud proposals.
9 H. C. Deb., vol. 768, col. 460.
10 For discussion of this Act see, pp. 124–8.
11 See F. Stacey, op. cit., pp. 305–6.
12 Marcia Williams, *Inside Number 10* (Weidenfeld and Nicolson, 1972), pp. 1–12.
13 For an explanation of random and quota sampling, see F. Stacey, op. cit., pp. 303–5.
14 Hugh Berrington, *Public Opinion Polls, British Politics, and the 1970 General Election* (a paper read to the British Political Studies Association Annual Conference at Edinburgh in March 1972), p. 5.
15 R. Rose (ed.), *The Polls and the 1970 Election* (University of Strathclyde Research Centre Occasional Paper, no. 7), p. 34.
16 Michael Steed, 'An Analysis of the Results', Appendix II in D. Butler and M. Pinto-Duschinsky, *The British General Election of 1970*, p. 392.
17 Butler and Pinto-Duschinsky, op. cit., p. 185, and Hugh Berrington, op. cit., p. 11, agree in attributing the failure of the polls in 1970 largely to 'late swing'.

CHAPTER III

Parliamentary Reform: Specialist Committees and the Scrutiny of Administration and Expenditure

WE have seen that before 1966 the main hope of many advocates of reform of the House of Commons lay in the creation of specialist committees of the Commons. For commentators like Bernard Crick, who claimed to see a major decline in the role of the Commons as a critic of the executive, specialist committees would be the means of restoring some of this lost influence. Not all the members of this school were agreed on the exact function of such specialist committees. Crick's original proposal, advanced in 1959, was that specialist committees should inquire into the activities of departments, take the Committee stage of legislation, examine the departmental estimates, and scrutinize delegated legislation issued by the department.[1] This was the most ambitious proposal for such committees, envisaging a legislative and financial, as well as an inquiring role. A. H. Hanson and H. V. Wiseman favoured specialist committees whose chief role would be to inquire into the activities of departments. The committees would only consider legislation in draft, when consulted by Ministers about draft Bills or statutory instruments.[2] The common element in all the proposals, however, was that there should be a series of committees of the Commons concerned with overseeing the work of all central departments, either taken singly (for example, the Foreign Office would be the concern of a Committee on Foreign Affairs), or in cognate groups.

The opposition to this idea came not only, as one would expect, from Ministers (for example, R. A. Butler in 1958 opposed Jo Grimond's suggestion for a Committee on Colonial Affairs), but also from some active back-benchers. For example, Michael Foot argued that such committees would lessen, not enhance, parliamentary control of the executive because they would reduce the importance of debates on the floor of the House.

The Procedure Committee of the House of Commons had examined suggestions for specialist committees in the session

1964–65, and in July 1965 reported on the matter to the House.[3] It did not support the idea of specialist committees, as such, but recommended that the Select Committee on Estimates should have a series of specialized sub-committees which would perform some of the functions of specialist committees, in inquiring into the activities of government departments and providing information for Members of the Commons and for the public. The Estimates Committee had been working through sub-committees ever since 1946 and some of its sub-committees had produced notable reports, for example the report on Trunk Roads in 1959 and the report on Recruitment to the Civil Service in 1965.[4] But its sub-committees were not specialist in the sense of having a continuous oversight of a group of designated departments. In December 1965 the Estimates Committee was reorganized in this way. It was divided into six sub-committees, five of which were given specific sectors of government for scrutiny. Besides the steering sub-committee, the sub-committees were allocated respectively: Defence and Overseas Affairs, Economic Affairs, Social Affairs, Technological and Scientific Affairs, and Building and Natural Resources.

This partial reform did not satisfy the advocates of specialist committees. The general election of 1966 brought an influx of new M.P.s many of whom, like John Mackintosh and David Marquand, were already convinced of the need for specialist committees of the Commons. The Labour leadership took note of this tide of opinion, particularly evident among the new Labour Members, and, shortly after the general election of 1966, the Prime Minister, Harold Wilson, announced that there would be an experiment with specialist committees. The Government, he said, would discuss the idea with the Conservative and Liberal Parliamentary Parties. He himself favoured specialist committees on Home Office affairs, education and housing, and local government.

In fact, the Conservative Opposition favoured, instead, a Committee on Science and Technology; there was also support among Members for a Committee on Agriculture. In December 1966 the Leader of the House, Richard Crossman, announced that these two committees were to be set up on an experimental basis. They would be given power to examine witnesses and to hear evidence in public. This last was an interesting new departure which owed much to Crossman's own conviction of the advantages of openness in politics. Previously, committees like the Estimates Committee, and its sub-committees, had always met in private. The prospect that specialist committees would hold most of their meetings in public might take the sting from some of the opposition to such committees. Critics had argued that, since proceedings in specialist committees would be private, only members of the committees would become well informed about the activities of government departments. Debates in the full House would be drained of interest, and parliamentary control, in practice, would become less effective. Since debates in the committees would now normally be in public, all Members, and some of the interested public, would be able to take account of what went on. Debate in the House might therefore be enriched rather than being partially denuded of interest.

The Select Committee on Agriculture was set up by the Commons on 14 December 1966, and the members of the Committee were nominated on 30 January 1967. It consisted of 14 members: 8 Labour, 5 Conservative, and 1 Liberal. Its chairman was a Labour back-bencher, Tudor Watkins. The choice was an obvious one since it is the convention for committees concerned with policy to be chaired by Government supporters. A Labour chairman was needed since Labour was in office, and Watkins was one of the few Labour Members who represented a largely rural constituency, Brecon and Radnor, in mid-Wales. A month later, two Scottish Members were added to the Committee: Alick Buchanan-Smith (Conservative) and John Mackintosh (Labour). The Committee chose as its first inquiry to look into the measures which were being taken by the Ministry of Agriculture to prepare for entry into the European Economic Community. This was in some ways an unfortunate first choice since it was a highly controversial subject. On the other hand, it was an extremely topical subject, about which many Members were concerned, and these were the kind of criteria which had often been used in the past by sub-committees of the Estimates Committee in choosing their fields of inquiry.

The Committee soon ran into difficulty. The Foreign Office objected to its intention to visit the British delegation to the European Economic Community in Brussels. Eventually, the Committee got its way and not only visited the British delegation in Brussels but also had informal meetings with Dr. Mansholt, the Commissioner in charge of agriculture, and members of the E.E.C.

staff. But relations with the Foreign Office and with the Ministry of Agriculture were strained.

In December 1967 Richard Crossman told the House that the Committee on Agriculture was to be wound up, and that a new specialist committee, on Education and Science, was to be appointed. In fact, the Agriculture Committee was reappointed for the session 1967–68 and was allowed to complete its second inquiry, into horticulture. The advocates of specialist committees naturally protested about the short life given to the Committee. In their view this did not give a fair trial to the idea of a specialist committee. Crossman retorted that since specialist committees were experimental it was appropriate that the Commons should experiment with committees on different departments, giving each committee a limited life. The early demise of the Agricultural Committee was perhaps also due in part to the poor relations which it enjoyed with the departments. Another possible cause was that the Committee was not very popular with Labour back-benchers, few of whom had a keen interest in farming, which made it difficult to man the Committee on the Labour side. We will return later to this question of the difficulty of manning the committees.

The Committee on Education and Science chose as its first topic of inquiry Her Majesty's Inspectorate of Schools, and published its report in September 1968. Its main finding, that primary responsibility in the field of inspection now lay with inspectors employed by the local authorities rather than with Her Majesty's Inspectors, was useful but not exciting. Not surprisingly, the report was not given much coverage in the Press.

The Committee then turned to the burning issue of student unrest in universities, art colleges and other places of higher education. In 1968 there was much turmoil and revolt in French universities which seemed to spark off a bush fire of discontent among students in Britain and the United States. The Select Committee on Education set up a sub-committee to take evidence from students and staff in institutions where there was student unrest. It visited first the Guildford School of Art, where numerous staff had been dismissed following controversy with the controlling local authority. It compiled volumes of evidence here and elsewhere. The Committee's reception varied widely: at Essex University student militants refused to allow the Committee to take evidence, while at Swansea University College a fruitful interchange developed between members of the sub-committee and spokesmen for different elements in the student body, as well as with members of staff. The Committee's voluminous report was, however, little noticed, although the sub-committee's visits to places of higher education may well have had some therapeutic effect.

Meanwhile, the Select Committee on Science and Technology had undertaken two useful inquiries. Its report on the Nuclear Reactor Programme was well received. Replying to a well-informed debate in the Commons on this report, the Parliamentary Secretary to the Ministry of Technology, Dr. Jeremy Bray spoke of the 'penetration and effectiveness' of the Committee's inquiry.[5] The second inquiry, on Oil Pollution, was stimulated by the wreck of the giant oil-tanker the *Torrey Canyon* in 1971. The Committee's report on this subject was given wide coverage in the Press and received favourable comment in editorials.

The Committee on Science and Technology was to acquire a long-term status, as was the Committee on Race Relations and Immigration set up in 1968. The formation of this Committee was due to an initiative of the Home Secretary at the time, James Callaghan. Its terms of reference gave it the task of reviewing the operation of the Race Relations Act of 1968 and the work of the Race Relations Board and the Community Relations Commission. It was also instructed to review policies for the admission into the United Kingdom of Commonwealth citizens and foreign nationals wishing to settle there. Its chairman from 1968 to 1970 was Arthur Bottomley who had been Secretary of State for Commonwealth Relations from 1964 to 1966. After the 1970 general election his place as chairman was taken by William Deedes who had been a Conservative Minister without Portfolio from 1962 to 1964.

The Committee has published several useful reports, for example on the Problems of Coloured School Leavers (1969), Housing (1971), and Relations between Immigrants and the Police (1972). Each of these reports has been well prepared. The Committee has visited places with a high proportion of immigrants to make its own first-hand inquiries, and has also heard evidence from experts, and from representatives of immigrant associations. Its reports have done a great deal to encourage among M.P.s a fair-minded and cool appraisal of the problems of race relations in Britain.

Another committee which was to prove more than a temporary phenomenon was the Select Committee on Scottish Affairs, first appointed in March 1969. It must be distinguished from the Scottish Grand Committee, which includes all Members representing Scottish constituencies and is a debating forum on Scottish issues. The Select Committee on Scottish Affairs has sixteen members only and its task is to inquire into the activities of the Scottish departments. Its first inquiry was concerned with the plans for economic development in Scotland.

Only a few months after the appointment of the Scottish Select Committee, the Procedure Committee of the Commons completed a report which was to have far-reaching effect on the future of specialist committees. This was its report on Scrutiny of Public Expenditure and Administration, ordered by the Commons to be printed on 23 July 1969.[6] Perhaps the key finding in the Committee's report was its conclusion that the introduction of specialist committees had 'depleted the membership of the Estimates Committee and reduced the scope of its examination of Departmental spending'.[7] Since one of the main themes of the Procedure Committee's report was that the Commons should improve its scrutiny of Government expenditure, this finding gave cause for concern.

The Procedure Committee had heard evidence from the Chairman of the Estimates Committee, William Hamilton, from Treasury Ministers and leading Opposition spokesmen, from the Clerk of the House, and from Permanent Secretaries of some of the key Ministries. The statistics of decline in the activities of the Estimates Committee were given in a memorandum prepared for the Procedure Committee by the Clerks Assistant of the House.[8] We have seen that, following a recommendation of the Procedure Committee in 1965, the Estimates Committee had set up five specialized subcommittees in December of that year. At the time the Estimates Committee had a total of 43 members.

Only two years later, in the session 1967–68, the Estimates Committee was reduced to 36 members. It decided in this session to appoint four instead of five sub-committees, and to end the shortlived practice of giving specialized functions to sub-committees. It reverted to the previous practice of designating the sub-committees by letters of the alphabet, and allowed them a wide range of freedom in choosing their fields of inquiry. One reason given for this change was the apparent duplication between the sub-committees of the Estimates Committee and some of the new specialist committees. For example, the Estimates Committee had a sub-committee on

Technological and Scientific Affairs which seemed to parallel the work of the specialist committee on Science and Technology. In practice, the chairmen of the two bodies had consulted to ensure that they did not both inquire into the same subject at the same time, but the apparent duplication was none the less confusing.

In the following session, 1968–69, the Estimates Committee was reduced in size again to 33 members, and therefore decided that it could only maintain three instead of four investigating committees. Owing to the difficulty of manning the Committee the scope of its inquiries was necessarily being curtailed. The statistics showing the increased number of committee sittings in this period give one indication of the reason for this difficulty: in 1964 there were 240 sittings of select committees, in 1968 no less than 555. During the same period, the number of sittings of the Standing Committees, which consider the committee stage of legislation, had also risen from 205 in 1964 to 330 in 1968.[9] Sufficient members had to be found to attend 880 sittings of committees in 1968, as compared with only 445 sittings in 1964.

It might be thought that since there are 630 Members of the Commons it would still be possible to find enough Members to attend this greatly increased number of sittings. In fact, as H. V. Wiseman pointed out, more than 100 Members of the Government (Ministers and junior Ministers) and more than 40 Opposition front-bench Members do not serve on specialist committees. This leaves 490 Members who are theoretically available, but about 190 of these do not serve, leaving the whole burden of manning committees to the remaining 300 Members.[10]

Why is it that some Members who are theoretically available do not serve on committees, and others who do some service on committees show a marked disinclination to spend much of their time in this way? There is a variety of reasons. Some Members still combine membership of the House with another occupation, such as barrister, company director, journalist, etc. Nearly all Members give up a great deal of their time to constituency business, taking up with Ministers or with other government agencies the problems raised by their constituents.

Finally, for those Members, and there are many, who aspire to Ministerial office, service on committees is not very attractive. It is still in the Commons Chamber that reputations are usually made and that young members are 'spotted' by Ministers or Opposition front-benchers for their potential as future Ministers. Service on a specialist committee may be interesting, and is certainly valuable, but it is not likely to be a road to glory in the sense of singling out a Member as a potential Minister. The extent to which Members find specialist committee work interesting also varies a great deal from one individual to another. John Mackintosh, for example, has expressed a preference for serving on a specialist committee rather than on one of 'those boring standing committees'. On the other hand, Members who are particularly concerned to try and influence the detail of legislation which affects them, or their constituents, are often keen to serve on standing committees, but may not be at all enamoured of the long process of hearing evidence which is unavoidable on a specialist committee.

The main proposal put forward in 1969 by the Procedure Committee, in its report on Scrutiny of Public Expenditure and Administration, was that the Estimates Committee should be replaced by a new Select Committee on Expenditure. It was envisaged that this would be a large committee, with a suggested membership of 80. It was to set up eight sub-committees, each with nine members, and each sub-committee was to be allocated a sphere of government. Thus there might be one sub-committee concerned with Trade and Agriculture, another with Defence, and another with External Affairs.

The terms of reference proposed for the Expenditure Committee and its sub-committees were much wider than the terms of reference for the Estimates Committee. It was suggested, for example, that the sub-committees should be empowered to consider the activities of the departments of state within the field allocated to the sub-committee, as well as the department's estimates of expenditure. They would also be responsible for examining the implications of the policy chosen by Ministers, and of assessing the success of departments in attaining these objectives.[11]

When the Commons debated this report on 21 October 1969 the Leader of the House, Fred Peart, gave a general welcome to its proposals. He also said that the Wilson Government was reviewing the operation of specialist committees. The general election of 1970 was, however, held before this review was complete and it was left to the Heath Government to make proposals for the future of specialist committees, and for the implementation of the Procedure Committee's 1969 Report. In October 1970 William

Whitelaw, the new Leader of the House, published a Green Paper setting out the Heath Government's proposals on these questions. As regards specialist committees, the Green Paper proposed that the 'subject' committees on Nationalized Industries, Science and Technology, Race Relations and Immigration, and Scottish Affairs should continue. The Government thought, however, that the committees which were overseeing the work of specific departments should be wound up, and that this task be taken over by a new Expenditure Committee working through a series of specialized sub-committees.

When the Green Paper was debated in the Commons on 12 November 1970, Whitelaw said that in his view they had to find the right balance between what could be the conflicting interests of select committees and the Chamber of the House. The select committee system could be valuable to debates in the Chamber, but if too many Members were engaged on select committee work the Chamber could be denuded. The Government thought that it would not be possible to have the sort of Expenditure Committee which the Procedure Committee had proposed, and at the same time maintain the 'subject' committees on such matters as the Nationalized Industries, Science and Technology, and Race Relations. The Government proposed that the Expenditure Committee should therefore have 45 members instead of the 80 suggested by the Procedure Committee. It would work through specialized sub-committees, and the Committee and its sub-committees would have wider powers than those previously enjoyed by the Estimates Committee. It would be empowered to consider the policies implied in the Estimates and would be able to examine Ministers when necessary.[12] The Green Paper was welcomed by Fred Peart, speaking for the Opposition, and it was clear from the debate that there was majority support in the House for the Government's proposals.

Before going on to consider the new Public Expenditure Committee which then emerged, it is appropriate to assess what was achieved by the experiment with specialist committees from 1966 onwards. The three 'subject' committees on Science and Technology, Race Relations and Immigration, and Scottish Affairs had become an accepted feature of the machinery of parliamentary scrutiny and were reappointed each session. The 'departmental' committees on Agriculture, Education, and Overseas Aid were transitory. The first had been terminated by the Wilson Government. The other two were finally wound up after the Conservative Government's Green Paper in 1970.

The experiment and its outcome could not, therefore, be to the liking of those, like Crick, who had advocated a full series of 'departmental' committees of the Commons. The experiment had, however, been a limited success in that it had led to the establishment of the three effective 'subject' committees on Science and Technology, Race Relations, and Scottish Affairs. It also had some valuable by-products. As we have seen, Crossman had at the outset suggested that specialist committees should normally sit in public. Not only was this suggestion taken up by the specialist committees but, in the session 1967–68, the Estimates Committee decided that, as an experiment, one of its sub-committees would hear evidence in public wherever practicable. This was such a success that from the following session it became normal practice in all the sub-committees of the Estimates Committee.

The principle that select committees could ask Ministers to give evidence also came to be accepted. Before 1966, the Estimates Committee, and the Public Accounts Committee, had heard evidence from senior Civil Servants and not from Ministers. By this means the fiction was maintained that the committees were not inquiring into Ministerial policy, but were gaining information about administration in the departments. Crossman suggested that the specialist committees should hear evidence from Ministers. By 1970 this had become so much an accepted and useful practice that the Conservative Government proposed that the Expenditure Committee should have power to examine Ministers.

Two further points about select committees deserve to be considered: first, how to assess the effectiveness of a committee's report. And second, related to this, how to measure its effect on Parliament. On the first point, one method would be to check how many of a committee's recommendations were accepted by the Government. For example, Sir George Sinclair, Conservative Member for Dorking, told the Commons in the debate on the Whitelaw Green Paper, that he had been a member of the Committee on Race Relations, which in its recent report had made about 40 recommendations, nearly all of which were accepted by the Government.[13] But it would not be true to say, by contrast, that a committee whose recommendations were not accepted by the

Government was not effective. For example, the recommendations on governmental dispositions for scientific research and development, made in 1973 by the Select Committee on Science and Technology, were rejected by the Heath Government. Again, this does not reflect on the thoroughness of the Committee's report .The Committee heard evidence from a wide range of expert witnesses and reported in favour of appointing a Minister for Research and Development, supported by a council for science and technology. The Government rejected these recommendations but it was not clear, when the issue was debated in the Commons, that the Government's arguments were more cogent than those put forward by the Committee.[14]

As regards the second point, it is equally difficult to measure the impact which a committee's report makes on Parliament. It used to be a cause for complaint that the reports of the Estimates Committee, and of the Public Accounts Committee, were rarely discussed in the Commons. Nowadays time is quite often found for debates on reports from specialist and other select committees, but these debates are rarely well attended, and many Members who speak in the debates are themselves members of the reporting committees. For example, during debate on 25 May 1968 on the Science and Technology Report, Wedgwood Benn said that it was impressive for a Minister to take part in a debate in which so many contributors were so well informed on the subject. But H. V. Wiseman pointed out that of 17 speakers in this debate, 11 were members of the Committee, and 2 were Ministers, while only 4 were neither Ministers nor members of the Committee.[15] One is led to wonder, in this instance, how many M.P.s outside the Committee had read and mastered the Committee's report. Was the Committee producing information which was useful to the House, and contributing in an important way to the debate on nuclear energy policy? The answer is probably yes. But a committee's influence cannot be satisfactorily measured by the number of non-members of the committee who attend and speak in the debate on the committee's report. The specialized nature of the subject-matter of a report must often mean that a report appeals to a specialized public, and there may not be many M.P.s outside the committee with a specialist interest in that subject. The report may, however, be very influential among the specialized interested public outside the House, and may also influence opinion in the government department concerned, even if it is not immediately implemented by the government of the day.

We can now return to the Select Committee on Public Expenditure and assess its role. The Committee was first set up early in 1971. William Whitelaw was better than his promise, for whereas he had said that the Committee would consist of 45 members, 50 members were in fact appointed. The Committee's first action was to set up a 15-strong steering committee and 6 sub-committees. These were given the following areas: Public Expenditure (General), Defence and External Affairs, Trade and Industry, Education and the Arts, Environment and Home Office, Employment and Social Services. The chairmanships of the sub-committees were equally divided between Conservative and Labour Members. The Labour chairmen appointed were Dick Taverne, to head the Public Expenditure (General) Sub-Committee, William Rodgers, to head the Trade and Industry Sub-Committee, and Mrs. Renée Short, to head the Employment and Social Services Sub-Committee. The Conservative chairmen were Colonel Sir Harwood Harrison for the Defence and External Affairs Sub-Committee, Neil Marten for the Education and the Arts Sub-Committee, and John Hall for the Environment and Home Office Sub-Committee. Edward du Cann, a Conservative, and former Economic Secretary to the Treasury, was elected chairman of the whole Public Expenditure Committee.[16]

The terms of reference of the Committee were similar to those of the Estimates Committee, except that they gave the Committee power to consider policy in the departments. Most of the sub-committees have, on the face of it, operated very much as the sub-committees of the Estimates Committee did. We can take as an example the Environment and Home Office Sub-Committee into Urban Transport Planning, whose report was published in December 1972. It recommended in strong terms that there should be a major attempt to improve public transport, and to discourage the use of cars for the journey to work in city areas.[17] It added that the present road system in towns should be put to the best possible use before substantial additions were made to it. The report was very well received in the Press and was an important contribution to the debate currently raging about whether to build urban motorways in the centre of cities or to make a significant reduction in the use of cars in city centres.

Before drawing up its report, the Committee heard evidence from senior Civil Servants in the Department of the Environment, from representatives of some of the larger local authorities, including the Greater London Council, and of the Passenger Transport Authorities in Merseyside, the West Midlands, Tyneside, etc. It collected the views of planning consultants, of British Railways, and the National Bus Company, and, at its final session, cross-examined the Minister responsible, Peter Walker, Secretary of State for the Environment. These sessions were similar in kind to the hearings undertaken by sub-committees of the Estimates Committee. The one difference was that the Minister himself gave evidence, at the end of the sequence of hearings.

The sub-committee made special visits to the cities of Hamburg and Munich, and discussed with the city authorities the approach they were taking to urban traffic problems. This kind of overseas visit had been difficult before 1965 for sub-committees of the Estimates Committee, but since October 1965 they had been able to make such visits.[18] Another point about the inquiry was that Mr. David Starkie, a Lecturer in Geography in the University of Reading, had been appointed to advise the sub-committee for the duration of the inquiry. This kind of appointment was another recent development, but had already been made use of by sub-committees of the Estimates Committee. For example, Sub-Committee E of the Estimates Committee had the assistance of a specialist adviser in transport economics for its inquiry into Motorways and Trunk Roads in the session 1968–69.[19]

The power which select committees now have to appoint specialist advisers in this way, makes up to some extent for the absence of full-time specialist advisers on the staff of the Commons. There are indeed certain advantages in the appointment of such *ad hoc* advisers, provided they can be found, and are able to take up part-time appointments with select committees, yet there remains a need for more full-time staff. One of the difficulties experienced with specialist committees was the shortage of clerks to act as secretaries to committees. There is also need for full-time specialist advisers to assist such committees as the Public Expenditure Committee, and the Committee on Nationalized Industries.

Many of the other inquiries undertaken by sub-committees of the Expenditure Committee have been similar in type to the inquiries previously undertaken by sub-committees of the Estimates Committee. For example, in 1972–73 the Employment and

Social Services Sub-Committee inquired into Youth Employment Services, and published its report in March 1973.[20] The same sub-committee had earlier inquired into the provision of beds for private patients in National Health Service Hospitals.[21]

The Trade and Industry Sub-Committee inquired into Government Aid for Private Industry and followed this up by inquiring into Incentives for Regional Development in Britain. As part of this latter inquiry, the sub-committee visited Brussels in February 1973, and heard evidence on the regional and competition policies of the European Economic Community from two members of the Commission, George Thomson and Albert Borschette. Members of the sub-committee said they were well satisfied with this interchange.[22] They did not experience ministerial hostility to the visit as had the Agriculture Committee when it visited Brussels in 1967.[23]

One sub-committee of the Expenditure Committee which has a different function from any sub-committee of the Estimates Committee is the Public Expenditure (General) Sub-Committee. It is this sub-committee which has been attempting to scrutinize the 'forward look' which the Government now takes over projects for expenditure several years ahead. The Select Committee on Procedure, in its 1969 Report on Scrutiny of Public Expenditure and Administration, had emphasized the unsatisfactory nature of a situation in which the House of Commons was still considering Departmental Estimates of Expenditure on an annual basis, while for some years the Treasury had been considering expenditure on a five-year basis. This forward planning of expenditure was one of the reforms suggested by the Plowden Committee in 1961.[24] The Plowden Committee had originally been set up following a suggestion made in an Estimates Committee Report.[25]

The system of 'forward looks' had been considerably developed and modified since 1962, as we shall see in Chapter VI. From the point of view of the Procedure Committee, in 1969 parliamentary control of expenditure was lagging behind. One of the reasons for advocating a new Expenditure Committee instead of an enlarged Estimates Committee was to facilitate parliamentary scrutiny of expenditure on a long-term basis. In the event, the Public Expenditure (General) Sub-Committee was given this task.

The sub-committee began by making three interrelated inquiries: first, into Changes in Public Expenditure, second, into Public Expenditure and Economic Management, and third, into the

Relationship of Expenditure to Needs. The sub-committee clashed with the Treasury in 1972, in the course of these inquiries, over the Treasury's refusal to reveal to the sub-committee its own assessment of medium-term economic prospects. The Government now publishes annually a White Paper giving long-term projections of public expenditure. In peacetime, the Departments' annual estimates of expenditure are of course also regularly published and presented to Parliament. What was missing was a statement of medium-term economic projections. The sub-committee's specialist adviser, Mr. Wynne Godley, and the Department of Applied Economics of Cambridge University, of which he is a member, were asked to prepare medium-term economic assessments and these were used by the sub-committee.

This one dispute does not mean that the sub-committee's relations with the Treasury have generally been strained, in fact they have mostly been very good. The Treasury has found that the sub-committee has been able to point in a useful way to deficiencies in government planning, particularly in relating expenditure to needs. For example, the sub-committee found that the Department of Health and Social Security had no idea of the amount spent on old people by government services in the country as a whole. Similarly, it found that the Department of Education and Science did not have an over-all plan for developing nursery education in the areas where it was most needed. In fact, it emerged generally that in those areas where the need for nursery education was greatest, there was also the least provision. Subsequently, the Department of Education and Science published a major programme for the expansion of nursery education.

In this kind of way, therefore, the General Sub-Committee has been making observations which are helpful to the Government in planning the over-all allocation of resources, just as the other sub-committees, like the sub-committees of the Estimates Committee in the past, advance recommendations about changes of policy regarding urban traffic problems, development of the youth service, and so on. The General Sub-Committee has not, however, been very successful in its wider aim of contributing to a meaningful discussion in the Commons of the Government's long-term strategy for expenditure. Although, in theory, the sub-committee's reports should provide valuable material for critical discussion of the Government's annual White Paper on Expenditure, debates in the

Commons on these White Papers have been poor as very few Members take an interest in them, or have much grasp of the issues. In 1971 two days were allocated for the debate, but it collapsed on the second day because there were not enough Members who wanted to speak. In 1972 only one day was set aside for the debate.

This relative failure does not mean that the whole idea of scrutiny by the Commons of the Government's long-term strategy for public expenditure should be abandoned. The point is that the Government is now, by means of its annual White Paper, lifting the corner of the veil on its internal planning processes. Not much interest has been aroused, as yet, because what can be seen does not make much sense without a wider knowledge of the issues involved. The move towards 'open government' is the logical development of this; we will return to this in Chapters VI and VII.

NOTES

1 Bernard Crick, *Reform of the Commons.*
2 A. H. Hanson and H. V. Wiseman, 'The Use of Committees by the House of Commons', *Public Law*, 1959, pp. 277–92.
3 H.C.303 of 1964–65, Fourth Report from the Select Committee on Procedure.
4 H.C. 223 of 1958–59, First Report from the Select Committee on Estimates: Trunk Roads; H.C. 308 of 1964–65, Sixth Report from the Estimates Committee: Recruitment to the Civil Service, which led to the setting up of the Fulton Committee. See p. 97.
5 H.C. Deb., vol. 765, col. 1071 (23 May 1968).
6 H.C. 410 of 1968–69, First Report from the Select Committee on Procedure: Scrutiny of Public Expenditure and Administration.
7 Op. cit., para. 10, p. viii.
8 Op. cit., pp. 241–2.
9 Op. cit., p. 247.
10 H. V. Wiseman: 'The New Specialised Committees' in A. H. Hanson and B. Crick (eds.), *The Commons in Transition* (Fontana, 1970), p. 215.
11 H.C. 410 of 1968–69, pp. xv-xvi, paras, 34–35.
12 H.C. Deb., vol. 806, col. 620.
13 H.C. Deb., vol. 806, col. 642.
14 H.C. Deb., vol. 849, cols. 47–164 (22 January 1973).
15 H. V. Wiseman in A. H. Hanson and B. Crick (eds.), op. cit., p. 216.
16 In the session 1972–73 Edward du Cann was succeeded by Sir Henry d'Avigdor Goldsmid as chairman of the Expenditure Committee. This followed du Cann's election as chairman of the Conservative 1922 Committee, the organization of back-bench Conservative M.P.s.
17 H.C. 57–I of 1972–73, Second Report from the Expenditure Committee: Urban Transport Planning, pp. xix-xx, paras. 26–9.
18 See F. Stacey, *The Government of Modern Britain*, p. 144.
19 H.C. 475 of 1968–69, Sixth Report of the Select Committee on Estimates: Motorways and Trunk Roads.

20 H.C. 148 of 1972–73, Fourth Report from the Expenditure Committee: Youth Employment Services.
21 H.C. 172 of 1971–72, Fourth Report from the Expenditure Committee: National Health Service Facilities for Private Patients.
22 Report in *The Times*, 20 February 1973.
23 See above, pp. 23–4.
24 Cmnd. 1432, Control of Public Expenditure; Report of the Plowden Committee.
25 H.C. 254 of 1957–58, Sixth Report from the Select Committee on Estimates: Treasury Control of Expenditure. See F. Stacey, *The Government of Modern Britain*, pp. 361–62.

CHAPTER IV

Parliamentary Reform: Improvements on the Floor of the House, Legislation

WHILE many academic reformers have been concerned to impress upon parliamentarians the need to set up specialist committees of the Commons, many of the parliamentarians themselves have wished to improve procedures on the floor of the House. Since, to them, the real forum for challenging the government is the floor of the House, the most important reforms are those which remove some of the frustrations and inconveniences of procedures in the House itself.

Improved Procedures: Some Successes, Some Failures

One procedure long in need of reform was that relating to emergency debates. In theory, debates under Standing Order No. 9 provided a valuable opportunity for Members to challenge and cross-examine the government on a 'matter of urgent public importance'. Any Member could move the adjournment after question time under this Standing Order and, if the Speaker accepted the motion, and if forty Members showed their support by rising in their places, a debate would be fixed for 7 p.m. that day, interrupting the scheduled business of the House.

In practice, the precedents which surrounded the use of the Standing Order had become so complicated and restrictive that it had grown increasingly difficult to get an emergency debate. The Speaker had to consider whether the subject-matter for debate was definite, whether it was urgent, whether it was of public importance, whether it was the responsibility of a Minister, whether there would be another opportunity in the near future of raising the matter in the House, and so on.

Since holding an emergency debate was highly disruptive to ordinary business, and since there was increasing pressure on the time of the House, Speakers tended to become more cautious in accepting motions under the Standing Order; restrictive precedents increased this caution still more. When the Select Committee on

Procedure looked into the question in 1966 it found that there had been a spectacular decline in the number of emergency debates in the House since the beginning of the century. In the first twenty years there had been 102 such debates, whereas in the twenty years between 1946 and 1966 there had only been 15.[1]

The Procedure Committee recommended that the rules should be changed 'to relieve Mr. Speaker of the need to be bound by previous interpretations of the standing order'.[2] In 1968 this was done and the Speaker does not now have to give his reasons for not accepting a motion under Standing Order No. 9. This allows him to judge each case for an emergency debate on its merits, without being bound by an accumulation of restrictive precedents. Another change, made at the same time, provides that the emergency debate can take place on the day following acceptance of the motion. This gives Ministers more notice and a better opportunity to acquaint themselves with the facts, and also causes less disruption to the scheduled business.

Reliance is also placed on the Speaker for preventing Members from making tedious and over-long speeches. There had been a considerable campaign by some Members in the 1950s and 1960s for introducing a time-limit on speeches;[3] experiments have not found permanent favour. The present Speaker, Selwyn Lloyd, prefers to encourage short speeches by making Members aware that if their contributions are not lengthy they are more likely to catch the Speaker's eye in debate. If a Member goes on for too long he is liable to be interrupted by the Speaker, who reminds him that, although the Chair has no sanctions against long speeches, provided they are relevant, 'it has a memory'.[4]

An experiment made in the session 1966–67 was to have morning sittings of the Commons, but this proved a failure. In August 1966 the Procedure Committee had suggested that the House should sit on Wednesday and Thursday mornings with the aim of providing more time for debates and, if possible, bringing the parliamentary day forward so that Members would less frequently be kept at the House late in the evening, or into the night. The days chosen in the session 1966–67 for morning sittings were Mondays and Wednesdays, to avoid conflict with the sittings of Standing Committees, which are held on Tuesday and Thursday mornings. No votes were taken during these morning sittings; divisions which were called in the morning were held over until the afternoon.

The snag was that only Labour Members were in favour of it. The Conservatives, almost to a man, had opposed the suggestion when it was discussed by the Procedure Committee in 1959, and proposed by the Committee in 1966. More Conservative Members than Labour Members have professions such as those of barrister, stockbroker, or merchant banker, which can be combined with membership of the House. These Members are anxious to keep their mornings free and resist any suggestion that the M.P.'s job should become a full-time one. The morning sittings were therefore poorly attended by Conservatives and, with no votes being taken, had a certain air of unreality and lack of purpose. The experiment was not repeated.

In the following session, 1967–68, another experiment was tried, also without success, although it did have some useful long-term effects. The Procedure Committee had for some time been considering the suggestion that more time could be found for debates on the floor of the House if the Finance Bill were to be taken in Standing Committee at Committee Stage. Discussion of the Finance Bill takes up a lot of time, and much of it is technical. There seemed to be a good case for taking it off the floor of the House and entrusting it to a Standing Committee, which would include in its membership all the main experts on financial and taxation matters. The experiment was tried in the session 1967–68, but, like the experiment with morning sittings, was much disliked by the Conservatives.

Leading Conservative spokesmen, such as Iain Macleod, found themselves cooped up for long hours in Standing Committee, unable to attend to their other concerns. The Standing Committee had to sit for some of the time while business was proceeding on the floor of the House. When this was contentious and caused divisions, the members of the Standing Committee had to commute hurriedly by lift from the committee corridor, to vote in the division lobbies, and then return to their committee room. The whole experience was not appreciated by Conservative Members, who were emphatic that the experiment had not been a success.

Procedure reforms are not normally adopted unless there is a substantial measure of agreement on them between the two main parties. But in this case a compromise was arranged. It was decided that, in future, the Finance Bill would be split into two parts: one part, which would include the larger changes and issues of principle in the Bill, would be taken on the floor of the House, and the other part, which would include most of the more technical aspects of taxation, would be taken in Standing Committee. This would allow the leading Opposition spokesmen to appear from time to time on the floor of the House, while the technical experts would do the donkey work in Standing Committee.

This device proved successful and has been repeated in subsequent sessions. The Leader of the House told the Procedure Committee in 1970 that taking part of the Finance Bill in Standing Committee had saved about five days on the floor of the House in the sessions 1968–69 and 1969–70.[5]

A proposal for reform which, while not causing contention between the parties, has proved highly controversial and has not yet won approval, is the suggestion for televising proceedings in the House. On 19 October 1972 a Conservative Member, Brian Batsford, introduced a motion recommending an experiment with 'the public broadcasting' of the proceedings of the House 'by sound and television'. He was supported in the debate by William Hamilton, Michael Foot, Tom Driberg, Hugh Jenkins, and Philip Whitehead, on the Labour side. Other Labour Members, Charles Pannell, Alexander Lyon, and John Mendelson, were against the proposal. The Conservative Members who took part in the debate were also split: Norman St. John Stevas and David Crouch, for example, supported the proposal. Angus Maude, Sir Harmar Nicholls, Norman Tebbit, and Neil Marten were among the many Conservatives who opposed it. One of the Liberals who took part in the Debate, David Steel, was in favour. The Government did not commit itself on the issue and allowed a free vote which resulted in the defeat of the motion by 191 votes to 165.

The arguments put forward on both sides were presented with great conviction. Those who argued against televising proceedings maintained that it would alter the character of the House and put an undesirable power in the hands of the television producer in presenting the debates. The advocates of television argued that it would be a means of restoring people's interest in Parliament. Michael Foot also contended that it would increase the power of back-benchers, and the Opposition, against governments of the day.

The proposal was defeated again in the Commons on 30 January 1974. The general elections in February and October 1974 altered the composition of the House considerably and strengthened the case of those who argued that another debate should be held on the subject, and should be followed by a free vote. A debate was planned for December 1974, but the pressure of other business forced it off the agenda. The advocates of televising proceedings had mixed feelings about this postponement. Unfortunately for them, when the Queen's speech was televised at the opening of the 1974 session, the brightness of the lights of the camera crews annoyed many parliamentarians. This was a tactical blunder because it had always been argued that specially bright lights were not technically necessary for televising proceedings of the House. Postponement of the debate could therefore be an advantage, since it would allow the memory of the annoyance caused by the special lighting to recede.

The debate eventually took place on 24 February 1975. There were two motions before the House. The first proposed an experiment in sound broadcasting, and the second in televising proceedings of the House. The second motion was rejected by a majority of twelve, but the motion to allow an experiment in sound broadcasting was carried by a majority of 172.

The experiment was carried out during the four weeks beginning 9 June 1975. On the first day the B.B.C. broadcast the whole of question time and questions to the Prime Minister. It proved a dramatic beginning because on this day the House was resuming after the referendum campaign. There was therefore a special interest in the Prime Minister's statement on the result of the referendum and in the interchanges which followed. At question time Tony Benn was the Minister down to answer questions. Added point was given to the lively exchange which then took place between him and Conservative back-benchers by the fact that it was widely expected that the Prime Minister would move him from the Department of Industry, following his vigorous criticisms of the European Community during the referendum campaign.

The most important feature of the experiment, however, was the use made of recorded extracts in news bulletins and in 'Today in Parliament'. To give time for the recorded material, this programme and its companion 'Yesterday in Parliament' were expanded from fifteen minutes to thirty minutes each. The longer period also made it possible to put in more explanation of proceedings in the House than was customary before.

Public reaction to the broadcast extracts was mixed. Many people disapproved of the barracking and 'baying' by Members during statements from Ministers and Opposition front-bench speakers.

The microphone may have magnified the sound of interruptions and given a more exaggerated impression of unruliness than someone actually present in the House would have gained. It can be argued that televising proceedings would give a more balanced impression to the viewer. For anyone at all familiar with proceedings in the House the broadcasts were sheer gain. The ability to hear extracts from speeches and comments, exactly as made in the House, made news bulletins and the 'Today in Parliament' programmes much more interesting and informative.

Legislation

When we turn to the way in which legislation is considered in the Commons, we find a somewhat confused situation. Have governments become more, or less, high-handed in the last nine years in their attitude towards back-benchers in their role of scrutinizing and amending government bills? Evidence can be presented for each case. Have back-benchers played an increasing part, in this period, in introducing their own legislation and getting it on to the statute book? There is some evidence that they have, although again the situation is not altogether clear.

Let us look first at legislation introduced by back-benchers. Was the period from 1964 to 1969 a Golden Age for private Members' legislation? We can point to the series of reforms achieved by back-benchers in the Commons in these years: in 1965, Sidney Silverman's Death Penalty (Abolition) Bill became law. In the session 1966–67, after a long struggle, two minor reforms sponsored by private Members reached the statute book. One was Leo Abse's Sexual Offences (No. 2) Bill which made homosexual practices in private between consenting adult males legal in England and Wales. The other was David Steel's Abortion Bill which legalized abortion, on health or social grounds, provided that two registered medical practitioners concur in the opinion that an abortion is necessary, and that the operation is carried out in a National Health Service hospital, or in some other place approved by the Minister of Health (now the Secretary of State for Social Services); where an emergency operation is necessary to save a woman's life, the decision to undertake an abortion can legally be made by one doctor. In 1968 the Theatres Bill, introduced by George Strauss, abolished control of theatres in London by the Lord Chamberlain, thus effectively ending censorship of plays. Finally, in 1969, the Divorce Bill, introduced by Alec Jones, brought about a major change by re-establishing the law on the principle that a divorce can be obtained when it can be shown to the satisfaction of a court that a marriage has broken down.[6]

There would seem to be a spectacular divergence here from the view advanced by Peter Bromhead in his study *Private Members' Bills in the British Parliament*.[7] Whereas Bromhead commented that the only reforms which back-benchers could achieve were, with rare exception, small-scale non-controversial reforms, we find five major reforms, all of them controversial, being carried through by private Members in as many years. Has there been a major change, giving the private Member enhanced opportunities for sponsoring legislative reforms?

In considering this question, a special factor in the reforms carried between 1965 and 1969 should be noted, namely that the government of the day, led by Harold Wilson, had had a benevolent attitude towards all the five issues. The Government did not officially support any one of the reforms, and some government back-benchers were opposed to each reform, although in the case of abolition of the death penalty, the extent of opposition on the Labour side was quite small. Only one Labour M.P. voted against the Death Penalty (Abolition) Bill at Second Reading in 1964.[8] The Government was prepared to allow a free vote in each case and, even more importantly, to find additional parliamentary time to allow the necessary stages of legislation to be completed. At the same time, we should recognize that the supporters of each reform had to organize their own *ad hoc* parliamentary machine to try to ensure that a large enough body of sympathetic Members was present in the Chamber, or near to hand elsewhere in the House, at each stage of the debate.

Although there were some Conservative Members in each of the *ad hoc* organizations, working for abolition of the death penalty, homosexual law reform, etc., their numbers in each case were relatively small in relation to the total number of Conservative M.P.s, except on the issue of abolition of the death penalty. Thus 51 Conservatives voted, in 1966, for the introduction of the bill reforming the law on homosexuality, 32 for the Abortion Law Reform Bill, on Third Reading, and 24 for the Divorce Reform Bill, on Second Reading. Even the 81 who voted for the Death Penalty (Abolition) Bill, on Second Reading, were only a minority of the 253 Conservative M.P.s.[9]

A considerable section of Conservative Members disapproved of the assistance given to these private Members' bills by the Wilson Government. For example, Sir Lionel Heald argued that in the case of the Divorce Bill, the Government was pretending to be neutral and taking no responsibility, although it was assisting the case by finding additional time to enable it to pass all its stages in the Commons. His motion of protest on this matter was defeated on 12 June 1969 by 166 votes to 62. But after the 1970 general election, the Heath Government took account of this feeling and let it be known that it would not find extra parliamentary time for controversial private Members' bills as the Wilson Government had done.

The Heath Government did not, however, hold strictly to its resolve in every case. For example, when the National Health Service Family Planning Amendment Bill, introduced by the Labour M.P. Philip Whitehead, seemed to have failed at the very last stage of consideration, the Government intervened to secure its passage. This Bill provided that vasectomy operations could be carried out under the National Health Service for men wishing to limit their families in this way. The Bill was widely supported in both main parties, but also had its opponents, some vocal and determined, one of whom was the Conservative Member for Yarmouth, Anthony Fell. When the Lords amendments to the Bill were being discussed in the Commons on 16 June 1972, Anthony Fell spoke for an hour and succeeded in delaying the Bill, so that not all the amendments had been voted upon by the end of the time allotted to private Members' bills. The Bill seemed to be lost. The Government decided, however, to intervene on the side of the Bill's sponsors.

It is interesting to note the position adopted by the Leader of the House at the time. In a letter to Philip Whitehead, quoted in *The Times* of 18 October 1972, Robert Carr said that the Government would table a motion to enable a division to be taken in the House on the outstanding Lords amendments to the Bill. He emphasized that he fully recognized 'the importance of the need to avoid any repetition of the situation which developed under the last Government in connection with the provision of government time, on a selective basis, for private Members' bills'. He said that his decision was a breach in the line that the Government had been taking but that he was satisfied that 'the House can be given an opportunity to come to a conclusion here without jeopardizing our position in relation to private Members' bills generally'.

Robert Carr was therefore saying that the Government was, exceptionally, giving assistance to the Bill on the grounds that it had so nearly completed all its stages and that it enjoyed a wide measure of support. But the Heath Government was also to relax its stand, in the following session, on William Hamilton's Anti-Discrimination Bill. This Bill had been talked out on Second Reading on 2 February 1973, as had already occurred at Second Reading in the previous session. The Bill proposed to make it illegal to discriminate in employment, or training, on grounds of sex, and provided for the establishment of an Anti-Discrimination Board which would attempt to bring about conciliation between complainants and employers, or, if this failed, to prosecute employers. The Bill was actively supported by many women's organizations and had the approval of a large section of Labour Members and of a significant proportion of Conservative Members.

The Labour Opposition decided to give time for discussion of the Bill on one of its 'Opposition Days' in the week following 2 February. This would not, however, have secured the Bill a second reading without the co-operation of the Heath Government. Ministers agreed to put down a formal vote for a small sum of money to be paid to the Department of Employment. This procedural device allowed the Bill to be debated and secured its second reading.

The Government then asked the Commons to appoint a select committee to consider how discrimination between the sexes in matters such as employment and education could be eliminated. The Government undertook itself to introduce legislation following the report from the select committee. In July 1973 the six-man Select Committee, which included William Hamilton, reported that legislation on the lines of his Bill should be introduced. In the same month the House of Lords gave a third reading to Lady Seear's Sex Discrimination Bill. The change of government after the February 1974 general election gave the Wilson Government the opportunity to introduce a reform of this kind. In October 1974 the Queen's speech announced that a bill to end sex discrimination would be introduced in the session 1974–75.

On two occasions, therefore, the Heath Government departed from its announced policy of not finding extra time for controversial private Members' bills in the way the Wilson Government had done. These were clearly exceptions since we find Douglas Houghton,

Labour Member for Sowerby and Chairman of the Parliamentary Labour Party, writing to *The Times* on 24 July 1973 to protest against the Government's failure to find time to complete discussion of two private Members' bills which were not able to secure a third reading owing to the obstructive tactics of their critics. These were Houghton's own Bill to improve control over experiments on live animals and Neil McBride's Bill to provide for more effective control of atmospheric pollution.[10]

There was clearly a broad party division between Labour and Conservative Members in the House on this matter. Labour Members in the main argued in Douglas Houghton's words that if the House of Commons approved 'the general objects of a particular measure on second reading, Parliament should not be frustrated by procedural stratagems or deliberate obstruction from reaching a final conclusion on the bill'.[11]

Many Conservative Members, on the other hand, argued that for governments to do this was to take sides and, in effect, to sponsor legislation which was then only in a formal sense private Members' legislation. That, in practice, this was government legislation flying under false colours. In view of this divergence of opinion it is likely that we shall see a different attitude towards controversial private Members' bills during the lifetimes of Labour and Conservative governments. During Labour periods it may be easier for private Members to get controversial bills on to the statute book than during Conservative periods of office. In real terms, however, this does amount to an increased role for private Members in introducing legislation.

When we look at legislation introduced by the government the picture is also unclear. Between 1966 and 1970 some of the measures introduced by the Wilson Government were extensively amended during their passage through Parliament. For example, the Transport Bill was modified by around 700 amendments carried in the Commons and the Lords. Many of these, of course, were government amendments, but the legislative process did facilitate very thorough consideration of the Bill and incorporation of numerous changes to meet points raised by back-benchers. Certain other major government measures, or projects for legislation, were withdrawn in response to criticism. The Parliament (No. 2) Bill, which proposed a number of major changes in the composition and powers of the House of Lords, was withdrawn after it had run into heavy opposition from the left-wing of the Labour Party, led by Michael Foot, and from right-wing Conservatives, whose outstanding spokesman was Enoch Powell.[12] In the same session, 1968–69, the Wilson Government's original project for trade-union legislation, embodied in the White Paper 'In Place of Strife', was abandoned in the face of concerted opposition from a large majority of the Parliamentary Labour Party, from the trade unions, and from a section within the Government itself. Back-bench Members seemed at this time to be assertive in their attitude to government proposals and remarkably effective in securing their modification, or abandonment.

The relationship between the Government and the Commons seemed to change radically after the Conservative victory at the 1970 general election. The new Prime Minister had indicated that in his view some of the concessions made by the Wilson Government to back-bench opinion were a sign of weakness. In his foreword to the Conservative Party's Election Manifesto in 1970 Edward Heath had said, 'Once a decision is made the Prime Minister and his colleagues should have the courage to stick to it. There has been too much running away lately. Courage and honesty are essential in politics, and it is high time that we saw them again.'[13]

In conformity with this attitude, the Heath Government took up an inflexible position on two of the main government measures introduced in its first two years of office. Thus, the Industrial Relations Bill, which was a complicated and highly controversial bill, fiercely opposed by the Labour Opposition and the trade unions, was passed without any substantial concession to its critics. The Bill was subjected to a drastic guillotine (allocation of time order) at Committee Stage in the Commons. When the final guillotine fell, on 24 February 1971 at the end of the committee stage, less than 50 of the Bill's 150 clauses had been debated. This was the most drastic use of the guillotine in the Commons since the Second World War.

On the other hand, it could be claimed that the Parliamentary Labour Party had made its root-and-branch opposition to the Bill clear from the outset, and it was to be expected that Labour Members would use every possible parliamentary device to try and prevent the Bill from becoming law. A guillotine would therefore have had to be imposed at some stage. The fact that the Bill was taken at Committee Stage on the floor of the House necessitated imposition of a more drastic guillotine, since protracted debates on the floor of the House hold up the whole parliamentary timetable, whereas long days of debate in Standing Committee are not such a serious problem from the government's point of view.

It was surprising, in fact, that the Heath Government agreed to take the Bill on the floor of the House, as the modern convention is that only bills of constitutional importance need to be taken there. The Industrial Relations Bill was not a constitutional bill although it was of first-rate political importance. However, other highly controversial bills, such as the measures nationalizing transport, and iron and steel, had been taken in standing committee since 1945.

What we must note was that the Industrial Relations Bill was not adequately debated in the Commons, owing to the intensity of Labour opposition and the imposition of the guillotine. Thus, when the Bill became law and went into effect, it could be argued that it was an imposed measure, in the sense that it had not undergone the regular parliamentary process of discussion and compromise to which a measure of major reform is normally subjected. Furthermore, the proposals in the Bill had not been discussed by the Department of Employment and the trade unions before the Bill reached the House. It is true that the Government had offered consultation on its proposals and that the T.U.C. had rejected this. But then, was the Government wise to go ahead with proposals which made such fundamental changes in the law relating to trade unions and collective bargaining?

In the short term, the operation of the new Act led, in the summer of 1972, to a fine of £55,000 being imposed on the Transport and General Workers Union by the Industrial Relations Court which had been set up by the Act, and to the imprisonment of five dockers who defied an order of the Court. This provoked a national dock strike and a wave of sympathy strikes by other unions. The crisis was only brought to an end by the intervention of the Official Solicitor who secured the release of the imprisoned men.

In April 1973 the Commission on Industrial Relations in its annual report took stock of the operation of the Act in its first year. It concluded, in the words of *The Times*, that the Act had 'not produced the expected results in two key areas: abolition of the "closed shop" system and legal enforceability of labour contracts'.[14] Closed-shop agreements continued to be widespread, and effective, although they were void under the Act. The great majority of labour agreements were not legally enforceable because the unions saw to it that a clause was inserted in each agreement making it not legally binding. The Act seemed therefore to be largely inoperative, and to constitute a cause of friction in industrial relations, rather than a means of improving them.

Was the Industrial Relations Act, and the manner of its passage, a special case, or were there similar examples of inflexibility on the part of the Heath Government regarding its legislative programme? In a sense, the European Communities Bill provides a further example. This Bill, which was of the most far-reaching constitutional importance since it gave legislative effect to Britain's adherence to the European Economic Community, was discussed at great length in the Commons in the session 1971–72, but was not amended in any way. There were some close divisions, and throughout the proceedings the Heath Government faced the threat that the Bill might be thrown out, or emasculated, by the combined action of Conservative Anti-Marketeers and Labour Members, the majority of whom were consistently opposed to the Bill. But the Labour Pro-Marketeers, by abstaining, or in some cases voting with the Government, helped to ensure the Bill's passage.

These two examples of major government measures which were forced through with little or no concession to Opposition opinion might be held to indicate that the Heath style of government was more authoritarian than that of his immediate Prime Ministerial predecessors, whether Labour or Conservative. There was, in fact, a good deal of talk in the first two years of the Heath administration of 'the end of consensus government'. The abolition of the Prices and Incomes Board, soon after the Heath Government took office, and the apparent policy of confrontation with the trade unions were a marked breach of continuity with the previous government, and seemed to give little scope for compromise or the attainment of anything near consensus.

On some issues, however, the Government's attitude became more conciliatory, and on a number of government bills it proved willing to accept important amendments. For example, the Local Government Bill was extensively amended in its passage through Parliament in the session 1971–72. A valuable new provision was written into the Bill to ensure that all committees of the new county and district authorities would normally be open to the public. Numerous changes of detail were also made in the geographic pattern of new counties and districts established by the Bill. For example, after a campaign in the Commons and the Lords, the Government bowed to the opinion that the Isle of Wight should remain as a separate county in the new local government structure.[15]

In the session 1972–73, a major amendment was inserted in the Government's Bill at Report Stage to establish a new airport and seaport at Maplin in the Thames estuary. The amendment provided that the whole project should be reconsidered if the Civil Aviation Authority recommended that technological and other developments made it unnecessary. The amendment was moved by Conservative back-benchers and carried, against the Government, by the combined vote of the Labour Opposition and 17 Conservatives. After the general election of February 1974 the Wilson Government decided to abandon the project.

From February to October 1974 Labour formed the Government but could not command a majority in the Commons. We might expect to find that this would be a period of low legislative output, but in fact the output was considerable. No fewer than 35 government bills were passed in this short session. Some of them, such as the Trade Union and Labour Relations Bill, which repealed the Conservatives' Industrial Relations Act, were highly controversial. There were special reasons for the success of the minority Labour Government in getting much of its legislation through

For some months after the general election the Conservative Opposition was in a low state of morale. Edward Heath had gambled for high stakes in calling an election well before expiry of the Parliament, and specifically on the issue of 'Who governs?'—the lawful government or the miners, who by their industrial action were, in his view, challenging the government's authority. The fact that he lost the election and that the incoming Labour Government speedily settled with the miners and ended the three-day week which the Conservative Government had imposed in order to conserve fuel, undermined Heath's popularity severely. By contrast, the minority Labour Government stood high in the opinion polls and could in effect say to the Conservative Opposition, 'We dare you to throw out our legislation, if you do we will go to the country and come back with a big majority.'

Significantly, when in June 1974 the Labour lead in the opinion polls began to decline, the Conservative and Liberal Oppositions became much more active. They carried some major amendments to the Trade Union and Labour Relations Bill, and prevented the Commons from striking out certain further amendments which the Lords had inserted against the wishes of the Labour Government. These amendments had the effect of frustrating the Labour Government's desire to legalize the 'closed shop' in industry.

The Wilson Government also suffered several defeats at the hands of the Conservatives and Liberals on the Finance Bill. In June the Government's proposal to refund £10 million of tax paid by the unions who had failed to register under the Conservatives' Industrial Relations Act was thrown out. Other amendments to the Bill which were carried against them included provisions reducing corporation tax liability for small companies, and a reduction in the rate of pool betting duty on sporting organizations and charities.

When Labour won an over-all majority in the October 1974 general election, it set about reversing some of these defeats. The Trade Union and Labour Relations (Amendment) Bill, which was given a second reading in the Commons on 3 December 1974, proposed to make the closed shop legal again. It also repealed certain other provisions of the Trade Union and Labour Relations Bill which had been inserted by the Opposition parties in the 1974 session. For example, workers were accorded the right to strike over events in other countries, even in cases where they were only indirectly affected by the action of international companies. Similarly, in the 1974–75 session, the Finance Bill revived the provision for repayment of tax to the unions which did not register under the Industrial Relations Act.

The Queen's speech at the opening of Parliament in October 1974 had envisaged an ambitious programme of legislation, including measures to regulate extraction of oil from the North Sea, to nationalize the shipping and aircraft industries, to establish planning agreements with industry, and to set up a National Enterprise Board. With the small over-all majority of three or four which the Wilson Government then enjoyed it was doubtful whether this legislation would be passed without the Government having to make some concessions to the Opposition and to minority views. On the other hand, Labour Governments with small majorities have, on previous occasions such as in the 1964–66 Parliament, shown that they can often organize steady support in the lobbies for their measures because they have a higher proportion of full-time M.P.s in their ranks than the Conservatives have. Any whittling-away of the Labour majority through defeats at by-elections might, however, seriously weaken the Government's position.

Therefore, when we survey the relationship between governments and the Commons on government bills, during these nine years from 1966 to 1975, what emerges is that the high-handed behaviour of the Heath Government on its Industrial Relations and European Communities Bills was exceptional. On several of its other measures, the Heath Government was ready enough to make concessions and, on some bills, concessions were forced upon it by the action of its own back-benchers. The Labour Government of 1966–70 had even more trouble from its back-benchers, and had to withdraw its initial proposals for trade union legislation and its Bill reforming the House of Lords. Since the February 1974 general election, Labour's lack of an over-all majority, and then its small majority, have strengthened the possibility of defeats for the Government in its legislative programme. We may sum up by saying that in relation to private Members' bills the back-bencher now enjoys, particularly during Labour administrations, a more important initiating role than he did in the twenty-year period following the Second World War. In relation to government bills he can still play an important part in the legislative process.

Party Discipline in this Period

We may well reflect that it could scarcely be otherwise, since back-benchers continue to be generally more active and assertive than back-bench Members were before the Second World War, and certainly than they were in the nineteenth century. In this period back-benchers have continued to play a lively part in party specialist groups and committees, and in the Parliamentary Labour Party, and the Conservative 1922 Committee. What is more, the ties of party discipline have, if anything, been loosened rather than tightened since 1966.

When Richard Crossman was Leader of the House between 1966 and 1968, he and the Labour Chief Whip, John Silkin, made a conscious effort to lessen the impact of party discipline in the Parliamentary Labour Party. In so doing he was putting into practice the view he had advanced in his preface to the Fontana edition of Bagehot's *The English Constitution*, that party discipline in the Commons provided too powerful a buttress for the power of the Prime Minister, and needed to be relaxed.[16] In February 1968, at the suggestion of Crossman and Silkin, and with the active support of Douglas Houghton who had become chairman of the Parliamentary Labour Party the preceding year, the P.L.P. approved a new Code of Conduct. This provided for a less strict system of internal discipline on P.L.P. Members than had applied in the past.

The Code distinguished three degrees of discipline. The mildest was a reprimand which could be issued by the Chief Whip alone. More serious was suspension of the whip, which had to be approved by a full meeting of the P.L.P. acting on the recommendation of the P.L.P. Committee, when Labour is in Opposition, or of the Liaison Committee, when the Party is in office. Most serious of all was withdrawal of the whip, which could result in expulsion from the Party. Withdrawal of the whip could be decided on under the same conditions as suspension of the whip. Suspension or withdrawal of the whip could only be applied against Members who voted against the Party decision, and not against those who abstained.

In fact, even this more relaxed code of discipline was not applied in the fierce controversies which were to divide the P.L.P. over 'In Place of Strife' in 1969, and over entry into the European Economic Community in 1971 and 1972. The Wilson Government's White Paper, 'In Place of Strife', was so strongly opposed by elements in the P.L.P., as well as by the trade unions, that it had to be abandoned. It was apparent that the P.L.P. would not support legislation which could involve the fining and imprisonment of strikers. The Code of Conduct could not have been invoked because the vote in the Parliamentary Party meeting would have gone against the Prime Minister. Wilson had therefore no alternative but to beat a strategic retreat on the question, particularly since a number of his Cabinet colleagues were opposing him.

On the Common Market controversy the majority of Members of the P.L.P. were opposed to entry into the European Economic Community on the terms negotiated by the Heath administration. This was the position taken by Wilson as Labour Leader and it had the support of a large majority in the P.L.P., and of a majority at the Labour Party Conference. The P.L.P. did not, however, invoke the Code of Conduct against Labour Members who voted to approve the Heath Government's decision to join the E.E.C. On 28 October 1971 no less than 69 Labour Common Marketeers voted with the Government on this issue, and against the Labour leadership. There was safety in numbers, particularly since the 69 included the Chairman of the P.L.P., Douglas Houghton, and several former Ministers, including Roy Jenkins, Harold Lever, Michael Stewart, and Shirley Williams. The minority was clearly too large and influential to be coerced.

The Common Market episode, whatever one may think of the merits of the arguments for and against entry, helped to make the Labour Parliamentary Party less monolithic than it had been previously. Only one constituency party attempted to apply sanctions against one of the pro-Common Market minority, and this was the Lincoln Labour Party. Its announcement that it would not readopt Dick Taverne at the next general election initially rebounded on its own head. Taverne resigned his seat, and fought and won the ensuing by-election against the official Labour candidate. He held on to the seat at the February 1974 general election, but was defeated in October 1974 by the official Labour candidate.

On the Conservative side of the House a similar degree of tolerance extended to the minority of Conservative Members who consistently campaigned and voted against entry into the Common Market. Thus on 28 October 1971 a group of 39 Conservatives voted against the European Economic Communities Bill. This group opposed the Bill at every stage, but there was never any question of disciplinary sanctions being used against them by the Conservative Party. Moreover, no Conservative Association in the constituencies refused to readopt a Member on account of his anti-Common Market position.

Reform of the Legislative Process

There has been a good deal of discussion of reform of the legislative process in these years, but few changes of note have been made. The major changes were made in the years immediately following the Second World War, when the Attlee Government decided to put into effect a scheme prepared by a group of Ministers in the wartime Coalition for sending all major bills, except constitutional bills, to standing committee at committee stage. The implementation of this reform led to a great increase in the output of legislation, without lowering the effectiveness of parliamentary scrutiny. Indeed, it came to be accepted that discussion of a bill in standing committee often resulted in a closer scrutiny of the bill and in the introduction of more useful amendments than was possible in committee of the whole House.[17] This intensive use of standing committees soon became an accepted practice and, as we have seen, it was an exceptional step to take the Industrial Relations Bill at Committee Stage on the floor of the House in the session 1970–71.

Yet a number of questions regarding the legislative process remain controversial. Should better methods be employed of allocating time on a bill which is guillotined? Should the Commons give less attention to the detail of legislation? Should the Commons be given a bigger part in the pre-legislative process, before bills are drafted? Should the scope for private Members' bills be increased? Does the Commons have adequate control over delegated legislation? All these issues have been discussed by the Select Committee on Procedure in recent years. The conclusions of the Committee appeared in July 1971 in the important report, 'The Process of Legislation'.[18]

Although it is a long report, which with minutes of evidence and appendices runs to 358 pages, and although it makes many detailed suggestions for improvement, it cannot be said to have had as yet much impact on the way in which the Commons deals with legislation. The Procedure Committee looked with favour on the idea of pre-legislation committees. It reported that evidence given to them (notably by the Study of Parliament Group), had made a strong case for the regular use of pre-legislation committees to enable Parliament to exercise influence on the Government at an early stage in the process of decision-taking on legislation.[19] It recommended that in future regular use should be made of such committees.

However, this recommendation has only been followed on two occasions in this period. First, when a joint committee of the Commons and the Lords considered the whole question of the censorship of stage plays before George Strauss introduced his Bill for the abolition of censorship, which became law as the Theatres Act in 1968. Second, as we have seen, when a government bill to end discrimination on grounds of sex was preceded by examination of the question in a select committee of the Commons, in 1973. These were, however, both rather exceptional cases.

The report made three constructive suggestions for easing the path for private Members' bills. It suggested that the ballot for private Members' bills should be held before the summer adjournment of the House instead of in the autumn at the beginning of the new session.[20] This would give the lucky Members who come high in the ballot much more time to decide their topic of legislation and to prepare the content of the bill. The report also proposed that government draftsmen should draft the bills being prepared by the ten leading Members in the ballot. As an alternative, 'the Government should reimburse to those private Members the fees charged by outside draftsmen'.[21] Finally, they proposed the abolition of counting the House, so that opponents of a private Members' bill could not bring about its defeat by calling a sudden count, thus ending the business of the day if forty Members could not be found to go into the division lobby. As a safeguard the Committee recommended that if it should appear at a division on a bill that forty Members were not present, the next business would be taken and the bill would not proceed.[22] At the end of 1974 action had been taken on two of these proposals. Financial assistance was being provided by the Government to the ten leading private Members in the ballot to assist them in drafting their bills, and the old rule which enabled a sudden count to be called to defeat bills had been abandoned.

Another recommendation made in the report was that the Government should appoint a committee including Members and Officers of both Houses to review the form in which legislation is drafted.[23] The aim was to get greater simplicity and clarity in the language of legislation and in this way to assist Members in understanding the content of bills and in moving appropriate amendments. The Heath Government acted on this suggestion in 1973. In May of that year a Committee on the Preparation of Legislation was appointed with Sir David Renton as chairman. The Committee reported in May 1975, making many proposals for improved drafting of statute law to make it more intelligible to the ordinary citizen. It emphasized the need for the recruitment and training of more parliamentary draftsmen. It warmly approved of the increasing readiness of governments to issue Green Papers, in advance of legislation, and recommended that the practice should be further extended.

Delegated Legislation

The Procedure Committee was concerned about the control of delegated legislation. The author concluded in 1967 that at that time the House of Commons exercised more effective control over delegated legislation than it had in the 1920s.[24] This control was maintained by the activities of the Select Committee on Statutory Instruments, scrutinizing delegated legislation lying before the House, and by the readiness of back-benchers to put down 'prayers' to annul instruments, some of which the Select Committee had reported to the House as being procedurally dubious (exceeding the powers given to a Minister, having retrospective effect, imposing a tax, etc.).

By 1971 the situation had deteriorated considerably because, in the words of the Procedure Committee's report, the

> failure of Governments of both major Parties to find time to debate Prayers has led to a breakdown of part of the process of legislation—as Parliament is not being given the opportunity to consider negative Instruments made under Acts which were passed on the understanding that such an opportunity would exist in every case. The problem, although already serious, will become worse as more and more legislation is passed providing for its detailed implementation for which in turn the flood of legislation leaves annually less and less time for debate. . . . Your Committee believe it to be of cardinal importance that the House should appreciate the gravity of the inroads into its power of control of legislation.[25]

The Procedure Committee recommended that a joint committee of the Commons and Lords should be appointed to 'inquire into the procedures and practice by which the control of each House over delegated legislation is exercised, and to report on how they might be improved'.[26] Such a committee was set up with a former Conservative Home Secretary, Lord Brooke, as its chairman. Six other peers were members of the committee, including Lord Diamond, who had been a Labour M.P. from 1945 to 1970 and Chief Secretary to the Treasury in the Wilson Government, Lord Diplock, who is a Lord of Appeal in Ordinary, Baroness Sharp, who was Permanent Secretary at the Ministry of Housing and Local Government from 1955 to 1966, and Lord Wade, who was the Liberal M.P. for Huddersfield West from 1950 to 1964. The 7 peers on the committee were matched by 7 Members of the Commons, 4 of whom were Conservatives, Brian Batsford, Michael Hamilton, James Ramsden, and David Walder, and 3 Labour, Albert Booth, Denzil Davies, and George Lawson.

The Joint Committee issued its report in August 1972, from which emerged two principal features of interest.[27] First, the committee confirmed that the time given to delegated legislation in the Commons had been severely 'squeezed', so that a considerable proportion of prayers to annul was not being discussed. In 1953 a Committee of the Commons under the chairmanship of Clement Davies had recommended that debates on prayers to annul statutory instruments should be terminated at 11.30 p.m. This was to prevent the Commons from having to sit late into the night, or through the night, discussing prayers. The recommendation was accepted by the Commons and effectively countered a means of obstruction, and harassment of the Government, which had been employed both by the Conservative Opposition between 1950 and 1951 and by Labour in Opposition between 1951 and 1953.[28] The 11.30 rule did, at that time, give adequate scope for discussion of statutory instruments since they are 'exempted business', that is they can be discussed after 10.00 p.m., the time at which the House normally ends its scheduled business, unless Standing Orders have been suspended. The Brooke Committee found that by 1971 government business was so often being taken after 10.00 p.m. that the time which theoretically was available between 10.00 and 11.30 p.m. was frequently already filled up. The Committee suggested various ways in which more time could be found in the Commons for discussion of prayers.

The second principal finding of the Committee was that there was a lack of co-ordination between the work of the House of Lords Special Orders Committee, which examines certain types of statutory instrument, and the Select Committee on Statutory Instruments in the Commons. The Brooke Committee recommended that a joint committee of the two Houses should take over the work of the two committees in considering whether the proper procedure had been applied in the making of statutory instruments: whether there had been an unusual or unexpected use of ministerial powers in making an instrument, whether the instrument claimed to have retrospective effect when this power had not been given to the Minister in the statute, and so on.

In addition to this joint committee of the Lords and Commons, to consider the procedural aspects of delegated legislation, the Brooke Committee also recommended that there should be a Commons Standing Committee to consider the merits of statutory instruments. This committee would debate prayers to annul instruments in certain cases, and debate some, but not all, instruments which require an affirmative resolution in order to come into effect, or to remain in operation. It was proposed that the decisions as to which instruments would be referred to the standing committee would be made in the following ways. All negative instruments which are subject to annulment by a prayer would be referred to the standing committee, unless the Opposition front bench objected through its whips, or 20 or more Members objected in the House. The Government would be empowered to refer affirmative resolutions to the committee, unless objection was made by the Opposition front bench or by 20 Members.

Following the report of the Brooke Committee, in the late summer of 1972 there was an extraordinary hiatus in parliamentary scrutiny of delegated legislation. The Select Committee on Statutory Instruments was not appointed by the Commons at the beginning of the 1972–73 session. The reason for this was that the Government was anticipating that a joint committee of the two Houses would be set up, although this did not in fact take place until February 1973. The committee was given the range of powers recommended by the Brooke Committee, but the Select Committee on Statutory Instruments was not completely superseded by the creation of a joint committee. It still continued to consider those statutory instruments which have a financial aspect, since this is not a matter for the Lords. Thus, in May 1973 the Statutory Instruments Committee reported to the Commons that it had examined instruments regulating import duties, value added tax, etc.[29]

There remained the Brooke Committee's recommendation for a standing committee of the Commons to debate the merits of certain statutory instruments. In a debate on 18 December 1972 the Leader of the House, James Prior, told the Commons that the Government intended to propose the setting-up of such a committee.[30] The idea was given a mixed reception by Members. There was understandably a feeling that the proposed merits committee might be an unsatisfactory substitute for debate in the House on prayers to annul delegated legislation. To meet this feeling James Prior told the Commons that the Government would be prepared for instruments to be discussed in the whole House, where desirable, after 11.30 p.m., provided that there was a time-limit for any such debate of 1½ hours. The standing committee of the House to debate statutory instruments was first set up in 1973 and has since met regularly.

European Community Secondary Legislation

The Brooke Committee had given some consideration in its report to the problems which would be created for the House by entry to the European Economic Community, in its scrutiny of legislation issued by the Commission and Council of Ministers of the E.E.C. When the European Communities Bill became law in 1972 these problems tended to overshadow the difficulties which the British Parliament was experiencing in controlling delegated legislation issued by its own government. It was soon realized that once the United Kingdom had become a full member of the Community, legislation decided in Brussels would determine important areas of life in this country. Regulations made by the Council of Ministers, which are of general application, are binding in their entirety and are directly applicable in all Member States. The Council of Ministers, and the Commission, also issue Directives which Member States are expected to put into effect through their own legislation. However, regulations are of main concern to the Commons because the only way in which M.P.s can influence Community regulations is by finding out what the Commission is proposing to the Council of Ministers, and trying to induce United Kingdom Ministers in the Council to urge modifications to the Commission's proposals.

A Commons committee was therefore set up with a well-known Conservative back-bencher, Sir John Foster, as chairman, to advise the Commons how information about Community legislation could best be secured and transmitted to M.P.s.[31] The committee, known as the Select Committee on European Community Secondary Legislation, included among its members both leading supporters and opponents of entry into the E.E.C. For example, Michael Foot and Peter Shore, on the Labour side, had been prominent in opposing British entry, while Shirley Williams was a committed pro-Marketeer. The committee published its first report early in 1973.[32] This was debated in the Commons on 18 April 1973.

James Prior, the Leader of the House, told the Commons in this debate that the Heath Government accepted two of the committee's recommendations. The first was that the Government should provide explanatory memoranda relating to each legislative proposal made by the Commission to the Council of Ministers. These proposals are available to Members in the Vote Office. It is obviously helpful if the relevant British Ministry can attach to each proposal a statement of its likely effect on this country if adopted. The Government also accepted the recommendation that it should publish, each month, a list of the subjects likely to be dealt with at the next scheduled meetings of the Council.

The Heath Government did not, however, accept two of the committee's recommendations, namely, that there should be a regular statement in the Commons by the Government on the agenda of the Council of Ministers, and that there should be a monthly statement by the Government on the proceedings in the

Council of Ministers. Prior argued that to have a regular statement in the Commons on the agenda of the Council of Ministers would not only be time-consuming, but might diminish the necessary freedom of action of Ministers in negotiations in the Council of Ministers. The Government was opposed to a monthly statement on proceedings in the Council of Ministers because it claimed that it was better for Ministers to report to the Commons when a decision had been reached in the Council, for example on the level of farm prices, rather than to report after each meeting regardless of whether agreement had been reached or not.

This statement did not satisfy the chairman of the committee, Sir John Foster, and many M.P.s spoke of their keen dissatisfaction with the situation. More than one M.P. referred to the fact that the Council of Ministers is, in practice, the legislature of the E.E.C. although it does not meet in public and its debates are not published. Neil Marten commented: 'I regard this as a mild form of scandal. We should have a full Hansard-type report of what the Ministers of Agriculture have been saying.'[33] The objection to this proposal would be of course that as the Council of Ministers is a place for negotiation between Ministers of the participating States, if its meetings were open to the public, what would happen in practice is that the real negotiations would go on in private before the Council met.

Several Members also voiced dissatisfaction with the European Parliament. Its chief role is to scrutinize the activities of the Commission and the Council of Ministers but, as Sir Geoffrey de Freitas pointed out, the official report of debates in the European Parliament is not published until 4 to 6 weeks after a session of the Parliament.[34] Neil Marten commented that 'the documents which we receive from the European Assembly are largely incomprehensible.' The remarks of the British representative are printed in English, and those of the Dutch representative who follows him are printed in Dutch, without translation. Further, the text of parliamentary questions raised in the Assembly is given, but the answers to parliamentary questions are not printed until months later. In short, the European Parliament at present leaves much to be desired as a channel for information about the European Commission's proposals to the Council of Ministers.

James Prior, in winding up the debate, looked forward to the second report of the Select Committee on European Community

Secondary Legislation which, it was hoped, would suggest new machinery in the Commons for scrutinizing proposals made by the Commission to the Council of Ministers. The report, covering the session 1972–73, was published on 25 October 1973, and its main recommendations were soon put into effect. It suggested that a new committee should be set up with the function of sifting all the draft proposals made by the Commission of the E.E.C. to the Council of Ministers, and of informing the Commons of those proposals which in its opinion were of legal or political importance and worthy of further consideration by the Commons.[35] This would be a new type of committee, neither a standing committee, nor a select committee, for its essential role would be participation in legislation. It should have not less than 9, and not more than 15, members and should meet at least fortnightly during sittings of the House, and perhaps once or twice during the summer recess. It should be served by Clerks of the House, and also have the advice of an official with the status and qualifications of the Speaker's Counsel. This official would assist the committee in determining which of the Commission's proposals would effect, or require, changes in United Kingdom law, and what those changes would be.[36]

A committee on these lines was appointed by the Commons on 7 May 1974. Its terms of reference were 'to consider draft proposals by the Commission of the European Community for secondary legislation and other documents published by the Commission for submission to the Council of Ministers and to report their opinion as to whether such proposals or other documents raised questions of legal or political importance . . .' The fact that the Committee was instructed to consider such 'other documents', including the general budget of the E.E.C., gave rise to its somewhat curious title, the 'Committee on European Secondary Legislation etc.'

The Committee has 16 members. As its first chairman it chose John Davies, Conservative M.P. for Knutsford, who, as Chancellor of the Duchy of Lancaster from 1972 to 1974, was the Minister in the Heath Government with special responsibility for European affairs and was the British representative on the Council of Ministers of the E.E.C. After the October 1974 general election, the Committee was reappointed, and again elected John Davies as its chairman. The Committee includes supporters and opponents of continued British membership of the E.E.C.: John Mackintosh, for example, Labour M.P. for Berwick and East Lothian, is an ardent supporter of the E.E.C., and Neil Marten, the M.P. for Banbury, is one of the most active opponents of British membership on the Conservative side of the House.

The Committee completed three reports during the short 1974 session and recommended that twenty draft proposals by the E.E.C. Commission were of such importance that they should be given further consideration by the Commons. It also examined a large number of other proposals and recommended that they did not raise questions of legal or political importance. The Committee is working effectively, but the worrying feature is that the Commons has been finding it very difficult to set aside time to debate draft E.E.C. proposals which the Committee has recommended as worthy of further consideration. James Callaghan told the Commons in June 1974 that normally all such designated proposals would be discussed in the Commons and that the government would not allow them to progress in the Council of Ministers until they had been debated in the Commons. The main category which might have to be exempted from this undertaking would be provisions on agriculture which sometimes have to be put into effect too quickly to permit prior discussions in the House.

In practice, the time allocated for debate in the Commons has been far from satisfactory. One and a half hours are provided for this purpose at the end of some parliamentary days. When, for example, some important E.E.C. proposals for a Community energy policy were discussed in the Commons on 3 December 1974, John Davies, the chairman of the Committee on European Secondary Legislation etc., described the debate as 'manifestly inadequate'. After the allotted ninety minutes were up, there had been only a sketchy discussion of what were far-reaching and important proposals, and no member of the committee had been called to speak in the debate.

The House of Lords also has a European Communities Committee with very similar terms of reference to those of the Commons Committee on European Secondary Legislation etc. The Lords Committee, which was first appointed on 10 April 1974, has 17 members and has Lord Diamond as its chairman. The Lords Committee works through five sub-committees concerned with E.E.C. proposals in the following areas: finance, economics, and regional policy; external trade and treaties; environment, social, health, employment, education, and research; agriculture, fisheries and food, energy, and transport; law. Each sub-committee has co-opted other peers with specialized interests in the area covered by the sub-committee.

In a special report published on 18 June 1974 the Lords Committee described its organization and activities.[37] It pointed to the large number of draft proposals which the Committee had had to consider, a total of 403 by the end of July 1974.[38] The Committee commented that although this did constitute a heavy work load it was not beyond its capabilities. The Lords and Commons Committees on E.E.C. draft proposals make available to each other the text of evidence submitted to them by Ministers and civil servants, thus avoiding some duplication of work. There is also a certain element of division of labour between the committees. Thus, the Lords Committee has decided, in principle, to leave to the Commons Committee the task of scrutinizing the Community budget, and other Community proposals of a fiscal nature.

The Referendum Issue

The question whether parliamentary sovereignty could be reconciled with membership of the E.E.C. became a major issue in the referendum campaign in the summer of 1975. This referendum was of such great constitutional interest that it is valuable to consider the circumstances in which it took place, and to try to assess its effect on the British political system.

To hold a referendum on a constitutional issue was a major innovation in Britain. There had been such a referendum recently in Northern Ireland. In the 1970 Parliament legislation was approved for a referendum in which the people of Northern Ireland were asked to say whether or not they wished to remain in the United Kingdom; the result was a large majority for staying in. Furthermore, Parliament had on a number of occasions authorized the holding of referenda on local issues. For example, legislation still in force provides for local referenda at periodic intervals in the Welsh counties on the issue of whether or not public houses may open on Sundays.

No referendum on a national issue had, however, been held in Britain. The principle of consulting the people directly on constitutional questions was, of course, well established but such consultations had taken place previously through a specially called general election. Thus in 1832 William IV agreed to a second general election being held to decide whether there was sufficient support among the electorate for the Reform Bill. Similarly in 1910 a second general election was held to determine whether George V should be ready to create sufficient peers to secure the passage of the Parliament Bill, limiting the powers of the House of Lords.

The Labour Party had committed itself to consulting the British people on continued membership of the E.E.C. in its manifesto at the February 1974 general election. It left open, however, the question as to whether the consultation would take place 'through a General Election or a Consultative Referendum'. The Labour criticisms of the Heath Government's actions on the E.E.C. were two. First, Labour claimed that the Conservative Government had not negotiated satisfactory entry terms and second, that Edward Heath, as Prime Minister, had taken the United Kingdom into the E.E.C. without gaining 'the full-hearted consent of the British people' which he had undertaken to secure. Heath's position was that this consent had been made clear by the majorities accorded in Parliament to the European Communities Bill in 1972. The Labour leadership claimed that the vote in Parliament did not necessarily reflect the views of the British electorate who should have an opportunity to make their views known, particularly since at the 1970 general election both the major parties were committed only to negotiate entry into the E.E.C., not to legislate for entry.

Soon after the minority Wilson Government was formed in March 1974 James Callaghan, as Foreign Secretary, began renegotiation of the terms of Britain's accession to the Community. In March 1975 the process of renegotiation was completed and the Wilson Government announced that it would recommend to the British people that the terms were acceptable and that they should approve continued United Kingdom membership of the E.E.C. At the October 1974 general election Labour had still kept open the possibility that consultation might take place either through a general election or a referendum. In February 1975 a White Paper announced that legislation would be introduced into Parliament to provide for a referendum on continued membership of the E.E.C. The Referendum Bill was approved by Parliament in May 1975 and the referendum took place on 8 June 1975.

The decision to hold a referendum had been strongly opposed on many sides. Within the Labour Party Roy Jenkins had resigned from the Labour Shadow Cabinet when it decided to propose a referendum as a possible method for consulting the people on the E.E.C. question. He subsequently came to accept the referendum and campaigned strongly for a 'Yes' vote. John Mackintosh, from the Labour back-benches, maintained all along that the referendum was constitutionally a nonsense. On the Conservative side the majority of Conservatives were also critical of the idea of a referendum, although the anti-Common Market minority was enthusiastic for it. The majority of Liberal M.P.s took the view that a referendum was unnecessary.

The criticism of the referendum on constitutional grounds took two main lines of argument. The first was that a referendum was incompatible with the 'Burkean' interpretation of the role of an M.P.: that he is elected to make up his own mind according to his conscience and his conception of the public interest. He is not subject to recall by his constituents but is only held responsible at election time for the way in which he has represented the constituency during the lifetime of a Parliament. Linked with this view is the argument that on an issue as complicated as the Common Market, it is appropriate for an M.P. to decide and not the ordinary person who is relatively ill-informed and ill-equipped. The second main line of argument was that for the Government to take the Common Market issue to a referendum was to abdicate responsibility.

The first line of argument was contested on the grounds that the question of continued membership of the E.E.C. was of such fundamental importance to each elector, since it affected the whole future of the country and its constitutional arrangements, that each elector should have the right to take part in the decision. Since experts of all kinds, whether economists, lawyers, political scientists etc., were divided on the merits of the issue, it could scarcely be argued that this was an occasion when the experts should decide. The supporters of the referendum conceded that it was important that the public should receive the maximum possible information on the issues and that a major attempt should be made to secure as high a poll as possible.

Many advocates of a referendum were aware that referenda work best in countries like Switzerland where a high degree of interest is normally shown in the issues and the media give good coverage to their discussion. On the other hand, in certain states of the United States where referenda are used, the poll is normally very low and interest groups often play an undue part in influencing the result.

Nearer home the periodic referenda on Sunday-opening in Wales do not excite much interest or a high poll. But part of the reason for this is that the local authorities do not inform each elector that the referendum is taking place, and virtually the only media for informing the public of the issues are the local pub or the pulpit in the nonconformist chapel.

A great deal of care was taken at the 1975 referendum to see that the public was informed and to try to ensure a high poll. Local authorities sent every elector a 'where to vote card' with the question he would be asked to reply to in the referendum. Each household was sent, at public expense, three pamphlets: one a statement from the Government recommending a 'Yes' vote, one from the Britain in Europe organization recommending 'Yes', and one from the National Referendum Campaign asking people to vote 'No'. The Government bought a great deal of advertising space in the newspapers to publicize the mechanics of the referendum.

Each of the 'umbrella' organizations, Britain in Europe and the National Referendum Campaign, received £125,000 from public funds towards its campaign. In fact, Britain in Europe clearly had much more to spend than its opponents, as evidenced by the greater number of Britain in Europe advertisements appearing in the Press and its more lavish and professional programmes on television. Nevertheless, an equal amount of time was allocated to both organizations on television. Some of the discussion programmes organized by the B.B.C. and ITV were of exceptional interest. The final B.B.C. discussion on Panorama between Roy Jenkins and Tony Wedgwood Benn was at a high level, as well as being compulsive viewing for anyone at all interested in the campaign. The final programme on ITV, which was in the form of a parliamentary debate between the advocates and opponents of staying in the E.E.C., provided the fascinating spectacle of Peter Shore and Enoch Powell appearing on one side of the 'House' and Edward Heath, David Steel, and Roy Hattersley on the other.

All this information and discussion on the media had the intended effect of heightening interest in the referendum. The poll on referendum day, at 63·2 per cent, was much higher than many had expected. In view of the fact that in most areas the party organizations were not in action getting out the vote, this percentage poll was surprisingly high. A clear majority of voters in the United Kingdom as a whole, 67·2 per cent, voted for staying in the E.E.C. In only two areas were there majorities for the 'Noes': these were the Shetland Islands and the Western Isles. Every other county and region in England, Scotland, and Wales had a 'Yes' majority varying from the 56·3 per cent majority in Fife to the 76·2 per cent in Surrey. Scotland, Wales, and Northern Ireland all produced a majority for 'Yes' although the majority in Northern Ireland, at 52·1 per cent, was much lower than in the United Kingdom as a whole.

The high poll and the comfortable majority in favour of staying in the E.E.C. produced a dramatic change of opinion in the minds of many people about the utility of referenda. But before we consider the possible use of referenda in the future in the United Kingdom, we should examine the other criticism of the referendum: that it represented an abdication of responsibility on the part of the Government. Undeniably it did involve a breach in the convention of collective responsibility. The Wilson Government decided to allow an agreement to differ on the Common Market comparable to the agreement to differ on the introduction of a general tariff in the Ramsay Macdonald Coalition Government in 1932.[39] Members of the Wilson Government were given *carte blanche* to speak in public for or against the referendum, for the duration of the campaign. Roy Jenkins became the president of the Britain in Europe movement, and Tony Wedgwood Benn and Peter Shore, with Enoch Powell, were easily the most prominent exponents of the anti-Common Market case. When Roy Jenkins exclaimed during the campaign that it was hard to believe in Tony Benn's credibility as an economic Minister, it seemed as if a major split in the Labour Cabinet might result. Following the referendum, Harold Wilson carried out a skilful reshuffle in his Cabinet, moving Benn to the Department of Energy, but replacing him at the Department of Industry by another anti-Marketeer, Eric Varley. Defeat in the referendum did not therefore result in victimization of the anti-Marketeers. The one anti-Marketeer who left the Government, Judith Hart, could, it seems, have stayed if she had been willing to accept the Ministry of Transport, in place of the Ministry of Overseas Development.

The breach of collective responsibility was therefore temporary and did not, at any rate in the short run, result in a wholesale resignation of the dissenting Ministers. Such departures from the convention are likely to recur when and if major issues are again decided by referendum. Whether the referendum will be used much in the future is an open question. The Common Market issue was a special case. It was an important constitutional question on which both the major parties were divided. There was a strong argument, therefore, for resolving the issue by means of a referendum. The argument for referenda on ordinary legislation, or on its far-reaching constitutional issues, is not so strong.

NOTES

1 H.C. 282 of 1966–67, Second Report from the Select Committee on Procedure.
2 Op. cit., p. viii.
3 See F. Stacey, *The Government of Modern Britain*, pp. 123–4.
4 *Guardian*, 8 June 1972, report of an interview given by the Speaker to Donald Chapman.
5 H.C. 538 of 1970–71, Second Report from the Select Committee on Procedure: The Process of Legislation, p. vi, para. 4.
6 For an excellent account of the passage of all these private Members' bills see: Peter G. Richards, *Parliament and Conscience* (Allen and Unwin, 1970).
7 Routledge and Kegan Paul, 1956, p. 193.
8 See Peter Richards, op. cit., p. 180.
9 Ibid.
10 Neil McBride was Labour Member for Swansea East from 1963 until his death in 1974.
11 Letter to *The Times*, 24 July 1973.
12 See also on this Bill, pp. 72–81.
13 Conservative Central Office, *A Better Tomorrow:* The Conservative Party Manifesto for the 1970 General Election, p. 1.
14 27 April 1973.
15 For further discussion of the Local Government Act and its provisions see pp. 124–31.
16 Fontana, 1963, pp. 42–56.
17 See on this period, K. C. Wheare, *Government by Committee* (Clarendon Press, 1955), chap. VI; also F. Stacey, op. cit., p. 101. The author has shown in his study of the passage of the Parliamentary Commissioner Bill, 1967, how close a consideration was given to that Bill in Standing Committee, whereas it received only a relatively superficial consideration in the whole House at Report Stage. See F. Stacey, *The British Ombudsman* (Clarendon Press, 1971), pp. 95–191.
18 H.C. 538 of 1970–71, Second Report from the Select Committee on Procedure: The Process of Legislation.
19 Op. cit., p. viii, para. 8.
20 Op. cit., p. xxxv, recommendation (25).
21 Ibid., recommendation (26).
22 Ibid., recommendation (27).
23 Ibid., recommendation (28).
24 F. Stacey, *The Government of Modern Britain*, p. 208.
25 H.C. 538 of 1970–71, p. xxii, para. 42.
26 Op. cit., recommendation (24), p. xxxv.
27 H.L. 184 and H.C. 475 of 1971–72, Report from the Joint Committee on Delegated Legislation.
28 See F. Stacey, *The Government of Modern Britain*, esp. pp. 205–6.
29 See for example, H.C. 185–vi of 1972–73, Sixth Report from the Select Committee on Statutory Instruments.

30 H.C. Deb., vol. 848, col. 1004.
31 Sir John Foster, Q.C., Conservative Member for Northwich, was first elected to the Commons in 1945 and was Under-Secretary for Commonwealth Relations from 1951 to 1954. He is chairman of the executive committee of Justice, the all-party association of lawyers concerned with the liberties of the individual.
32 H.C. 143 of 1972–73, First Report from the Select Committee on European Community Secondary Legislation.
33 H.C. Deb., vol. 855, col. 584.
34 Op. cit., col. 571.
35 H.C. 463–I of 1972–73, Second Report from the Select Committee on European Secondary Legislation, p. xix, para. 69.
36 Ibid., p. xviii, paras. 63–6.
37 H.L. (139), Special Report of the House of Lords European Communities Committee (H.M.S.O., 1974).
38 Ibid., p. vi, para. 4.
39 See F. Stacey, *The Government of Modern Britain*, p. 237.

CHAPTER V

The Attempt to Reform the House of Lords

THIS was the major attempt at reform which failed in these years. The main lines of the White Paper on House of Lords Reform, published by the Wilson Government in November 1968, had been agreed between the leaders of the Labour, Conservative, and Liberal Parties.[1] Yet the Parliament (No. 2) Bill, which was based on the White Paper, was abandoned in April 1969 after protracted discussion at Committee Stage in the Commons in which vigorous opposition to the Bill had been expressed by back-benchers on both sides of the House. Was it precisely because the front-benchers were agreed, that back-benchers were not enamoured of the Bill? Did the Bill fail because the party leaders were themselves not enthusiastic about details of the reform? Were there other factors which contributed to its abandonment? We will try to elucidate these points.

After the constitutional crisis of 1909–11 the Parliament Act of 1911 took away the power of the Lords to defeat or amend financial legislation, and provided that other public bills could become law after two years' delay, without the consent of the Lords. The preamble to the 1911 Act had implied that this was only an interim reform, and that 'a Second Chamber constituted on a popular instead of a hereditary basis' would be established as soon as was practicable.

While no thoroughgoing reform of the Lords has been carried through three partial reforms have been made. The Parliament Act of 1949 reduced the period for which the Lords can delay legislation from two years to one. An all-party conference which had attempted to reach agreement on the composition and powers of a reformed House had broken down in 1948. The Life Peerages Act of 1958 gave the Queen power to create life peers, either men or women. The Peerage Act of 1963 gave to hereditary peers the right to renounce their peerages.[2]

The Labour Manifesto at the 1966 general election stated that a Labour Government, as part of its programme for modernizing Parliament, would introduce legislation 'to safeguard measures approved by the House of Commons from frustration by delay or defeat in the House of Lords'. Discussions on reform of the Lords began in November 1967 between leaders of the Labour, Conservative, and Liberal Parties, and had reached a substantial measure of agreement when, in June 1968, they were called off by the Prime Minister, Harold Wilson. The occasion was the rejection in the Lords of the Southern Rhodesia (United Nations Sanctions) Order, 1968. The Prime Minister was incensed at this refusal by the majority in the Lords to implement United Nations decisions on sanctions against Rhodesia. He took the view that the Conservative leadership in the Lords could have restrained Conservative backbench peers. He has claimed since that 'not since the Parliament Act of 1911 had the Lords deliberately set themselves out to frustrate in this way the executive actions, and in this case actions to fulfil international commitments, of the elected Government'.[3]

The Government then proceeded to round off the nearly completed work of the all-party conference, and in November 1968 published its White Paper on Lords Reform. The composition of the House of Lords as it stood in August 1968 was as follows: 736 hereditary peers by succession, 122 hereditary peers of first creation, 155 life peers (created under the Life Peerages Act, 1958), 23 serving or retired law lords, and 26 bishops.[4] The 736 hereditary peers by succession were therefore more than double the combined figure of hereditary peers of first creation and life peers. In the total membership of the House of 1,062 there was, of course, a very large Conservative majority.

The White Paper proposed that the hereditary basis of membership should be eliminated and that no one party should possess a permanent majority in the Lords. To achieve this, an ingenious system of two-tier membership of the House was suggested. One tier of the House would consist of 'voting' members who would be entitled to speak in debates and vote in divisions. The voting members would comprise hereditary peers of first creation and all the life peers, including the life peers created under the 1958 Act, who regularly attended in the House, the law lords, and the bishops.[5] To them would be added a few of the hereditary peers by succession who, by their previous record, had shown themselves to be active in proceedings of the House. They would be made life peers and thus join the ranks of voting members.

The remainder of the hereditary peers by succession would

become 'non-voting' peers. They could speak in debates but could not record a vote in divisions. This would have been a sensible and civilized arrangement as it would have eliminated the huge, and overwhelmingly Conservative, hereditary vote. At the same time, it would not have excluded hereditary peers altogether from the business of the Lords.

The White Paper also proposed that in normal circumstances the government of the day should be able to secure a working majority in the Lords. To achieve this it suggested a complicated procedure, which was to prove the most controversial feature of the scheme. This was that after each general election the incoming government would be entitled to at least a 10 per cent majority over the combined strengths of the Opposition parties in the Lords, excluding the votes of the cross-bench (non-party) peers. To achieve this, the Government would be entitled to appoint sufficient of its own supporters as life peers. This need not mean a continual increase in the number of voting peers as the White Paper proposed to introduce a retiring age of 72. After a general election all voting peers who had reached the age of 72 in the preceding Parliament would lose their voting rights and be able to attend and speak, but not vote.[6]

The aim would be to have a House of Lords consisting of between 200 and 250 voting peers, not counting the law lords and bishops. Thus, in a House of 230, the Government might have 105 peers, the main Opposition party 80, and the other parties 15. The cross-benchers might number 30 (excluding the law lords and bishops). The cross-benchers would therefore be able to intervene to defeat the government of the day, but it was thought that they would be unlikely to do so frequently, although their intervention could be a safeguard against hasty or high-handed action by the Commons.

The implications of this proposed new system were to come under heavy criticism both in the debate on the White Paper, on 19 November 1968, and in the debates on the Parliament (No. 2) Bill. Criticism in the debate on the White Paper was levelled particularly at the wider powers of patronage given to the Prime Minister under the proposed new system. There were two features of the system which invited attack. First, the procedure for securing a majority for the government of the day, after each general election, would sometimes involve the Prime Minister in creating a larger batch of life peers from his own party than had normally occurred since the passage of the Life Peerages Act, 1958. There would need to be a fairly large creation of Labour peers under the Wilson Government's proposed timetable. Under its proposals, the new system would have come into effect immediately after passage of the Parliament (No. 2) Bill. The section of voting peers in the reformed House would then have had to include 105 Labour peers (following the figure of 230 voting peers taking a Labour, Conservative, or Liberal whip, instanced in the White Paper). Since some of the older Labour peers would lose their voting rights, there would need to be a sizeable creation of Labour peers in order to make up the necessary 105.

The Conservative front-bench favoured a different timing for implementation of the reform, and argued that it should come into effect after the next general election. This they hoped would result in a majority for their own Party in the Commons, entitling the Conservatives to a majority of voting peers in the Lords over all other parties. There would not then have to be such a large creation of Labour peers and, correspondingly, the number of Conservative peers given voting rights would be a good deal larger. This would not cause such a traumatic change in the composition of the Lords from the Conservative point of view: a small majority would replace the previous overwhelming majority, but would still be a Conservative majority.

The second feature of the system which, in the view of critics particularly on the Conservative side, undesirably widened the powers of patronage of the Prime Minister was the proposal in the White Paper to pay voting peers a salary. Harold Wilson, as Premier, would therefore find himself not only recommending the appointment of more Labour supporters as life peers than ever before, but each of these appointments would carry a sizeable salary. There was, in fact, so much criticism of the proposal in the debate on the White Paper that the Wilson Government decided to modify it. In the debate on the second reading of the Parliament (No. 2) Bill, Harold Wilson told the House that the Government had decided, at this stage, not to go ahead with the idea of paying a salary to peers. Instead, the existing system of tax-free expenses for peers would continue. This would give more time to see how the new system worked in practice, and 'what form of remuneration is best fitted to give the necessary time to the work of the reformed House'.[7]

This statement pleased no one. The opponents of a salary for peers were not satisfied by the statement that there would not be a salary at this stage. Those who favoured a salary for members of the

Upper House on the grounds that otherwise only well-to-do or retired people could accept membership, considered the Prime Minister's statement an unjustified retreat.

There are, in fact, good grounds for saying that much of the criticism directed against the patronage power given to the Prime Minister under the scheme was misconceived. Since 1958, Prime Ministers have on the whole used their power to recommend the creation of life peers in a fair way. Harold Macmillan and Sir Alec Douglas-Home were particularly concerned to strengthen Labour representation in the Lords. A high percentage of the life peers created between 1958 and 1964 were Labour supporters, whose names were suggested to the Premier first by Hugh Gaitskell, and then by Harold Wilson as Labour Opposition Leaders. The one significant incidence of unfairness during this period was the failure on the part of Macmillan and Douglas-Home to nominate even one Liberal as a life peer. Harold Wilson as Premier repaired this omission and the Liberal Leader, Jeremy Thorpe, commented in the debate on the second reading of the Parliament (No. 2) Bill that 'On that ground, and on wider grounds he [The Prime Minister] has been scrupulous in his exercise of patronage in regard to another place.'[8]

The criticism of the wider power of patronage given to the Prime Minister also ignored the safeguards proposed in the White Paper. It was suggested that a committee be created to

> review periodically the composition of the reformed House and report, either to the Prime Minister or to Parliament, on any deficiences in the balance and range of membership of the House. Its members would include representatives of the political parties and persons without party political affiliations; a person of national standing but not necessarily with party political affiliations would be its chairman. Its reports would enable Parliament and the country as a whole to satisfy themselves that the powers of patronage were not being abused.[9]

The burden of criticism from the Left in the debate on second reading was that the reformed Upper House would have too much power. Michael Foot argued that in the all-party conference on reform of the Lords the Conservatives had got the better of the bargain. The 'powers of the Lords are to be retained pretty well as they are, but the possibility of using them will be greatly enhanced because the place will have been made much more respectable'.[10] He was in favour of abolishing the Lords and having a single-chamber system.

It is appropriate at this point to look at the powers which the Bill would have given to the Lords. As regards delegated legislation, the Bill proposed to take away the power of the Lords to throw out such legislation. Any subordinate legislation defeated in the Lords would become law if approved by vote in the Commons. As regards ordinary legislation, the Lords would have been given power to delay Public Bills (but not, of course, Money Bills) for six months. The delay would run from the date of disagreement between the two Houses.

Although, on the face of it, this was a reduction from the twelve months delay which the Lords could impose under the Parliament Act of 1949, the Labour Left argued that in practice this amounted to an increase in the power of the Lords, since the reformed House would be much more inclined to use its powers of delay. Although the government of the day, under the Bill, would have a majority over all other parties in the Lords, it would be dependent on carrying a majority of the cross-bench peers. Michael Foot spoke of the possibility that there would be 'crypto cross-benchers', meaning clearly from his point of view cross-benchers who were undeclared Conservative sympathizers.

The weakness of the abolitionist case, as was pointed out by a Labour Member, Fred Blackburn, in the second reading debate, is that it ignores the problem of the extra legislative burden which would then be placed on the Commons, and the valuable roles which the House of Lords performs. But before we examine this question more fully it is necessary to trace briefly the fate of the Parliament (No. 2) Bill. The Bill was taken in committee of the whole House at Committee Stage, as it had to be since it was pre-eminently a constitutional measure, and bills of constitutional importance are not sent to standing committee. The whips were not on on either side of the House and the Bill was opposed most effectively by back-benchers on the Conservative side, led by Enoch Powell, and by Labour back-benchers, ably led by Michael Foot. Their reasons for opposing the Bill were different, but they were united in heartily disliking its provisions. As a result of this 'union of opposites' led by two of the most brilliant parliamentarians in the House, progress on the Bill was very slow and, since the committee stage was on the floor of the House the whole business of the session seemed to be threatened. On 17 April 1969 the Wilson Government gave up the struggle and announced that the Bill was being abandoned.

We put these questions at the beginning of this chapter: did the Bill fail because back-benchers were suspicious of a compromise reached by their party leaders? Were the party leaders themselves not enthusiastic about the details of the reform, or were there other factors which led to the failure of the Bill? Unrest on the back-benches was undoubtedly a factor. As we have seen, this was a period when back-bench opinion was particularly assertive. Some of the party leaders were not enthusiastic about certain aspects of the reform. Leading Conservatives were opposed in particular to the timing of the introduction of the new system. There were, however, intrinsic weaknesses in the proposed system which laid it open to criticism.

That there is a strong case in favour of some kind of Upper House in Britain was underlined by the experience of the first years of the Heath administration. In these years the Lords played a most important part in legislation and several bills were considerably improved by amendments which they inserted. For example, the Housing Finance Bill was modified to provide for better rebates for disabled tenants, and an amendment was inserted to require local authorities to send out a notice of fair rent to each tenant individually instead of the notices merely being available for inspection at local authority offices, as the Bill proposed. The Local Government Bill was extensively amended in the Lords. The Industrial Relations Bill was fully scrutinized in the Lords whereas, as we have seen, it was so heavily guillotined in the Commons that less than two-thirds of the Bill was debated there at Committee Stage. No less than 351 amendments were made to the Bill in the Lords. The National Health Service Reorganization Bill was amended in important ways. In response to pressure from Labour peers and from other sections of the House, the Government introduced an amendment at report stage which gave the Health Service Commissioner power to investigate directly a complaint made by a member of staff on behalf of a patient. This enables the Commissioner to bypass the provision in the Act requiring him to see that all complaints have been made in the first instance to the relevant health authority.[11]

The National Health Service Reorganization Bill was also important in relation to the Lords since it was a major scheme for reform which was taken first in the Lords before being introduced in the Commons. This step was taken in the 1972–73 session because the Lords had been working long hours at the end of sessions in order to deal with major bills like the Local Government Bill which only reached the Upper House towards the end of the summer of 1972 and required prolonged scrutiny and debate. Leaders of all sections in the Lords therefore asked the Heath Government to send some major legislation to the Lords first in order to try and lessen over-crowding of business in the Lords at the end of the session. The Government agreed to do this in the case of the National Health Service Reorganization Bill. This was recognized as an advantageous move and the major part being played by the Lords in the legislative process was therefore highlighted.

In this period the Lords also continued to play a major part in discussing public issues, and reports of Royal Commissions and Committees for which the Commons could find no time. Thus on 6 June 1973 the Lords discussed the Report of the Younger Committee on Privacy, many peers expressing concern over the fact that although the report had been published in July 1972 no action had been taken by the Government, nearly a year later, to implement its major recommendations.[12]

Such debates are important not only because they actually take place, and are taken account of by the government of the day, but because some of the speeches made by peers are of high quality. The life peers, in particular, include among their number nowadays not only many experienced parliamentarians who formerly made their mark in the Commons, but also many distinguished men and women who have an unrivalled knowledge of medical, industrial, scientific, architectural, educational, or theatrical matters, to name only some of the fields from which eminent people have been appointed to the Lords since 1958.

An elected Upper House would be a very different sort of chamber; it would be more subject to party discipline. If it had the same party majority as the Commons, it might be something of a carbon copy of the Commons. If, because it was chosen by different electoral processes (for example, by proportional representation), or because it had a longer term, it had a majority for the Opposition parties it could be a cause of frustration and parliamentary deadlock. There is much to be said for the existing working House of Lords, which consists of life peers and an admixture of hereditary peers. But the large 'tail' of hereditary peers who attend rarely but can be brought in to sway the vote, at a time of high excitement, is both an embarrassment and an anachronism.

The Parliament (No. 2) Bill was therefore on sound lines in its proposal to create a small working house of voting members, all of whom would be life peers. The proposals for a retiring age and for a salary for voting peers also had much to commend them. The weakness in the proposed system lay in the idea that the government of the day should always be given a majority among the voting peers who take a party whip. This would necessitate more creations of life peers and a rather complicated juggling process of creations and retirements after each general election.

The proposal appeared necessary, however, because of the desire, presumably among Conservatives, to retain a significant delaying power for the Lords. If the power to delay legislation were retained, then it would be manifestly unfair to give it only to Conservative majorities in the Lords, hence the complicated adjusting procedure which it was proposed should operate after each general election. If, however, the idea of giving a substantial delaying power to the Lords were abandoned, this adjusting procedure would be unnecessary, since it would not matter very much which party had a majority in the Lords. The Upper House would retain its power to revise and improve legislation, and would be empowered to require the Commons to reconsider legislation, but would not be able to impose a delay. It would retain its valuable function of debating public issues and reports of Commissions and Committees.

This is, in practice, the role which the Lords plays in its partially reformed state. But the failure of the more thoroughgoing reform which the Parliament (No. 2) Bill proposed in 1969 has left the Lords still in an unsatisfactory condition. The existence of a large body of hereditary peers, with the right to vote in divisions, means that at any time a Labour, or even a leftish Conservative Government, could be obstructed by the majority of hereditary peers. Similarly, private Members' bills from the Commons could be defeated or emasculated in the Lords by a largely uninformed majority. The other defect remaining in the Lords is its dependence on people who can afford to give their time with very little financial reward. Although not such a major defect it must to some extent narrow the basis of membership of the Lords.

When will reform of the Lords now come? Michael Foot made a telling point during discussion of the Parliament (No. 2) Bill. He said that reform of the Lords has never come about by agreement between the parties. The 1911 reform was pushed through by the

Liberals, supported by Labour and the Irish Members. The Life Peerages Act of 1958 was introduced by a Conservative administration, as was the 1963 Act, although this was in response to an individual campaign waged by Wedgwood Benn to renounce his peerage. It is probable that further reform of the Lords will have to be carried through by one of the major parties, taking account of the views of the other parties, but not accepting a compromise which makes a laughing-stock of the whole plan for reform.

NOTES

1 Cmnd. 3799, House of Lords Reform (H.M.S.O., 1968).
2 For a discussion of these earlier reforms see F. Stacey, *The Government of Modern Britain*, pp. 213–24.
3 Harold Wilson, *The Labour Government 1964–1970. A Personal Record* (Weidenfeld and Nicolson, 1971), p. 537.
4 Cmnd. 3799, p. 3, para. 9.
5 The White Paper stated that the number of bishops sitting in the Lords would be reduced gradually from 26 to 16; Cmnd. 3799, p. 2, para. 6.
6 Harold Wilson told the House, when introducing the Second Reading of the Bill, that Ministers and those holding high judicial office would be exempt from the retirement provisions and from the proposed requirement that voting peers should attend one-third of all sessions of the Lords or lose their voting rights.
7 H.C. Deb., vol. 777, col. 54.
8 H.C. Deb., vol. 777, col. 81.
9 Cmnd. 3799, p. 14, para. 31.
10 H.C. Deb., vol. 777, col. 87.
11 For further discussion of this amendment and its importance, see chapter XI, p. 193.
12 For discussion of these recommendations see F. Stacey, *A New Bill of Rights for Britain* (David and Charles, 1973), pp. 109–13.

CHAPTER VI

Reform at the Centre of Government

THERE were two main strands of reform running through the organization of central government in this period: the attempt to improve co-ordination in the machinery of government, and the attempt to provide more effective instruments for policy planning at the centre. Neither of these objectives is new. The debate about Cabinet organization which had gone on briskly in the 1940s and 1950s, from the date of the publication of L. S. Amery's *Thoughts on the Constitution*, had been concerned with both these questions.[1] Amery advocated a small Cabinet of Ministers without departmental responsibilities, who would have to devote themselves to forward policy planning.

He argued that this would be much more efficient than the large Cabinet consisting mainly of ministers with departmental responsibilities whose time is dominated by the affairs of their departments. The type of Cabinet organization which Amery advocated had been used by Lloyd-George, as Premier, between 1916 and 1918, but was never to be used in peacetime. However, Winston Churchill, as Prime Minister between 1951 and 1953, made what might be termed a 'limited Amery experiment' by appointing two non-departmental Ministers with the task of co-ordinating groups of departments whose Ministerial heads were excluded from the Cabinet. Thus Lord Woolton was given the task of co-ordinating the Ministries of Food and Agriculture, while Lord Leathers co-ordinated the Ministries of Transport and Fuel and Power.

The experiment was not a success and was quietly dropped in 1953. Instead, what may be called the 'Anderson model' of Cabinet organization, which had been developed in the Attlee Government, was readopted, and became the standard pattern in successive administrations. Sir John Anderson advocated a larger Cabinet than Amery had done, to include both non-departmental and departmental Ministries.[2] Co-ordination and forward planning were to be achieved by extensive use of Cabinet committees, chaired by Cabinet Ministers. These committees would include departmental

Ministers, some of whom might be members of the Cabinet, and some outside the Cabinet. He also favoured development of the Cabinet's own advisory and information services.

The advantages which this type of Cabinet seemed to show over the Amery type were that policy planning was not divorced from administration, that co-ordinating Ministers were often senior departmental Ministers who had the assistance of their top-level Ministerial staff, and that the large Cabinet could permit representation of key figures in the party, inclusion of departmental Ministers from the major departments and from the politically sensitive departments. The disadvantages were the additional strain which the system placed upon Ministers who were required to attend a plethora of committees, and the clogging of the government machine which could result from an over-elaboration of the committee structure.

The Merging of Ministries

Meanwhile, an evolution in the structure of government was taking place through the merging of Ministries. In 1953 the Ministry of Pensions was combined with the Ministry of National Insurance. In 1955 the Ministry of Food was merged with the Ministry of Agriculture and Fisheries. In 1964 the formerly separate Service Ministries were merged with the Ministry of Defence. This process was taken much further in the years 1966–70. In 1968 the Foreign Office and the Commonwealth Office were combined, and in the same year the Ministry of Social Security (formerly the Ministry of Pensions and National Insurance) was merged with the Ministry of Health to form one large Department of Health and Social Security.

The Ministries concerned with trade, industry, and the environment were consolidated by stages between 1966 and 1970. In 1967 the Ministry of Aviation was merged with the Ministry of Technology. In October 1969 the Ministry of Technology was expanded further when it absorbed the Ministry of Power, parts of the Board of Trade, and part of the Department for Economic Affairs. Just before the general election of 1970, the Wilson Government was planning to merge the Ministry of Housing and Local Government with the Ministries of Transport and of Public Building and Works. Immediately after the general election, the Heath Government announced that these Ministries would be merged into one huge Department of the Environment.

The Labour spokesman in the Commons, Anthony Crosland,

welcomed this decision and told the Commons that Labour had been planning just such a merger before the election. But he criticized the Government's decision to combine the Board of Trade and the Ministry of Technology into the vast new Ministry of Trade and Industry, particularly as he felt that it implied that the Government would follow an increasingly *laissez-faire* attitude towards industry.[3]

When the Wilson minority government took office in March 1974, it preserved the Department of the Environment intact but partially dismantled the Department of Trade and Industry. It is interesting that the Heath Government had itself begun the process in its dying weeks. During the winter fuel-crisis of 1973–74, precipitated by a steep rise in world oil prices and by industrial action by the miners, the Heath Government had set up a Department of Energy consisting of those parts of the Department of Trade and Industry which had dealt with fuel and power questions. The Wilson minority government kept this new Department in being, but also split off from the Department of Trade and Industry a new Department of Prices and Consumer Protection, headed by Mrs. Shirley Williams as Secretary of State, and a Department of Trade, with Peter Shore at its head. In December 1974 there were therefore four Ministries in place of the large Department of Trade and Industry, set up in 1970. These were the Departments of Industry, Energy, Prices and Consumer Protection, and Trade. Each was headed by a Secretary of State with a varying team of supporting ministers according to the scope of its functions. Thus the Secretary of State at the Department of Industry had two Ministers of State and two Under-Secretaries, at the Department of Energy one Minister of State and two Under-Secretaries, at the Department of Prices and Consumer Protection one Minister of State and one Under-Secretary, and at the Department of Trade two Under-Secretaries.

There has therefore not been a continuous development towards giant Ministries in the years between 1966 and 1974. The development was continuous until the end of 1973 when the splitting-off of Energy from Trade and Industry began a swing back towards smaller Ministries which was greatly accelerated by the chipping-away of two more departments from the Department of Industry in March 1974. The over-all trend has been, however, towards large and indeed, in some cases, 'giant' departments. This trend has had important consequences, some of which we will now examine.

One consequence has been that it has become possible to include all Ministerial heads of departments within the Cabinet without having a very large Cabinet. In 1966, immediately after the general election, there were five Ministerial heads of department not in the Cabinet. These were the Minister of Health, the Minister of Pensions and National Insurance, the Minister of Public Building and Works, the Minister of Aviation, and the Postmaster-General. By March 1974, as the result of the mergers we have noted, there was not one Ministerial head of department outside the Cabinet. From the point of view of co-ordination of the central machinery of government this development must have certain clear advantages. The position of a Ministerial head of department who was outside the Cabinet was never a satisfactory one. He would be brought into Cabinet consultation when his department's affairs were under consideration, but he only saw a corner of the Cabinet's activities, and did not have the right to continuous participation in Cabinet business.

Now all departments have their spokesmen in the Cabinet. The problem of co-ordination is therefore moved further down to within the giant departments. Some idea of the dimension of this problem can be gained from examining the Ministerial structure in the largest surviving giant department, the Department of the Environment. The Department is headed by a Secretary of State who is a member of the Cabinet. In December 1974 this was Anthony Crosland. He was assisted by three Ministers, each of whom had responsibility for a major area of the Department's work. These were, in December 1974, the Minister for Planning and Local Government, John Silkin, the Minister for Transport, Fred Mulley, and the Minister for Housing and Construction, Reginald Freeson. A Minister of State in the Department, Denis Howell, had responsibility for Sport and Recreation. Four Under-Secretaries completed the Ministerial team in the Department, which numbered nine in all.

The problem of internal organization in such a giant department is a formidable one. As Sir Richard Clarke has commented, the Ministers in a giant department 'must work as a team together, and this requires good temperaments and good organization'.[4] There is a danger of muddle and conflict between Ministers. At official level, it is difficult in a giant department to develop the kind of organization which will 'bring clear policy determination and rapid execution'.[5] But the giant department also has certain other potential advantages besides simplifying the Cabinet structure. 'The "giant" can develop its own strategy and decide its own priorities; it can settle problems itself instead of lengthy discussion in interdepartmental committees; it is big enough to have specialized services; it can support a clearer strategy at the centre.'[6] Sir Richard Clarke had himself been Permanent Secretary at the Ministry of Technology at the time of the 1969 merger. He said, in his lectures to the Civil Service College, that in his experience at that Ministry it was reasonable to hope that these advantages might in time be realized there. But he also thought that until more experience of the working of the giant departments was available, it would be wise to take the view that something near the maximum size of a large department had been reached with the creation in 1970 of the Department of Trade and Industry, and the Department of the Environment.

Policy Planning at the Centre

Between 1964 and 1970, Harold Wilson as Prime Minister sought to provide for more effective policy planning at the centre of government, partly through creation of the Department of Economic Affairs, and partly by bringing into the Cabinet Secretariat outside advisers to brief the Prime Minister. Let us follow each of these ideas in turn. In a radio conversation before the 1964 general election, Harold Wilson told Norman Hunt that it was his intention, if he became Prime Minister, to establish a new Ministry of Production, or Planning, which would take over from the Treasury and would have responsibility for economic planning, and be concerned with 'co-ordinating decisions about expansion in the physical field, deciding what industries we need to encourage, either by tax means or by other methods'.[7]

George Brown has described how, as Chairman of the Home Policy Committee of the Labour Party in 1963 and 1964, he was formulating a project for such a planning Ministry. His committee thought that the economy was being held back 'by reason of the orthodox financial policy of the Treasury. Out of this kind of thinking grew the idea that it would be better to have an economic department, which (as I always saw it) would be superior to the Treasury in determining the country's economic priorities.'[8] Immediately after the general election of 1964, Harold Wilson asked George Brown to set up a new Department for Economic Affairs. George Brown set about this task with immense enthusiasm, and the new Ministry won for itself a great deal of publicity; but it was not to prove a lasting innovation. In August 1966, George Brown left the D.E.A. to become Foreign Secretary, and in 1969 Harold Wilson decided to wind up the Department, distributing its personnel, some to the Ministry of Technology, some to the Treasury, and some to the Economic Section of the Cabinet Secretariat.

Two principal reasons have been advanced for the failure of the D.E.A. to establish itself in the Whitehall scene. The first, and probably the main reason, was that it was a department whose chief aim was to achieve economic expansion, set up at a time of economic stringency. The grave balance of payments difficulties which plagued the Wilson Government from 1964 right up until 1969 also frustrated the principal objectives of the D.E.A. Its National Plan was still-born and, although the economic planning councils which it set up in the regions were to outlast it, it was to have few other achievements.

The other reason advanced for the D.E.A.'s lack of success was that it was not, as George Brown had hoped, superior to the Treasury. Where there was a confrontation with the Treasury, the Treasury usually got its way. In his book George Brown suggests two different explanations for this. At one place he regrets his failure to invite Sir William Amstrong to become Permanent Secretary of the new Department. Sir William was, in 1964, Joint Permanent Secretary at the Treasury, and Head of the Civil Service. George Brown consulted him about who should be Head of the new Department, but did not think of asking him to take on the job himself. Looking back, in 1970, he wrote, 'Had I been even more conscious than I was of the battle that would have to be fought between the entrenched Treasury and our new department which was going to usurp some of its functions, the appointment of Sir William as the head of the D.E.A. might have resulted in that battle's being won before it started.'[9]

The other explanation which George Brown offered was that he did not have enough support from Harold Wilson in his contests with the Treasury. He says that he came 'to feel that the Prime Minister had never really intended to allow the degree of freedom from Treasury control which was imperative if our ideas were to be carried out'.[10] Harold Wilson in his personal record of the Labour Government from 1964 to 1970 said that in his view the D.E.A. failed to provide 'an adequate offset to the Treasury' not through any fault of the 'D.E.A. or D.E.A. ministers, nor, indeed of the Treasury'. The failure was due to 'an inherited balance of payments deficit and hostile speculative activity'.[11] He also said that he did not regret the original decision to set up the D.E.A., 'Having thought further on these matters, I still feel that something on D.E.A. lines, however constituted, may have a permanent and central role to play in Britain's future machinery of government.'[12]

While the D.E.A. was experiencing first eclipse, and then elimination, a new department was being established at the centre of government: the Civil Service Department. Discussion of this Department is largely a matter for the next chapter, since it was set up on the recommendation of the Fulton Committee on the Civil Service, but the important impact which it has made on the power structure at the centre must be mentioned here. Sir William Armstrong was appointed Permanent Secretary of the Civil Service Department when it was set up in 1968, and continued to be Head of the Civil Service. When he retired in 1974, his successor as Head of the Civil Service also became Permanent Secretary of the Department. Thus there are now three leading officials at the centre of government: the Permanent Secretary to the Civil Service Department, who has the title of Head of the Civil Service, the Secretary to the Cabinet, and the Permanent Secretary to the Treasury. The first two give advice directly to the Prime Minister, the third to the Chancellor of the Exchequer. One result, therefore, of the creation of the Civil Service Department has been to give the Prime Minister a powerful new source of advice.

We have seen that Harold Wilson had also wanted to strengthen the Cabinet Office. He told Norman Hunt in 1964 that he wanted, by introducing outside advisers and highly qualified Civil Servants from the departments, to provide 'a briefing agency' for the Prime Minister 'so that he is right up to date on top of the job in respect of all these major departments of State'.[13] On forming his government in 1964 Harold Wilson brought in one outside adviser into the Cabinet Office. This was Thomas Balogh, who was Reader in Economics at Oxford University, and a prolific author on economic policy and planning.[14] From 1964 until the 1966 general election, Balogh had a room in the Cabinet Office. After the 1966 general election he moved into No. 10 Downing Street. Marcia Williams, Harold Wilson's Personal and Private Secretary at No. 10, says of this move that 'Thomas was absolutely delighted and in his element.'[15] But although it was an improvement for him and made him more readily available to give advice to the Prime Minister, his position was not an enviable one. The great disadvantage which Balogh experienced was that he was not given access to all departmental information, nor does he seem to have been fully accepted in the Cabinet Office machine.

Marcia Williams and her assistants also experienced considerable difficulties, particularly at the outset. She had been Harold Wilson's Private Secretary when he was Leader of the Opposition, and she brought with her into No. 10 a small staff of Labour Party people. Together they dealt with the party political side of the Prime Minister's correspondence and daily programme. She describes in her book how, in her opinion, she was cold-shouldered and, at times, obstructed by the Civil Service staff. As a result, she claims, the channels of communication between the Prime Minister and his party were not always as open as they needed to be in the period between 1964 and 1970. In her view, Harold Wilson was to some extent insulated from party political contacts by the behaviour of some of his Civil Service staff at No. 10.[16]

Edward Heath, as Prime Minister, was also concerned about the problem of improving the quality of advice available to the Prime Minister and to the Cabinet, and was a major innovator in this field. He had been considering the question before taking office. In a Commons debate on 20 November 1968, speaking as Leader of the Opposition, he said that in his view the Prime Minister's planning and information staff should be strengthened. He criticized the fact that there was a variety of organizations, such as the Cabinet Secretariat, the Civil Service Department, and the office of scientific adviser, all responsible to the Prime Minister, but that there was no 'unifying force except the Prime Minister himself' at the centre of government.[17]

In a White Paper on *The Reorganization of Central Government*, issued in October 1970, the Heath Government announced that it would establish 'a small multi-disciplinary central policy review staff in the Cabinet Office'.[18] Edward Heath chose Lord Rothschild to head this new organization and by the summer of 1973 Rothschild had recruited another 14 members. The Central Policy Review Staff was given two principal functions. First, it reviewed the Government's over-all strategy in applying its programme. Every six months the members of the Heath Cabinet met to spend the whole day discussing a strategy paper produced by the C.P.R.S. This meeting was usually held at Chequers. The strategy paper, in the words of one of the members of the C.P.R.S., attempted 'to identify the objectives of the Government's programme', discussed in fairly broad terms the progress being made towards achieving them and suggested ways of filling any notable gaps.[19] The paper was then discussed at further meetings with the middle-ranking and junior Ministers.

The second main function of the C.P.R.S., under the Heath administration, was to undertake study projects with the aim of helping to evaluate the Government's policy, and the options open to the Government, in almost any area. Thus, if the Government wanted to know if the RB211 engine, or the Concorde, should be proceeded with, the C.P.R.S. might be asked to advise. During these years, it reviewed national energy policy and recommended that more emphasis should be given to the exploitation of coal resources. It was asked by the Heath Government to advise also on such varied matters as the control of inflation, on talks between the Prime Minister and trade union leaders, and on race relations.

With such a range of projects, it was obviously desirable to have a multi-disciplinary team, although there was quite a strong representation of economists. Lord Rothschild himself was a zoologist. He had been Assistant Director of Research at the Department of Zoology of Cambridge University. From 1948 to 1958 he had been Chairman of the Agricultural Research Council, and from 1963 to 1970 was Chairman of Shell Research Ltd. His second in command was Professor C. Richard Ross, who had previously been consultant to the Economics and Statistics Department of the Organization for Economic Co-operation and Development. Prior to that, from 1963 to 1969, he had been Professor of Economics at the University of East Anglia. Other economist members of the C.P.R.S. were Richard Crum and Brian Reading. Madeleine Aston was both a scientist and an economist. There were a number of senior Civil Servants on the review staff seconded from the Treasury, the Foreign Office, and the Ministry of Defence.

The C.P.R.S. met in full session every Monday morning. Otherwise, its members tended to work on projects in groups of three or four. The areas of these projects were determined either by specific inquiries directed to the C.P.R.S., or by a review of the papers prepared by government departments for Cabinet committees, or for the full Cabinet. One of the accepted functions of the C.P.R.S. was to act as a critic of the departmental view. A departmental Minister's Cabinet colleagues are rarely qualified, on their own, to assess the brief which a department has prepared. The C.P.R.S. was sometimes able to provide Cabinet Ministers with, so to speak, a 'counter-brief'. To do this, the C.P.R.S. had to have enough notice of agenda and enough time to examine departmental papers in advance of Cabinet meetings. This could cause problems and friction with the Cabinet Secretariat. The C.P.R.S. also needed sources of advice. These were found to some extent among outside experts and to some extent, at first sight surprisingly, within the departments themselves. Quite often the departmental view, as presented in a paper to the Cabinet, or to a Cabinet committee, has its critics within the department. If the C.P.R.S. had channels to opinion among middle-rank Civil Servants in a department, as was quite often the case, it could get an alternative view from inside the department.

It is difficult to estimate how successful the C.P.R.S. was in the Heath administration. We know that its advice was sought on a number of major issues, but we do not know how far its advice was taken. It is clear that from about the beginning of 1972 the Heath Government started to take up a more flexible position on a number of questions on which it had begun with a rather rigid policy in 1970. It is likely that assessments made by the C.P.R.S. played a part in bringing about a change of attitude in the Government towards, for example, energy policy, and on methods for combating inflation.

The structure and composition of the C.P.R.S. showed certain advantages over the machinery for advising the Prime Minister which had preceded it. For example, while Lord Balogh had access to Harold Wilson, as Prime Minister, he did not have access to all the files, nor, as a one-man advice team, could he possibly have sufficient time, or the expertise, to give effective advice over a wide field. The C.P.R.S. had the advantage of combining people with varied experience and specialist knowledge: economics, science, business, and administration. Since it included some senior Civil Servants, the unit as a whole could have ready access to official information. During the Heath administration, the Staff also included an element of active Conservatives. Thus Peter Bowcock had, at one time, been in Conservative Central Office, and, similarly, William Waldegrave was an active and well-connected Conservative. Men like these provided a channel to the Conservative Party. At that time, therefore, the C.P.R.S. combined outside experts, without a committed party affiliation, senior Civil Servants, and committed and active Conservatives.

After the general election in February 1974, there was speculation whether Harold Wilson, as incoming Premier, would dispense with the C.P.R.S., continue it, or continue it in a modified form. He chose the third alternative. The committed Conservative members of the C.P.R.S. left after the election, but the remaining members of the team carried on. Wilson did not replace the Conservative members with Labour men in touch with Transport House, as he might have done. Instead, he appointed a new policy unit headed by Dr. Bernard Donoughue, and including a number of committed Labour people, to work alongside the C.P.R.S. As regards the division of labour between the two units it was reported that the Donoughue unit would advise on short-term domestic policy, while the C.P.R.S., under Lord Rothschild, would advise the Cabinet on long-term strategy.[20]

Bernard Donoughue was, until his appointment, a senior lecturer at the London School of Economics, and a specialist in recent British history and politics. With George Jones he was part-author of a massive biography of Herbert Morrison.[21] Other members of the unit included David Piachaud, a lecturer in social administration at the London School of Economics, Mrs. Catherine Carmichael, lecturer in social work at Glasgow University, Andrew Graham, who taught economics at Balliol College, Oxford, Richard Kirwaun, also an economist, from the Centre for Environmental Studies, Richard Graham, manager of Domestic Trunk Services for British Airways, and Adrian Shaw, who had been research assistant for Harold Wilson from 1973 to 1974. When asked in the Commons on 2 May 1974 about the future of the C.P.R.S., Harold Wilson confirmed that it would continue. He said that he had been doubtful about it when it had been set up by the Heath Government, but now believed that it was a good development. 'It has a non-political role, and its duties are carried through with high distinction.'[22] It seems, therefore, that a C.P.R.S. in some shape or form has come to stay, in either Labour or Conservative governments.

On 1 October 1974 Lord Rothschild resigned his appointment as head of the Central Policy Review Staff, and was succeeded by Sir Kenneth Berrill. Sir Kenneth had been head of the Government Economic Service, and Chief Economic Adviser to the Treasury since 1973. From 1969 to 1973 he was Chairman of the University Grants Committee. He has been an economic adviser to the governments of Turkey, Guyana, and the Cameroons, and to the Organization for Economic Co-operation and Development, and to the World Bank.[23]

It is appropriate to consider the potential impact of the C.P.R.S. on the machinery of policy planning at the centre, particularly when seen in conjunction with recent developments in planning and analysing expenditure programmes. We have seen, in Chapter III, that the Treasury had been developing a system for long-term reviews of public expenditure ever since 1962, when the idea was first formulated by the Plowden Committee.[24] In the Treasury, these reviews were made the responsibility of the Public Expenditure Survey Committee (P.E.S.C.). The Heath Government brought another innovation: Programme Analysis Review (P.A.R.). The division of responsibility in the Health administration between P.E.S.C. and P.A.R., as defined by Sir Richard Clarke, was as follows. P.E.S.C. was concerned largely with allocating resources to departments, on a medium and long-term basis, taking into account the national economic resources likely to be available in the future. The function of P.A.R. was to assess the statements of priorities and objectives submitted by the departments, before the process of allocation began.[25] The functions of P.E.S.C. and P.A.R. therefore interlocked. There was also a potential overlap between P.A.R. and C.P.R.S. Nevertheless, their roles were different, and can be briefly summarized as follows. P.A.R. was concerned with reviewing departmental programmes and with assessing how effective they were in attaining their stated objectives. The C.P.R.S., in the words of William Plowden, was concerned, together with the Treasury, 'with choosing the programmes to be analysed and reviewed, with monitoring the progress of the review and with trying to ensure that in the end Ministers are presented with the right options for action'.[26]

The relationship between the agencies for policy and expenditure planning and review may clearly change from administration to administration. But it seems to be accepted that any administration will now attempt, when formulating the objectives of government, to take into consideration the resources which are likely to be available to the nation in the future. This will be done through P.E.S.C. It will also subject to critical examination the options open to government in the key areas. This will be done by the C.P.R.S., and a short-term policy team like the Donoughue unit, or by a further modified C.P.R.S.

This is all to the good, but has the disadvantage that the whole process of policy and expenditure planning and review takes place within the penumbra of Cabinet secrecy. Although outside individuals and organizations may be consulted on specific issues, the process, up until now, has not been one of open consultation. When a party that has been in Opposition comes to power after a general election, it can find itself presented with a carefully worked-out programme of expenditure and forward planning, in the making of which it has had no real say. Similarly, individuals and organized groups cannot be confident that all the alternatives have been fairly assessed by the Cabinet when considering the future of the Concorde, or plans for a Channel Tunnel, or the future of the steel industry, or the railways, for example. The logic of the new system, therefore, is that the informed public, and the Opposition party, should be brought into the P.E.S.C.-C.P.R.S. system. In other words, the options open to government, and the forward planning of expenditure, should be publicly debated. The papers which now go to the Cabinet from the C.P.R.S., for example, should be published wherever possible, as should those available to the P.E.S.C.

This would be a radical change and would mean the partial abandonment of Cabinet secrecy over a wide area of government, while affecting the doctrine of collective responsibility of Ministers. But if the whole operation is to be done well, if, as William Plowden suggests, the Cabinet is to be presented with 'the right options for action', those options should be fully and publicly discussed. Then all bodies of informed opinion would have their chance to influence the decision. The other great advantage is that the Opposition party which nowadays is in a relatively weak position when it enters upon government, because it lacks the research facilities which are available to government departments and the Cabinet, would be greatly strengthened. A party which had been out of office would, on taking power, be already briefed on many of the problems it would face as a government, since those problems would have been already under discussion publicly between the Cabinet, the C.P.R.S., and informed people outside government.

The logic of developments in the Cabinet in the last few years, then, is that there is a need for progress towards more open government at Cabinet level. The Heath Government had not fully accepted this logic, as was evidenced by Edward Heath's reaction to a speech by Lord Rothschild to a group of agricultural scientists at Wantage, in Berkshire, on 24 September 1973. Lord Rothschild told his audience that unless people in Britain 'give up the idea that we are one of the wealthiest, most influential and important countries in the world, in other words, that Queen Victoria is still reigning we are likely to find ourselves in increasingly serious trouble'.[27] He was arguing that expensive prestige projects should be subject to careful scrutiny if Britain was not to overextend itself. He also implied that more attention should be given to the needs of the elderly, the sick, and infirm, and those generally disadvantaged in society.

It was reliably reported that Lord Rothschild had been rebuked for his speech, both by the Prime Minister and by Sir William Armstrong, on the grounds that it infringed the Civil Service 'Estacode' which provides that Civil Servants should not make speeches indicating that they have major policy differences with their Ministerial superiors. Some leading scientists, however, sprang to Lord Rothschild's defence. For example, Sir Brian Flowers, the Chairman of the Science Research Council, when introducing the annual report of his Council at a press conference on 26 September 1973, said that he had every sympathy with Lord Rothschild. He thought that people should not be hauled over the coals for 'trying honestly to point out a situation which seems to them very true and which seems to be worth pointing out'. Such honesty was 'a concept of open government of which I approve and which has been approved by the Prime Minister'.[28]

The concept of 'open government' requires that in all areas where there is not an overriding need for secrecy, as in some aspects of Defence, the advice submitted to Ministers may be subject to public scrutiny. This means that disagreements between Ministers and their advisers will sometimes be known. The disadvantages of revealing such disagreements are considerably less than the drawbacks of the traditional secretive system. For in the traditional system, no one can really know how far government decisions are based on inadequate advice. One of the most notable features of the Fulton Report was its advocacy of open government, and it is to this report that we turn in the next chapter.

NOTES

1 Oxford University Press, 1946. For a discussion of the controversy in these years see F. Stacey, *The Government of Modern Britain*, pp. 265–77.
2 Sir John Anderson, 'The Machinery of Government', Romanes Lectures printed in *Public Administration*, 1946, pp. 147–56.
3 H.C. Deb., vol. 805, col. 886.
4 *New Trends in Government* (Civil Service Department and H.M.S.O., 1971), p. 3.
5 Ibid.
6 Ibid.
7 N. Hunt (ed.) *Whitehall and Beyond* (B.B.C. Publications, 1964), p. 17.
8 Lord George-Brown, *In My Way* (Penguin, 1972), p. 88.
9 Op. cit., pp. 89–90.
10 Op. cit., p. 104.
11 *The Labour Government 1964–1970. A Personal Record*, p. 710.
12 Ibid.
13 *Whitehall and Beyond*, p. 20.
14 His many books include *Dollar Crisis*, 1949, *Planning through the Price Mechanism*, 1961, and *Planning for Progress*, 1963. Balogh was made a life peer in 1968.
15 *Inside Number 10*, p. 141.
16 When Harold Wilson became Prime Minister again after the 1974 general election, Marcia Williams continued to assist him as Personal and Private Secretary. This time he decided not to live at 10 Downing Street. This decision was affected by the fact that he had recently bought a convenient London house, but it also meant that he would be less 'cocooned' within the atmosphere of No. 10. During the summer of 1974 Marcia Williams was made a life peer, taking the title of Lady Falkender. She continued to act as the Prime Minister's Personal and Private Secretary.
17 H.C. Deb., vol. 773, col. 1578.
18 Cmnd. 4506, The Reorganization of Central Government (H.M.S.O., 1970), p. 13.
19 William Plowden, 'The Central Policy Review Staff: the first two years' (unpublished paper read to the Political Studies Association Conference, Reading, 1973), p. 2.
20 Report in *The Times*, 16 March 1974.
21 Bernard Donoughue and G. W. Jones, *Herbert Morrison: Portrait of a Politician* (Weidenfeld and Nicolson, 1973).
22 H.C. Deb., vol. 872, col. 1320.
23 Sir Kenneth Berrill was a lecturer in economics at Cambridge University from 1949 to 1969; from 1967 to 1969 he was a special adviser to the Treasury.
24 Cmnd. 1432, Control of Public Expenditure (H.M.S.O., 1962).
25 Sir Richard Clarke, *New Trends in Government*, p. 7.
26 Op. cit., p. 3.
27 Report in *The Times*, 25 September 1973.
28 Report in the *Guardian*, 27 September 1973.

CHAPTER VII

Civil Service Reform

The Fulton Report and its Implementation

There were two principal reasons for the decision by the Wilson Government to set up the Committee under Lord Fulton which was to report, in 1968, in favour of major changes in the structure of the Civil Service. The most obvious reason was that such a committee had been recommended in a report of the Estimates Committee which appeared in 1965. This report suggested that a 'Committee of officials aided by members from outside the Civil Service, on the lines of the Plowden Committee, should be appointed to initiate research upon, to examine and to report upon the structure, recruitment and management of the Civil Service'.[1] One of the main findings of the Estimates Committee's report had been that there was a shortfall in recruitment to the Administrative Class of the Civil Service. In 1964 there were 88 vacancies, but the Civil Service Commission only felt able to fill 48 of them because, in its view, the other candidates were not of the necessary calibre. The problem of recruitment led the Committee to ask questions about many other features of the Service: its structure, the use of specialists in the Service, training, and management.

The other main reason for the decision to appoint the Fulton Committee was a spate of books and publications urging the need for reform in the Civil Service. Thomas Balogh, writing in 1959, described the Civil Service as 'The Apotheosis of the Dilettante'.[2] Professor Brian Chapman, in his short book, *British Government Observed* (1963), argued that the British Civil Service, at the higher levels, is 'a closed corporation' little influenced by other sections of the community. He claimed that many of the failings of British government in the 1950s and early 1960s, could be blamed on the narrow outlook of senior Civil Servants. Finally, in 1964, a group of Fabians produced a pamphlet advocating reform of the Civil Service. It was the work of a study group which had held a series of discussions over two years. Some of its members were themselves senior Civil Servants, but the names of the members of the group were not at that time revealed.[3]

Lord Fulton had himself at one time been a Civil Servant. From 1942 to 1944 he was Principal Assistant Secretary at the Ministry of Fuel and Power. After the Second World War he returned to academic life as Fellow in Politics at Balliol College; from 1947 to 1959 he was Principal of University College, Swansea, and from 1959 to 1967 Vice-Chancellor of the University of Sussex. Of the other members of his Committee, two were Permanent Heads of Government Departments, Sir Philip Allen and Sir James Dunnett. Two were academics, Norman Hunt and Lord Simey. Two were M.P.s, Sir Edward Boyle and Shirley Williams, who was replaced after only a few weeks by Robert Sheldon on Shirley Williams's appointment as Parliamentary Secretary at the Ministry of Labour. Two members of the Committee were industrialists, Sir Norman Kipping and Sir John Wall. There was one trade unionist, W. C. Anderson.[4] The Committee also included a senior scientific Civil Servant, Sir William Cook, the Chief Scientific Adviser to the Ministry of Defence, and the Economic Adviser to the Treasury, Robert Neild. The last-named provides a link with the Fabian study, *The Administrators*, since he was the chairman of the Fabian group which produced that pamphlet.

The Committee's investigations were carried on largely in the traditional way, by hearing oral evidence and considering written evidence. The Committee heard a great deal of evidence from senior Civil Servants, from the Civil Service staff associations, from bodies like the Confederation of British Industry, the Trades Union Congress, and the National Citizens Advice Bureaux Council, and from many individuals outside the Civil Service. Since all the members of the Committee were public men, with a heavy programme, they could not spare much additional time for the work of the Committee. But one member, Norman Hunt, was given leave by Exeter College for over a year so that he might devote his time to the Committee. He drafted the report and also headed a Management Consultancy Investigation which the Committee commissioned. He was assisted in this by a Civil Servant from the Treasury, a management consultant, and a specialist from British Petroleum. Twenty-three blocks of work in government departments were investigated, and 600 Civil Servants interviewed for this part of the inquiry.

The Committee also commissioned research from outside

academics and from within the Civil Service. A. H. Halsey and I. M. Crewe, of Oxford and Lancaster Universities, made a survey by questionnaire which was designed to provide a sociological portrait of the main general classes in the Civil Service. Richard Chapman, then at Liverpool University, surveyed by questionnaire and interview the men and women who entered the Administrative Class as Assistant Principals in 1956. Edgar Anstey, of the Civil Service Commission, made a follow-up study of members of the Administrative Class to compare their progress and performance, and check the validity of the selection procedures. Richard Chapman, who has written a good account of the work of the Committee, himself questions whether all of this research was adequately considered by the Committee.[5] In fact, the report of the Halsey–Crewe survey did not appear until after the Fulton Report was published. But the pressure on the Fulton Committee to report quickly must be borne in mind.

The Fulton Report maintained that the Civil Service was inadequate to face the problems of the second half of the twentieth century in six main respects.[6] First, the Administrative Class in particular was too much based on the philosophy of the 'generalist' or 'all-rounder'. Second, the system of classes in the Civil Service (there were then over 1,400) seriously impeded its work. Third, scientists, engineers, and members of other specialist classes were frequently not given responsibilities and opportunities commensurate with their abilities. Fourth, too few Civil Servants were skilled managers. Fifth, there was not enough contact between the Civil Service and the community. Sixth, personnel management and career planning were inadequate.

The principal recommendation of the Committee was that a new Civil Service Department should be set up with wider functions than those performed by the Pay and Management Group of the Treasury, which it would take over. The new department should be under the control of the Prime Minister, and its Permanent Secretary should be designated Head of the Home Civil Service. The second main recommendation was that in the non-industrial part of the Civil Service 'All classes should be abolished and replaced by a single, unified grading structure covering all civil servants from top to bottom.'[7] The Committee also thought that more emphasis should be given to in-service training and the development of management skills in the Service. They recommended that a Civil

Service College should be set up which should provide major training courses in administration and management, and a wide range of shorter courses. It should also have important research functions.

There were many more detailed recommendations in the report, but it is appropriate to consider first how far these principal recommendations have been acted upon. Harold Wilson, as Prime Minister, announced on the day of the report that a Civil Service Department would be set up on the lines recommended in the report. The new Department came into being in November 1968. Its first Permanent Secretary, as we have seen, was Sir William Armstrong, then Head of the Civil Service. The Prime Minister himself has ultimate responsibility for the Department but is assisted by another Minister who is concerned with the day-to-day operation of the Department.

Harold Wilson also said, on the day of publication of the report, that the Government had decided to implement the Committee's recommendation that it should set up a Civil Service College. The College is now established at three centres: London, Sunningdale, and Edinburgh. Its Principal is Dr. Eugene Grebenik, previously Professor of Social Studies in the University of Leeds. It has Directors of Programmes concerned with senior management training and the administration course for specialists, European training, specialized training in organization and methods and related fields, courses for Higher Executive Officers, and other middle management courses for administration training. There are five Directors of Studies: in Statistics and Operational Research, Economics, Personnel Management, Public Administration, Social Policy, and Social Administration. Some imaginative appointments were made for these posts. For example, Bernard Benjamin, the first Director of Studies in Statistics and Operational Research had, until 1973, been Director of the Research and Intelligence Unit of the Greater London Council, and before that Chief Statistician at the Ministry of Health. Henry Parris, the Director of Studies in Public Administration, had been Reader in Public Administration at Durham University. He is the author of *Government and Railways in Nineteenth Century Britain* (1965), *Constitutional Bureaucracy* (1969), and *Staff Relations in the Civil Service: Fifty Years of Whitleyism* (1973). Cyril S. Smith, Director of Studies in Social Policy and Social Administration, had been Director of Youth Leadership Training courses at Manchester University. His publications include *People in Need* (1957), *Adolescence* (1968), and, as a co-author, *Neighbourhood and Community* (1954) and *Leisure and Society in Britain* (1973). Most of the staff of the College are, of course, career Civil Servants.

The College provides at its three centres a wide variety of courses designed for Civil Servants at many different levels. What are chiefly of interest for the student of politics and administration are the courses provided for those Civil Servants who will man the senior posts in the departments. In 1963 a Centre for Administrative Studies had been set up in London. Before the Fulton Committee was appointed, the Centre had been running a three-week course for all Assistant Principals at the end of their first 6 months' service in the Administrative Class, and a second set of courses, lasting in all 20 weeks, which they attended in their third year of service. After publication of the Fulton Report, the Centre for Administrative Studies was embodied in the newly formed Civil Service College. The courses which it provided for Assistant Principals were developed and new elements were introduced. For example, the over-all training period was extended to 28 weeks and new courses in social administration were introduced.

In 1973 the structure of these courses had to be considerably modified following the decision to end the Administrative Class. We must look first at this decision before examining its consequences for the Civil Service College. We have seen that the Fulton Report had recommended the abolition of all classes in the Civil Service. The Government accepted this recommendation in principle. The Prime Minister announced on the day of publication of the Fulton Report that discussions would begin with the Staff Associations in the Civil Service to work out how a unified grading structure for the whole Service could be achieved. During 1970, a scheme was evolved in the National Whitley Council, on which the Official and Staff sides of the Civil Service are represented, for merging the old Administrative, Executive, and Clerical Classes into one Administration Group. On 1 January 1971 this scheme was put into effect. The Administration Group now comprises all grades from Assistant Secretary to the most junior grade of Clerical Assistant.[8] Whereas in the past it was possible, but difficult, to secure promotion from the Clerical Class to the Executive Class, and from the Executive to the Administrative Class, it is now hoped that the avenues of promotion in the unified Service will be easier. Some of the anomalies created by overlapping of the Classes have also been eliminated.

Once the decision had been taken to set up a unified Administration Group it was necessary to decide how promising university graduates could be brought in for training for the higher reaches of the Service, while at the same time improving the chances of promotion for people from the Executive grades. For this purpose a new grade of Administration Trainee has been created. Each year, between 250 and 300 men and women will enter this grade. At most, 175 of these will be recruited from outside the Civil Service, from honours graduates under 28 years of age who are successful in tests and interviews at the Civil Service Selection Board and the Final Selection Board. These tests are preceded by an initial written qualifying examination. The whole procedure is similar to the old Method II examination for selection to the Administrative Class.

The old Method I, consisting of a degree-type competitive examination, followed by interview at the Final Selection Board, was ended in 1969. The numbers taking Method I had declined steadily. When an inquiry, recommended by the Fulton Committee into the effectiveness of Method II, reported that it was a good system of selection, the Government decided to end Method I.[9]

Each year, around 125 men and women will be recruited to the grade of Administration Trainee from inside the Civil Service. They will be chosen by the same series of tests and interviews as those competing from outside the Service. The total number entering the Administration Trainee grade each year will be much greater than the number of between 70 and 90 previously recruited each year as Assistant Principals. The Civil Service will therefore be casting its net wider for recruits to the higher reaches of the Service than it did under the old system.

All the Administration Trainees will receive training at the Civil Service College. It is planned to give them courses lasting 15 weeks, broken by two periods of study leave. The subjects covered in the courses will comprise social administration, economics, public administration, and personnel management. The first Administration Trainees started on these courses in 1973.[10] The original intention had been that after serving for between 2 and 4 years in the Administration Trainee grade, about one-third of the A.T.s would be chosen for promotion to the new grade of Higher Executive

Officer (A). They would then receive further training in the Civil Service College. In 1973 it was planned that they would attend a 15 weeks course, 8 or 9 weeks of which would be a common core for all H.E.O.(A)s, plus 6 weeks given over to options. The first of these courses was to begin in the autumn of that year.[11]

An important modification of the original plan was made in 1973 when it was decided that two-thirds of the A.T.s would proceed to the grade of Higher Executive Officer (A). There were two main reasons for this change of plan. The first was that the general standard of intake of Administration Trainees had proved higher than was anticipated. This may partly have been because the job opportunities for university graduates in 1972 and 1973 were more restricted than they had been in previous years. It may also be that the larger intake encourages more able people from the universities to apply, as had been suggested to the Fulton Committee. The second main reason for the change of plan is that as there is a keen demand for Civil Servants at the Principal level a larger intake to the H.E.O. (A) grade is needed.

The consequences of this change of plan are important. The original concept had involved the idea of a 'fast stream' among the Administration Trainees who would be given accelerated promotions and so brought on at an earlier stage of their career to positions of considerable responsibility. Since they would only be one-third of the total intake of A.T.s they would be very much in the minority. A cogent criticism of the scheme was that the two-thirds not selected would lose heart and feel themselves 'shunted', as although they would still have a chance to work their way to the grade of Principal and above, it would be a slower process. Now that two-thirds of the A.T.s will be selected to become H.E.O. (A)s, the remaining one-third will not be such a significant element of 'slower streamers', particularly since there is always some wastage in the early years, as some individuals decide the Civil Service is not for them and leave to take up other careers.

There will be a further element of selection from the H.E.O. (A) grade. It is envisaged that after 2 or 3 years in the grade, many of the H.E.O. (A)s will be appointed Principals. Those who are not appointed will be transferred to the ordinary Higher Executive Officer Grade. This again is the concept of the 'fast stream'. But the total effect of the modified system is less drastic than had been originally proposed since the A.T.s who are promoted to the

H.E.O. (A) grade, and then transferred to the ordinary H.E.O. grade, will still have secured promotion, although they are not appointed Principals at that stage.

If we attempt an interim assessment of the system as it has been reformed since the Fulton Report the following advantages stand out: first, the creation of an Administration Group should improve opportunities for promotion. Second, the creation of the Administration Trainee grade should recruit more able people to the middle and higher ranks of the Civil Service. Those successful in entering the A.T. grade will not be such a small and exclusive élite as the small group of Assistant Principals were in the past.

A careful watch will be necessary of the operation of the 'fast stream', even in the less drastic form that it has now assumed. The method of selecting the successful two-thirds of the A.T. grade must be fair, and be seen to be fair. The opportunities for those not selected must be seen to be good, as well as for those transferred to the ordinary H.E.O. grade who miss early promotion to Principal.

These aspects of the new system will be very much a matter for the Civil Service Department to keep under review, and here we come to the third big advantage of the new system. The creation of the Civil Service Department means that there is now an influential department which can be continuously watching over questions of this kind. In the past when there was no organization to do this the Service became rather too rigid. It took one of the infrequent inquiries like the Tomlin Royal Commission in 1929–31, or the Fulton Committee, to hold the Service up to the mirror and see if its procedures and structure needed to be rethought. If it does its job properly, the Civil Service Department will now be doing this all the time.

Finally, the establishment of a Civil Service College should help to place a greater emphasis on training, and improve its quality. Already we can see that the period of training is longer. Under the new system, Administration Trainees who go on to become H.E.O. (A)s will receive 30 weeks training. The content of training is being modified by the Civil Service College as experience shows which aspects and methods are most successful. For example, in the economic and social administration course students have been given recently a wider range of options built around real problems or projects. Students have studied the work of the Industrial Reorganization Corporation, the Urban Aid Programme with special reference to Gateshead, labour mobility in the E.E.C., and environmental pollution.[12]

Numerous criticisms can of course be made of developments since Fulton. For example, the majority of members of the Fulton Committee recommend that, in recruiting from the universities, the Civil Service Commissioners should give 'preference to relevance'. That is, they should give preference in their selection to candidates who had studied in the social sciences or other relevant areas. The minority of the Fulton Committee rejected this proposal, and the Government followed the minority rather than the majority view. The argument which prevailed was that the Civil Service should draw from the best graduates whatever the subject of their degree course.

This is a topic on which the Civil Service College may in time be able to throw some light. In some continental countries, in France for example, the Civil Service does more than give preference to relevance, and in fact only selects entrants from those applicants who have specialized in appropriate fields. The entrants to the French École Nationale d'Administration have all studied in political science institutes and have a common background of such subjects as History, Economics, Sociology, Political Science, and Law. The courses in the École Nationale d'Administration (É.N.A.) can therefore assume a common background knowledge such as cannot be assumed by the courses held at in the Civil Service College. The College is now maintaining close relations with the É.N.A., with a regular annual exchange of groups between the institutions. It may therefore be possible, in time, to compare the advantages of the French specialized entry system with the open-competition system in the United Kingdom.

Open Government

We have seen that one of the criticisms of the Civil Service made by the Fulton Committee was that there 'is not enough contact between the Service and the community it is there to serve'. The Committee said that in their view the administrative process was surrounded by too much secrecy, 'The public interest would be better served if there were a greater amount of openness.'[13] The report then went on to say, in one of its most eloquent passages, 'Since government decisions affect all of us in so many aspects of our lives, consultation should be as wide as possible and should form part of the normal process of decision-making. It is an abuse of consultation when it is turned into a belated attempt to prepare the ground for decisions that have already been taken.'[14]

What has been done since 1968 to improve methods of consultation with the public and to reduce the secrecy which surrounds the processes of government? One important innovation has been the publication of 'Green Papers' by the Government. The traditional White Paper is a statement by the Government of the policy which it intends to follow. A Green Paper is a discussion document in which the Government outlines a problem, makes proposals for dealing with it, and invites public comment on the proposals.

The pioneering Green Paper was in fact published in April 1967, before the Fulton Report appeared, and proposed a regional Employment Premium for the Development Areas in Britain.[15] From 1968 onwards the Wilson Government made increasing use of Green Papers. Thus, Kenneth Robinson's proposals for reorganization of the Health Service in 1968 appeared as a Green Paper, as did Richard Crossman's proposals in 1970 which had been extensively modified to take account of criticisms made of the earlier Green Paper.[16]

The Conservative Party came to power in 1970 committed, in its Election Manifesto, to working towards greater openness in government. The Heath Government cannot be said to have extended the idea of Green Papers, indeed in some instances they retreated from it. For example, Sir Keith Joseph's proposals for Health Service Reorganization were not issued as a Green Paper but as a Consultative Document which was not given a wide circulation, or put on sale to the public.[17] Green Papers have nevertheless been issued, for example, the Heath Government published its proposals for the use of specialist committees by the Commons as a Green Paper in October 1970. Several alternative methods for reforming the system of local government finance were put forward as a Green Paper in 1971.

The publication of Green Papers is therefore a move towards taking the public into consultation about the policy options open to government departments. Yet this is only a beginning and the use of Green Papers would have to become the rule rather than the exception before it would be possible to say that the public was being taken fully into consultation.

Another essential reform, if open government is to be made a reality, is a repeal or drastic amendment of the Official Secrets Acts.

At present, the Acts make it an offence for Civil Servants to communicate to the Press, and for journalists to publish, unauthorized information about government departments. In practice, the letter of the law is often widely ignored by departments; information is often given to journalists on a 'non-attributable' basis, that is, the information may be published or used by journalists, but the source of the information may not be given. This is, however, a very unsatisfactory practice since it is often difficult for the reader to tell which unattributed reports in the Press are reliable and which are not. It is also far from satisfactory that Ministers and senior Civil Servants are able to 'fly kites' without taking any responsibility for the ideas they put forward on a non-attributable basis.

The Heath Government appointed a committee under Lord Franks to examine proposals for revision of the Official Secrets Acts. The Committee reported in September 1972 and recommended that it should no longer be an offence for a Civil Servant to communicate information about his work unless the information fell into one of the following categories: if it had been entrusted to the government by a private individual or concern; if it was likely to assist criminal activities or impede law enforcement; if it was classified information relating to defence, foreign relations, the currency, or reserves. The Committee also felt that the Press should continue to be denied access to Cabinet papers. However, the prohibition would not apply completely here, and an offence would only be committed if the Minister decided that disclosure of information, in one of the reserved areas, would cause 'at least serious injury to the interests of the nation'.

If the recommendations in the Franks Report were to be implemented they would open up very considerable areas of British government to public scrutiny. Even so, there are strong grounds for saying that they do not go far enough. In Sweden every member of the public has the right of access to government information, unless a Civil Servant can show that there are overriding considerations of national security etc. which preclude access. Thus anyone may inspect the files of government departments and can only be denied this right by a decision of the Civil Servant. Such a decision to withhold access can only be made on strictly limited grounds, and can be challenged in the courts.

This right of access to government documents has existed in Sweden since 1766. Recently, Denmark and Norway have passed similar legislation. Britain should follow their example and, as has been suggested above in Chapter VI, Cabinet papers should not be exempt from disclosure, apart from those papers which fall within the reserved categories where communication would not be in the national interest. In this way open government could really be achieved.

'Hiving Off' and the Nationalized Industries

One of the recommendations made in the Fulton Report which we have not so far considered was the suggestion that further inquiries should be made into the desirability of 'hiving off' certain areas of Civil Service work to autonomous public boards or corporations.[18] At the time of publication of the report, the Wilson Government was already preparing to 'hive off' the Post Office. In 1969 the passage of the Post Office Act converted the Post Office from a government department into a public corporation, headed by a chairman and with a board responsible to a Minister who was given a reduced department with the title 'Ministry of Posts and Telecommunications'. This Ministry was terminated in 1974.

Another form of hiving-off transformed the Department of Employment and Productivity. The Employment and Training Act of 1973 set up the Manpower Services Commission which was given responsibility for the Employment Service Agency, including all the former Employment Exchanges, now renamed local offices of the Employment Service. The Manpower Services Commission, which went into full operation in October 1974, is headed by a chairman appointed by the Secretary of State for Employment. Its first Chairman was Sir Denis Barnes, a former Permanent Secretary of the Department of Employment. Of the other members of the Commission, 3 are appointed in consultation with the T.U.C., 3 in consultation with the Confederation of British Industries, 3 in consultation with Local Authority Associations, and 2 in consultation with professional educational interests. The Manpower Services Commission is also responsible for the Training Services Agency which co-ordinates Industrial Training Boards, and develops training services for industry and for individuals in industry.

At the same time, the Conciliation and Advisory Service and the Safety and Health Executive were set up, leaving the Department of Employment with only residual functions. Five semi-independent agencies have in this way been created out of the old Department of

Employment, with the Department itself now exercising only a general oversight of their activities. The rationale of these reforms is largely to give a greater coherence to each of the services or agencies. The old Employment Exchanges, of which there were nearly 1,000 did not really constitute a unified service, but in practice were run by nine regional controllers. To revitalize the service, and make it more responsive to the needs of its users, it was unified and put under the control of a Chief Executive.

There were also interesting changes in the constitution of the group boards of the Iron and Steel Industry, which were renationalized in this period. The nationalization measures since 1945 have all provided for industry to be run by an appointed board, or boards, on Herbert Morrison's pattern of the 'efficiency board'. In Morrison's view, members of the board should be chosen for their personal ability and not as representatives of trade unions or employers' associations. Therefore, although many of the boards included members who were trade unionists, they were never considered to be representatives of trade unions, or in any way accountable to the workers in the nationalized industry concerned.

The Iron and Steel Act 1967 was no different from the earlier nationalization statutes in this respect. But two members of the British Steel Corporation, appointed under the Act, proved to have a particular interest in the idea of worker–directors. They were the chairman, Lord Melchett, and the board member responsible for industrial relations, Ron Smith. Melchett was the grandson of Lord Mond who as an employer had shown an interest in joint-consultation in industry, and Ron Smith had been General Secretary of the Post Office Union which has had a long record of pressing for industrial democracy.[19]

Melchett and Smith were both members of a committee which produced a plan to appoint worker–directors to each of the four group boards of the British Steel Corporation. In 1972 the experiment was assessed and was felt to be sufficiently successful to be extended and modified. The modifications are of considerable interest. Whereas originally the employee–directors were selected by the Corporation from a list of names put forward by the trade unions, in 1972 the Corporation decided that in future they would be selected jointly by a committee of the unions and the Corporation. The other important change was that, whereas previously worker–directors had not been allowed to hold trade union office when appointed to the board, this rule was now rescinded. Thus, as the Corporation's statement pointed out in March 1972, 'Links with unions are to be strengthened and employee-directors are to be given the right to hold union office.' The statement went on to say that there would be closer contact than before between the worker-directors and the Steel Committee of the trade unions, and with national and local full-time union officials.[20]

Not only has the Steel Corporation experimented with the idea of worker–directors, therefore, but, after five years experience, it has decided to appoint 16 such directors in place of the original 10 and to make them representative of the unions, and in continuous contact with union opinion. This may well prove to be the most significant development in the organization of nationalized industries in the last eight years. Although in this period there have been flurries of de-nationalization, of Thomas Cooks and the Carlisle public houses for example, and unexpected nationalization, for example of Rolls-Royce by the Heath Government, it is of much greater interest that, in the case of steel, the idea of the 'efficiency board' has been breached. It is particularly significant in the view of the interest now being taken in participation by workers in management in Western Germany, in both the state and private sectors. It may be that the concept of 'efficiency boards' for running nationalized industries is on the way out, and that they will be replaced either by representative boards, or by boards with a considerable element of trade union representation and perhaps also, in time, of consumer representation.

NOTES

1 H.C. 308 of 1964–65, Sixth Report from the Estimates Committee: Recruitment to the Civil Service, p. xxxv.

2 Hugh Thomas (ed.), *The Establishment*, pp. 72–115; Balogh's essay was republished in Hugh Thomas (ed.), *The Crisis in the Civil Service* (Anthony Blond, 1968), pp. 11–52.

3 Fabian Society, *The Administrators. The Reform of the Civil Service.*

4 Sir Philip Allen became Permanent Under-Secretary of State at the Home Office in 1966, and had previously been Second Secretary at the Treasury; Sir James Dunnett was Permanent Under-Secretary of State at the Ministry of Defence, and had previously been Permanent Secretary at the Ministry of Labour. Norman Hunt was Fellow in Politics at Exeter College, Oxford; Lord Simey was Professor of Social Science at the University of Liverpool. Sir Edward Boyle was Conservative M.P. for Birmingham, Handsworth, had been Minister of Education from 1962 to 1964, and from 1964 to 1966 was a member of the Estimates Committee; Shirley

Williams was Labour M.P. for Hitchin; Robert Sheldon was Labour M.P. for Ashton-under-Lyne. Sir Norman Kipping was former head of the Federation of British Industries; Sir John Wall was the Managing Director of Electrical and Musical Industries Ltd. W. C. Anderson was General Secretary of the National and Local Government Officers Association.

5 Richard A. Chapman (ed.), *The Role of Commissions in Policy Making* (Allen and Unwin, 1973). See his own chapter, 'The Fulton Committee on the Civil Service', pp. 18–19.

6 Cmnd. 3638, The Civil Service, vol. 1: Report of the Committee 1966–68 (H.M.S.O., 1968), pp. 104–6.

7 Ibid.

8 A unified grading system had already been agreed for the highest ranks of the Civil Service from Permanent Secretary to Under-Secretary.

9 See First Report of the Civil Service Department (H.M.S.O., 1970), pp. 25–6.

10 Civil Service Department, The Civil Service College 1971–72. Second Annual Report by the Principal to the Civil Service College Advisory Council (H.M.S.O., 1973), pp. 19–22.

11 Op. cit., p. 22.

12 Op. cit., p. 20.

13 Cmnd. 3638, p. 91, para. 277.

14 Ibid., p. 92, para. 278.

15 Department of Economic Affairs and H.M. Treasury, The Development Areas. A Proposal for a Regional Employment Premium (H.M.S.O., 1967).

16 See chap. X pp. 159–64 for a discussion of the content of these Green Papers.

17 See pp. 165–8.

18 Cmnd. 3638, pp. 61 and 106.

19 See G. Stuttard (ed.), *Teaching Industrial Relations: Industrial Democracy and Industrial Relations. A Report* (Society of Industrial Tutors, 1972), p. 8.

20 Op. cit., p. 12.

CHAPTER VIII

Local Government Reform

THIS was the reform which seemed to be longest in coming. It had been discussed for so long and proposals for change met with so much resistance that it seemed that it would never happen. Even when the Local Government Act became law in 1972, there was a certain air of unreality. It hardly seemed possible that an entirely new pattern of local authorities outside London would in 1974 take the place of the familiar system which had existed in England and Wales since the 1880s and 1890s.

From 1888 to 1965

The Local Government Act of 1888 set up county councils, the 1894 Act established urban and rural district councils, and an Act of 1899 established metropolitan borough councils within the area of the County of London, which was itself set up under the Act of 1888. This pattern of local authorities remained essentially unchanged until reorganization in 1974. By this time, many local authorities had become too small for the services they were required to administer. When the Acts of 1888 and 1894 were passed, counties and districts did not have responsibility for education and planning, two of the most complex services now administered by local government. The motor car was in its infancy, and the problems of urban planning which motor transport would create were still in the future.

It is therefore remarkable that a pattern of local authorities designed when conditions were so different should have survived with little change into the mid-1970s. The reasons for its survival must lie chiefly in the resistances to change which were built into the existing system. One of the principal causes of resistance was the conflict of interests between the county boroughs and the county authorities. The 1888 Act gave a special status to the larger boroughs in England and Wales which were in existence when the Act was passed. They were made into county boroughs, which meant that they became self-governing enclaves, exempt from county administration. So what were, in effect, two systems of local government were created side by side. In the county boroughs a single elected council was responsible for all the services, and there was no lower tier of local government. In the county areas, the county councils were responsible for one range of services, while the municipal borough and urban and rural district councils were responsible for a further range.

The distribution of services between counties and districts varied a good deal over the years. It is convenient to give the picture which existed in the years immediately prior to reorganization in 1974. In the early 1970s education was a responsibility of the counties, as was the provision of social services, the ambulance service, health clinics, and midwifery services; the counties were also responsible for the fire services, and provided libraries. They played a major role in planning the use of land, and shared responsibility for roads with the central government, which was responsible for motorways and trunk roads, and with the districts, which were responsible for the minor roads. The main responsibility of the district authorities and the municipal boroughs was the provision of low-cost housing for rent. Their other functions included care of environmental health, which embraced sewerage and sewage disposal, measures to avoid epidemics, and the inspection of slaughter-houses, and other premises used for the preparation of food. Street cleaning and the disposal of refuse were also their responsibility. They could provide libraries, parks, and entertainments of various kinds. Finally, in the rural areas, a third tier of local government existed, since parish councils were responsible for such things as village halls, footpaths, and lighting in the village.

The 1888 Bill, as originally drafted, provided for the creation of only ten county boroughs, all with populations in the region of 150,000 or above. During the passage of the Bill, the government of the day accepted the argument put forward by M.P.s representing boroughs, on both sides of the House, that many more towns should be accorded county borough status. As a result, the 1888 Act, in its final form, established 61 county boroughs in England and Wales. Between 1888 and 1926 the number of county boroughs rose to 83, as towns which increased in population applied for, and secured, county borough status. This process was alarming to the counties since each creation of a county borough denuded the surrounding county. Pressure from the counties led to the passage of the 1926 Local Government (County Boroughs and Adjustments) Act which raised the minimum population requirement for acquiring county borough status to 75,000. The Act also made the procedure for securing this status much more difficult.

The counties also contested proposals to extend the area of existing county boroughs. As the built-up areas spread out beyond their boundaries, the county boroughs sought to enlarge their geographic areas accordingly. But this would mean that in every case the counties would experience a loss of rateable value. Between 1926 and 1939 a number of county boroughs managed to secure substantial extensions to their boundaries. During the Second World War no boundary changes were made and after 1945 only minor changes were agreed. During this period many municipal boroughs grew to a size which they could expect would entitle them to county borough status, but nevertheless no new county boroughs were created. For example, between 1949 and 1953 Ealing, Ilford and Luton introduced Private Bills into Parliament to be accorded county borough status, but all three Bills failed because the government of the day was opposed to this kind of piecemeal reform. At the other end of the scale, county boroughs which had diminished in size were able to retain their county borough status. Canterbury, for example, remained a county borough although it had a population of little more than 25,000 while a number of non-county boroughs had a population four times as large. So the local government map became almost frozen in the outlines it had assumed in 1939.

Another major reason for resistance to change lay in the strong loyalties developed by councillors and officials to their authorities. The close links which often existed between local party organizations and the Members of Parliament for the city or county concerned helped to ensure that these loyalties were well understood in Parliament and in the central government departments. Councils in the county boroughs in particular came to be largely organized on a party basis. The Labour or Conservative groups on these councils would leave their M.P.s in no doubt as to their views on local government reorganization. But councillor opinion could be equally effective against reorganization in the many county areas where, nominally at any rate, few councillors had party affiliations.

Finally, the two systems of local government, one-tier and two-tier, developed their own partisans. Those who were familiar with the one-tier system in the county boroughs argued that their system was more efficient since it avoided conflicts between a number of authorities. They also claimed that it was better understood by the public since only one authority was responsible for all services. The advocates of the two-tier system in the counties, on the other hand, argued that a second tier brought local government nearer to the citizen, while the top tier, at county level, provided the larger scale and larger financial base which was needed for complex services such as education.

It is difficult, perhaps impossible, to prove the rights and wrongs of this controversy. The advocates of the one-tier system could point to some very efficient county boroughs, such as Coventry, which was also notably far-sighted in its development of consultation with the public on planning issues, for example.[1] On the other hand, many counties, such as Leicestershire and the West Riding of Yorkshire, were noted for their imaginative educational policies and efficient administration. In some respects, the most efficiently organized local authority in Britain was the London County Council. London stood outside the pattern of county boroughs, counties, and districts which covered the remainder of England and Wales. The London County Council, set up in 1889, and the Metropolitan Borough Councils, set up in 1899, provided a two-tier structure for London, making the capital city the only city in England and Wales not organized on a one-tier basis.

During the Second World War, it was recognized that many anomalies had developed in the local government map, and that some considerable changes would be necessary if a generally high standard of service from local authorities was to be achieved. In 1945 a Local Government Boundary Commission was appointed for England and Wales with Sir Malcolm Trustram Eve as its chairman.[2] In 1947 the Commission produced a report which advocated extensive changes in the local government system.

The Commission argued that a 'major defect of the present organization is the disparity between individual counties and individual county boroughs in the matter of population and resources'.[3] The counties then ranged in size from Middlesex, with a population of over 2¼ million, to Rutland, with a population of just over 18,000. The county boroughs varied from Birmingham, with a population of over 1 million, to Canterbury with a population of 25,000. Many non-county boroughs like Ilford, with a population of 182,000 and Walthamstow, with a population of 124,000, were far larger than a great many of the existing county boroughs.

To remedy this situation the Commission proposed a new system of one-tier and two-tier counties. Some of the larger county boroughs, like Birmingham, would become one-tier counties. Many of the medium-size and smaller county boroughs would go into two-tier counties as new county boroughs. Thus the County Borough of Oxford would be merged with the County of Oxford. The new county boroughs would, in the Commission's own phrase, 'be most purpose authorities'. They would continue to be responsible for such services as education and the administration of town planning. But the preparation of the over-all development plan would be a matter for the county council, as would control of the police. The Commission also recommended that some of the smaller counties should lose their separate identity. Thus Rutland would be combined with Leicestershire, and Herefordshire with Worcestershire. There was much to be said in favour of this plan, but it met with intense opposition, especially from those county boroughs which would become new county boroughs and lose their fully autonomous status, and from the counties which would lose their separate identities. As the scheme was generally so unpopular it was shelved by the Attlee Government, and the Commission was wound up in 1949.

So the picture of local government remained as it was until in 1954 the Conservative Minister of Housing and Local Government decided on a new approach. He invited representatives of the five local authority associations to meet him to see if some programme for reform could be mutually devised. The difficulty was that the Association of Municipal Corporations, representing the boroughs, on the one hand, and the County Councils Association, the Urban District Councils Association, the Rural District Councils Association, and the National Association of Parish Councils, on the other, presented diametrically opposing views. The Association of Municipal Corporations advocated the extension of the one-tier system to the whole country, as far as circumstances would allow. The other four associations adopted the opposite approach, favouring a reduction in the number of county boroughs, and possibly the creation of a two-tier system in the conurbations.

In 1956, after a series of meetings with the five local authority associations, the Minister published a White Paper under the title 'Local Government. Areas and Status of Local Authorities in England and Wales'.[4] This announced that the Government proposed to set up two Local Government Commissions, one for England (the

London area excluded) and one for Wales. The English Commission would be concerned with five main problems: creation of new county boroughs, extension of existing county boroughs, the revision of the county areas, the revision of county district areas, and the organization of the conurbations.[5] The Local Government Act, 1958, set up these Commissions. But the procedure under which the English Commission had to operate was so long-winded and cumbersome that only very slow and piecemeal progress was made in redrawing the local government map outside London.

More thoroughgoing changes were made in the London area. The 1956 White Paper had recognized that London was a special problem, and in 1957 the Government set up a Royal Commission 'to examine the present system and working of local government in the Greater London area'.[6] London had long outgrown the system set up in 1889 and 1899. By 1957 nearly two-thirds of the population of Greater London lived outside the County of London area. The government of the metropolis was therefore shared between the L.C.C., the metropolitan boroughs, and the City of London at the centre, five counties, Middlesex, Hertfordshire, Essex, Kent, and Surrey, and three county boroughs, Croydon, East Ham, and West Ham. Another anomaly was the great disparity which by then had appeared in the size of the metropolitan boroughs. For example, Wandsworth had a population of around 338,000 and Holborn only 21,000.

The chairman of the Royal Commission, Sir Edwin Herbert, was a solicitor, who had been President of the Law Society.[6] He was a director of Associated Rediffusion Ltd. He had been chairman of a Committee of Inquiry into the Electricity Supply Industry in 1954. The other members of the Commission were W. J. M. Mackenzie, who was at that time Professor of Government at Manchester University, Sir Charles Morris, the Vice-Chancellor of Leeds University, Sir John Wrigley, a former Deputy Secretary in the Ministry of Health, Paul Cadbury of Cadbury Brothers Ltd., the chocolate manufacturers, Alice Johnston, a member of the National Assistance Board, and William Lawson, a chartered accountant and past president of the Royal Institute of Chartered Accountants, who was a member of the Southern Electricity Board.

The Royal Commission reported in 1960, and its recommendations, with some major modifications, were embodied in the London Government Act, 1963. The Act abolished the L.C.C., the county of Middlesex, and the three county boroughs in the greater London area, and established a two-tier system for virtually the whole of the built-up area. At the top, the Greater London Council assumed responsibility for some planning functions, for main roads, and fire and ambulance services throughout the area. The second tier consisted of London boroughs, each with a much larger population than most of the old metropolitan boroughs. After some debate it was decided that the minimum population of the Greater London boroughs would be 200,000.

All the London boroughs have responsibility for the social services, for health, local roads, and libraries. Care of housing, planning, and highways is shared with the Greater London Council. The outer boroughs also have responsibility for education, but in the area of the old L.C.C. this is the concern of the Inner London Education Authority. This is a committee of the Greater London Council consisting of G.L.C. members from boroughs within the old L.C.C. area together with one member from each of the Inner London boroughs, and one from the City of London. Its creation was a concession to those who argued that the excellent machinery and traditions of the L.C.C. education service should be carried over into the new framework of London government.

The new system in London has its critics. For example, Professor Robson has argued that too much independence was given to the boroughs. In his view, the Greater London Council should have been given responsibility for making over-all development plans for the Greater London area, as was originally proposed by the Royal Commission. He also argued that the G.L.C. should have responsibility for further education.[7] But the members of the Greater London group found the system to be a qualified success in their study of Greater London in the first five years.[8] A similar view was put forward by Mrs. Enid Wistrich in her study of the first years of Camden, one of the new London boroughs.[9]

While London was being wholly reorganized in this way, the English Local Government Boundary Commission was proceeding with its seemingly endless examination of the special Review and General Areas outside London. The Commission did produce some results. For example, in the West Midlands a number of county boroughs were merged on the lines which it proposed, the counties of Huntingdon and Peterborough were combined, and the Isle of Ely was merged with Cambridgeshire. Teesside was reorganized.

However, large areas of the country, posing some of the most complex problems, still had to be dealt with. Eventually, Richard Crossman, as Minister of Housing and Local Government, decided to cut the Gordian knot. He told a conference of the Association of Municipal Corporations, in 1965, that the Government had decided to terminate the work of the Local Government Boundary Commission for England, and appoint a Royal Commission to make recommendations on both the functions and areas of local authorities in England.

The Redcliffe–Maud Commission on Local Government in England

Crossman explained to the conference that he expected the Commission to operate on the principle of the city region, which had recently been put forward by Derek Senior in an influential article.[10] The essence of Senior's argument was that around the major towns have developed what are in effect city regions, and that it is logical and appropriate to modify the local government map to fit in with the pattern of life which has been adopted by people living in these regions. Thus, Reading is a centre for shopping, recreational and business purposes for a wide population living outside the city, in what were at that time parts of the counties of Berkshire, Oxfordshire, Buckinghamshire, Wiltshire, and Hampshire. The whole local government map, he suggested, should be redrawn by identifying the city regional areas on the basis of the patterns of travel undertaken by the population to work, to shop, and for recreational purposes. In this way, sufficiently large and viable new top-tier authorities could be set up which would not seem remote for anyone living in the area, since they would already be the accepted, and accessible, centres for shopping and other purposes.

In this same speech Crossman spoke in a similar vein about Coventry, for which he was M.P., as the recognized centre for the whole surrounding region. He not only implied that the Royal Commission should make the city region its operating principle, but nominated Derek Senior to the new Commission. In the event, however, in its report of 1969 the Commission only followed his ideas to a limited extent, and Senior himself presented a minority report.

An explanation of this lack of accord between the Royal Commission and Richard Crossman can be found within the very composition of the Commission. Its chairman, Sir John Maud, was at that time chairman of another major inquiry into local government. This was the Committee on the Management of Local Government which was set up jointly by the Minister and the local authority associations in 1964, and reported in 1967.[11] Sir John Maud had been a Lecturer in Politics at Oxford University in the late 1930s. During the Second World War he was a Civil Servant, and stayed on in the Civil Service after the war. He was Permanent Secretary at the Ministry of Education from 1945 to 1952, and at the Ministry of Fuel and Power from 1952 to 1959. From 1961 to 1963 he was British Ambassador to South Africa. During the lifetime of the Commission he was made a life peer, with the title Lord Redcliffe-Maud. It is therefore convenient to speak of the report of the *Redcliffe-Maud* Commission on Local Government in England, as distinct from the report of the *Maud* Committee on Management of Local Government.

The Commission also included several members who were prominent in local government. Sir Francis Hill had been a member of Lincoln City Council since 1932, and from 1957 to 1966 was Chairman of the Association of Municipal Corporations. T. Dan Smith had been leader of the Labour Party on Newcastle City Council. Hedley Marshall had been City Treasurer of Coventry and was, at that time, Senior Research Fellow in the Department of Local Government and Administration at the University of Birmingham. Jack Longland was Director of Education for Derbyshire, and a well-known broadcaster. Peter Mursell had been a member of West Sussex County Council since 1947, and in 1969 became chairman of that Council. He is a farmer. Two members of the Commission who were not connected with local government were Victor Feather and John Bolton. Victor Feather was Secretary of the Trades Union Council, and John Bolton was a businessman, chairman of numerous companies and Vice-President of the British Institute of Management. Another member not strictly connected with local government, Dame Evelyn Sharp, had nevertheless had an extensive experience of dealing with local authorities as Permanent Secretary of the Ministry of Local Government from 1955 to 1966 and previously as Deputy Secretary of that Ministry dealing with local authorities.

It is apparent that the composition of the Commission was very different from that of the Herbert Commission on London Government. Whereas the Herbert Commission included no one who was closely identified with the existing system of local authorities, the

Redcliffe-Maud Commission included five members who were, or had been, associated with county boroughs or county councils. Three of them, Sir Francis Hill, T. Dan Smith, and Hedley Marshall, had a county borough background. The weight of county borough membership may have influenced the Commission towards recommending a largely one-tier system. Further influence was brought to bear by the evidence from central government departments which favoured drastically reducing the number of local authorities, and leaned to the view that one-tier local government would be more efficient than two-tier.

The Commission was assisted by L. J. Sharpe, who, as Director of Intelligence, organized its research programme.[12] Volume 3 of the report contains a series of appendices prepared by the research staff;[13] they include studies of aspects of the changing relationship of town and country, of migration between major centres and their surrounding areas, and an appraisal of three surveys of representation and community. How far this research was taken into account by members of the Commission was not made clear in the report.

The Commission recommended a one-tier system for the whole of England outside the conurbations; for the conurbations themselves they adopted what was essentially the Greater London model. Each of the conurbations centred on Birmingham, Liverpool, and Manchester should have a metropolitan authority responsible for planning, transport, and major development. In each of these areas there should also be district authorities concerned with education, the personal social services, health, and housing.

For the rest of England, the Commission recommended that there should be 58 unitary authorities responsible for all local government services. In place of a district tier within these unitary areas there should be local councils which, in the words of the Commission's own summary of its report, would 'be elected to represent and communicate the wishes of cities, towns and villages in all matters of special concern to their inhabitants'.[14] These local councils should have the duty to represent local opinion, the right to be consulted, and the power to provide amenities such as village greens and municipal parks and, where their resources permitted, to share in the provision of certain services such as house-building and house improvement.[15]

In his minority report Derek Senior proposed that, outside London, England should be divided into 35 regional areas. In 31 of these areas there should be a two-tier system. The regional authorities should be responsible for structure planning, transport, and education. The main responsibilities of the district authorities should be the provision of personal social services, housing management, local planning, and consumer protection. He also advocated what he called 'common councils', which would represent 'existing parishes and towns or parts of towns small enough to have a real feeling of community'.[16]

There were similarities between the majority report and the proposals in Derek Senior's memorandum of dissent. Both the majority and the minority report took account of the idea of the city region, although to a different extent. Some of the top-tier areas suggested in the reports were identical. Both reports proposed an almost identical city region around Carlisle consisting of Cumberland and the northern part of Westmorland. The proposals in the two reports for the Norfolk area were almost identical, although Senior's proposals would have taken in a slightly larger slice of East Suffolk than the majority proposals suggested. Both reports proposed a Reading city region on broadly similar lines, but with differences of detail; the majority proposals would have taken in a considerable part of Hampshire, but no part of Wiltshire, into the Reading authority. Senior proposed to take in less of Hampshire, part of Wiltshire, and, to the north-east of Reading, the southern section of Buckinghamshire, which the majority report would have excluded.

The key difference between the two sets of proposals was that the majority report advocated unitary authorities outside the conurbations in every case, whereas Senior proposed district authorities within nearly all the new areas. Thus Senior's Carlisle city region would contain two district authorities, whereas the majority report wanted it to be a unitary area. The Norwich city region would have three district authorities, whereas the majority report proposed none. The Reading city region would have three district authorities, while the majority report again proposed none.

There were also four interesting exceptions in Senior's plan. The regions which in his view should not have district authorities were the Leicester city region, and the city regions based on Lincoln, Peterborough, and Cambridge. The Leicester city region which he proposed was quite compact and therefore it could reasonably be argued that it did not need to be subdivided into districts. The

Lincoln, Peterborough, and Cambridge regions were somewhat larger in area but they were relatively thinly populated, and did not include other urban centres of any considerable size.

A possible objection to Senior's plan was that it was based on a principle which did not apply in the thinly populated rural areas. One cannot in any strict sense speak of a Norwich city region extending from the Wash to south of Lowestoft. Similarly, a city region based on Plymouth which includes Newquay and Land's End is an improbable concept. It is still true, no doubt, that for many people living at Land's End the obvious place for them to shop for clothes or consumer durables is Plymouth which is in some respects a centre for them.

More serious criticisms can be levelled against the majority Redcliffe-Maud proposals. Two objections stand out in particular: first, if it was wrong to have district authorities outside the conurbations, why was it right to have a two-tier system in the conurbations? Second, the attachment to the idea of having unitary authorities outside the conurbations meant the relegation of great cities like Bristol to the status of glorified parish councils. It was this absence of a district tier with any worthwhile functions which was to prove the most criticized of the Redcliffe-Maud proposals. But before we go on to examine the adoption of a general two-tier system by the Conservatives in the 1972 Act, it is important to note the reception given by the Wilson Government to the Redcliffe-Maud Report.

The Labour Cabinet accepted the report in principle, and announced that it intended to implement it with certain modifications of detail. In a Command Paper issued in February 1970 the Government announced that it intended to create two further metropolitan areas in addition to the three recommended by the Redcliffe-Maud Commission;[17] these would be West Yorkshire and South Hampshire. It had also been decided that responsibility for education should be given to the metropolitan area authorities instead of to the metropolitan districts, as the Redcliffe-Maud Report had proposed. The Government's reason for this was that the metropolitan areas would have larger resources, and would be able to appoint the specialized staff particularly necessary in the field of further and higher education.

The Heath Government's Proposals and the Local Government Act, 1972

The Labour Government's Command Paper was never implemented because the general election which followed in June 1970 brought the Conservatives to power pledged, in the local government field, to preserve the district tier throughout England and Wales.[18] The Conservatives, in Opposition, had been receptive to an imaginative campaign waged by many district authorities against the Redcliffe-Maud proposals. 'Don't vote for R. E. MOTE' was a slogan which needed no explanation. In February 1971 the Department of the Environment issued a White Paper outlining the new government's proposals for reorganization of local government in England.[19] Outside the metropolitan areas the old pattern of counties and county boroughs should be replaced by a system of enlarged counties, each with a lower tier of district authorities. The new districts would on average be much larger than the old since an extensive process of merging districts and boroughs would be undertaken, aiming at a population for each district of not less than 40,000, except in the sparsely populated areas.[20]

The pattern of counties which the Government proposed kept closer to the traditional county pattern than either the Redcliffe-Maud or the Senior proposals had done. One proposal was that Cumberland, North Lancashire, and Westmorland should be merged into one new county, later named Cumbria, whereas, as we have seen, both Redcliffe-Maud and Senior had suggested that Cumberland and the northern part only of Westmorland should be combined into a city region centred on Carlisle. Again, while Redcliffe-Maud had proposed that Kent should be divided into two unitary areas, the Government proposed to preserve it as a county authority. But the new proposals did not altogether ignore the idea of the city region. For example, the proposal for an authority called Avon, including Bristol, Bath, Weston-super-Mare, and their environs, was largely taken over from the Redcliffe-Maud proposals. The key difference, of course, was that under the White Paper Bristol and Bath would be district authorities, and that there were to be three other district authorities within the county.

The division of powers which the White Paper proposed gave the principal functions to the counties, including education, the personal social services, the over-all control of planning, highways, traffic and transport, police and fire, although in some cases counties could be amalgamated for the last two functions. The districts were also to have considerable powers, principally over housing, planning, development control, and environmental health, and concurrent powers with the county councils over museums, art galleries, parks and open spaces, playing fields and swimming baths.

As discussion of the White Paper continued, the powers allocated to the districts increased to some extent, perhaps not surprisingly since some of the largest and most powerful county boroughs were to be accorded district status. For example, the White Paper originally stated that all planning staffs would be part of a unified service administered by the counties. Under pressure, the Government changed its decision, promising that the districts would also employ planning staff, and would be given the function of drawing up local plans. Concessions were also made to the districts by providing that, through agency arrangements, the districts could carry out certain functions on behalf of the county councils. During discussion of the Local Government Bill in Parliament, the Department of the Environment agreed to arbitrate between districts and counties when they could not agree on agency arrangements.

In November 1973 the Secretary of State decided the first series of cases in which applications for agency arrangements had been in part refused, in this instance by the new Leicestershire county. Most of the applications concerned highway functions, and the Secretary of State in each case adhered to the county's view. Early in 1974, however, he decided a number of cases in which there were disputes between the new counties of Humberside and Warwickshire and some of the districts within those counties, ruling that the counties should surrender agency powers to the districts. For example, where the previous council had carried out highway-maintenance functions within urban areas the Minister ruled that it was reasonable that the new district council be granted agency powers to carry on these functions.

As regards the conurbations, the White Paper accepted the Redcliffe-Maud recommendations for metropolitan authorities for the Birmingham, Manchester, and Merseyside areas. It also took over the Labour Government's proposal for a West Yorkshire metropolitan authority including Leeds, Bradford, Wakefield, and Halifax. The White Paper envisaged two further metropolitan authorities, one for South Yorkshire, including Sheffield, Rotherham, Doncaster, and Barnsley, and one for Tyne and Wear, including Newcastle, Gateshead, and Sunderland. The Labour Government's proposal for a South Hampshire metropolitan authority was rejected.

The White Paper and the ensuing Local Government Act drew the boundaries of the new metropolitan areas more tightly than the Redcliffe-Maud Report had intended. The Act limits them in effect to the continuous built-up areas, giving the new metropolitan counties little room for expansion within their own boundaries. This change resulted from opposition from the surrounding counties, such as Cheshire and Lancashire, to the loss of present and potentially valuable land for rating. This feature of the White Paper has been particularly criticized by George Jones on the grounds that 'each conurbation hemmed into its urban straightjacket, is impeded in tackling its many social problems, especially housing'.[21]

Professor Robson has raised similar objections and is also critical of the division of functions between the metropolitan counties and the metropolitan districts.[22] The Redcliffe-Maud Report had proposed that the metropolitan district authorities should have responsibility for education. The Wilson Government proposed to alter this to give responsibility for education to the metropolitan area authorities. The 1972 Act went back to the Redcliffe-Maud proposals, and also gave the metropolitan districts responsibility for the personal social services. The metropolitan districts are therefore much more powerful than the district authorities outside the conurbations. The Act's provision for the metropolitan areas bears a strong family resemblance to the London Government Act, 1963. The new metropolitan districts have powers similar to those of the boroughs in the outer London area.

Before we go on to examine changes made during the passage of the 1972 Local Government Act it is appropriate to consider developments in Wales and Scotland. A Local Government Commission for Wales had been set up under the 1958 Local Government Act. In 1963 the Commission published proposals for local government reorganization in Wales;[23] these attracted considerable criticism largely on the grounds that they showed too little regard for existing county boundaries in proposing a new pattern of counties. In 1965 the Secretary of State for Wales, Jim Griffiths, decided to set up an Inter-Departmental Working Party to discuss the various possibilities for reform. These discussions were in progress when the decision was taken to set up the Redcliffe-Maud Commission, and the Wilson Government accepted the Secretary of State's view that Wales should be excluded from the terms of reference of the Commission.

In 1967 the Secretary of State issued a White Paper setting out his proposals for Wales. The Paper suggested a new system of enlarged counties for the whole of Wales, except for the predominantly industrial areas in South Wales. The new larger counties would consist of a combination of existing counties, instead of cutting across county boundaries as the 1963 scheme had proposed. In fact, in some cases the identity of existing counties would be preserved by transforming them into districts. Thus an extensive new county of Powys, in mid-Wales, would combine the counties of Brecon, Radnorshire, and Montgomery; each of these authorities would become districts within the new county.

In the south, the Paper proposed to keep intact the county of Glamorgan, making only minor changes in its borders. The county of Monmouthshire was also to be preserved largely intact although it was to acquire the Welsh name of Gwent. The county boroughs of Swansea, Cardiff, and Newport were to continue in being, but the smallest of all the South Wales county boroughs, Merthyr, was to be merged with Glamorgan. The proposals therefore took no account of the idea of the city region in South Wales, where it would have been particularly appropriate. It is possible to identify city regions based on Swansea, Cardiff, and Newport. The idea is not viable in the rest of Wales since there are few towns of any size and, in many areas, the population is very scattered. A pattern of enlarged counties and districts is more appropriate.

Although the 1967 White Paper made firm proposals, the Wilson Government decided to wait for the report of the Redcliffe-Maud Commission before introducing legislation for local government reform in Wales. When the report came it advocated, as we have seen, unitary areas, based to some extent on the idea of the city region. The Government then decided to modify the proposals for South Wales and announced that legislation would provide for three unitary areas in South Wales, one centred on Swansea, one on Cardiff, and one on Newport.

The Conservative Secretary of State for Wales, Peter Thomas, accepted these three areas in his Consultative Document, The Reform of Local Government in Wales.[24] But, in harmony with the scheme for local government reorganization in England, he announced that there would be a second tier of district authorities in each of the three areas. As far as the rest of Wales was concerned, he took over the 1967 proposals for a two-tier system of enlarged counties and districts. The scheme here differed in only one respect from the 1967 proposals. There had been opposition in North Wales to the suggestion that it should only contain one county. Peter Thomas, accepting the force of this criticism, opted for two counties in North Wales: a western county called Gwynedd to include the old counties of Merioneth, Caernarvonshire, and Anglesey, and an eastern county called Clwyd comprised of the old counties of Denbighshire and Flintshire.

This was not the end of the story, however. There was opposition in Cardiff to the suggestion that the capital city of Wales should be merged with the whole eastern part of Glamorganshire. A group of Conservative councillors in Cardiff campaigned strongly for a county authority separated from East Glamorgan, consisting of Cardiff and the area immediately to the west, which includes Barry, Cowbridge, and the predominantly rural and 'commuter country' zone which lies between them. The Heath Government accepted this proposal, despite very strong protests from the old Glamorgan county council. Glamorgan was eventually divided, like Gaul, into three parts. The 1972 Act brought into existence a West Glamorgan based on Swansea (with the boundaries first proposed by the Wilson Government), a South Glamorgan dominated by Cardiff, and the area in between known as Mid-Glamorgan.

This modification does not make much sense. The roads and the railway from the industrial settlements at the heads of the valleys run down to Cardiff which is therefore the natural centre for East Glamorgan. Lopping-off South Glamorgan has cut the city region in two, and left in Mid-Glamorgan an amorphous area which, although populous (531,000), has no natural centre and has a relatively low rateable value per head of population. The eventual outcome in Wales owes something therefore to the earlier Welsh proposals, something to the Redcliffe-Maud Commission, something to the 1971 Conservative Government's scheme, and something, at the last stage before legislation, to these curious modifications made in the Cardiff area.

Reorganization in Scotland has taken on a different character again. A separate Royal Commission was set up alongside the Redcliffe-Maud Commission to make proposals for Scotland. The

Wheatley Commission reported in favour of a two-tier system throughout Scotland, the top-tier authorities to be called regions and the second-tier districts. Action on the report was delayed because the Heath Government decided that it was not feasible to have a bill on Scottish local government reorganization proceeding through Parliament at the same time as the English and Welsh Bill. The Scottish Bill was therefore taken in the session 1972–73, and by that time pressure from various directions produced a number of changes in the original Wheatley proposals. The Commission suggested that the whole of Scotland should be divided into 7 regions and 37 districts, but in the final result, the number of regions rose to 9 and that of districts to over 50. Orkney, Shetland, and the Western Isles also managed to win exemption from the general system, being accorded the status of all-purpose authorities. The new system in Scotland was phased to come into operation in the spring of 1975, a year after reorganization in England and Wales.

We have been talking up to now of reorganization of local government almost entirely in terms of areas and boundaries, and sought to clarify this complicated picture. It would be wrong, however, to think of the reforms of 1972 and 1973 solely in these terms. For example, the 1972 Local Government Act made important changes in the powers of parish councils in England and of their equivalents in Wales, now known as community councils. There are more parish councils than before in England, since not only do previously existing parish councils continue to function, but many boroughs and urban districts which were merged into other authorities in April 1974 took on parish council status. The new district councils will be able to propose further parish councils, and must do so where a parish has 200 electors or more, and wishes to form a council.

The powers of the parish councils now extend much farther: they are able, with the consent of the county council, to provide off-street car parking; they are able to provide public conveniences; they are empowered to maintain bands and orchestras, and provide other kinds of entertainment; they can support and encourage local arts and crafts; they can provide facilities for recreation, conferences, trade fairs and exhibitions. These are all new powers arising from the 1972 Act and supplement the authority which they already had to provide street lighting, public footpaths, allotments, and so on.

Obviously, only the larger parish councils will be able to exercise some of the more ambitious new powers conferred by the Act.

However, all parish councils are now able to exercise the right to be notified of planning applications. This will enable parish councils to scrutinize planning applications made in their areas, and then to make representations to the district council. This is potentially the most important new function being given to parish councils since there is at present in many areas quite inadequate scrutiny of planning applications lodged with the planning authority. By and large, this can only be said to be really adequate where an active Civic Society regularly undertakes this scrutiny.

Another important change made by the 1972 reforms was the abolition of aldermen in the new authorities. The aldermanic system, if used well, could enable the elected members of an authority to add to their number non-elected members who would bring special knowledge or expertise to the work of the council. Thus Margaret Cole was for many years an alderman of the London County Council, and made a valuable contribution to the Education Committee of the L.C.C.[25] But the Maud Committee on Management, examining the appointment of alderman in a sample of authorities, found that many authorities used the aldermanic system merely to swell the majority of the party in power. Thus the Labour Party in Swansea, which normally won two-thirds of the seats in the borough, regularly increased its majority to give itself three-quarters of the seats on the council by appointing all the aldermen from among its own supporters. It also chose as aldermen exactly the same kind of person who was elected as a Labour councillor. In fact, the Labour councillors took turns to be aldermen. The abolition of aldermanic seats should in many areas, therefore, make for a closer contest between the parties, and do something to enhance local democracy.

One of the major changes made during the passage of the Bill was potentially even more important. The Bill, as introduced, provided that, in principle the committee meetings of all local authorities would be open to the public but that by resolution the public could be excluded for a period which could be as long as a year. After pressure during debate in the Commons, the Government agreed to introduce an amendment in the Lords which provided that a resolution to exclude the public must be made at each committee meeting and would only apply for that meeting. This means that the presumption will be that normally all committee meetings will be open to the public.

This is a significant reform in providing for more open government at local level. Previously, only education committee meetings were by law open to the public (as were meetings of committees including all members of the council), and in many localities members of the public were rarely seen, even at education committee meetings, because only few people knew of their right to be present. Now that all committee meetings will normally be open to the public it is likely that some interested members of the public will know about and exercise their right to attend. The Press will normally be able to report on the proceedings of all committees. More of the decision-making process in local government will come under public scrutiny, and this is all to the good.

As the provision in the Act unfortunately does not extend to sub-committees, this means that it will be possible for local authorities to exclude the Press and public from their meetings. Such action will obviously be against the spirit of the Act, but the only sanction against an authority which does not open its sub-committee meetings must, for the time being, lie in the public disapproval which this is likely to occasion.

The Local Government Bill was very fully discussed in both Houses of Parliament, and other important amendments were proposed from the back-benches and were accepted by the Government. For example, the Government conceded the strength of the case put forward by those who argued that the Isle of Wight should remain a separate county, and not be merged with Hampshire as the Bill, when introduced, had proposed.

Lord Redcliffe-Maud, speaking in the debate on the third reading of the Bill in the Lords, said that when the Act became law it would 'rank as the first major systematic and comprehensive measure which Parliament has placed on the Statute Book in the field of local democracy in this country'.[26] This was a generous tribute from the chairman of the Commission which had advocated reorganization on rather different lines. But his comments prompt one to ask how far the new system will be more efficient and more democratic?

These are difficult questions to which only time and much careful research and comparison can provide a proper answer, but some tentative comments can be made. One of the major defects of the old system was the extent to which elections to local councils were uncontested. Not only in the rural areas, but also in some boroughs, a proportion of seats was regularly uncontested. There is something more than a little absurd about a 'public representative' who rarely, if ever, has to answer to the electors because no one stands against him, either because his party has an unassailable position in the ward, or because sufficient interest cannot be generated among the electorate.

It is likely that reorganization will lead to fewer uncontested elections because in so many of the new authorities town and country are combined. As a great many of the towns are organized on party lines, where the contest in the town between the political parties is a close one the parties are likely to go out into the countryside to try and maximize their support there. This will mean that rural areas which had become accustomed to having many uncontested, or rarely contested, seats will find that local elections are becoming livelier. Or it may happen, for example, that a firmly entrenched Labour majority in a town will find that it has to fight to retain control because, in the rural area with which it is merged, Conservatives and Independents are strongly represented. Of course, there will be areas where a Labour majority in a town will merge into a Labour majority in the surrounding rural area (for example in West Glamorgan).

Although there may be fewer uncontested seats in the reorganized system, there will still be areas where one party predominates, and pockets in those areas where elections are not keenly contested. Only the adoption of proportional representation for local elections would be likely to promote a high degree of electoral participation almost everywhere. But any system of proportional representation would need to maintain the connection between councillors and electors at ward level. If multi-member constituencies were to be established on a wide basis, the contact between councillors and electors would become tenuous.

We have seen that reorganization under the 1972 Act involves in many cases the combination of town and country, both by the merger of former county boroughs with their surrounding counties and, at district level, by the creation of larger districts which combine rural and urban areas. On balance, this is likely to have good effects, not only in increasing interest in local elections. It is interesting to recall that as long ago as 1947 G. D. H. Cole advocated combining town and country in what he called 'town and country incorporations'.[27] These were to be in effect enlarged district authorities, each including a town, or towns, and the surrounding rural area. As a result of reorganization, these 'town and country incorporations' are now being established in many areas. Ending the separation of town and country in this way, may, in the short term, cause friction between the representatives of the urban and rural areas in the new authorities, but in the longer term, should have beneficial effects.

One of the avowed aims of Ministers in carrying through reorganization was to reduce central government control over local authorities. Peter Walker, as Secretary of State for the Environment, told the Commons, when opening the second reading debate on the Local Government Bill on 16 November 1971, that the larger, better staffed authorities which would result from reorganization would enable the central government to jettison 100 of the specific controls which had been felt to be necessary when departments were dealing with counties and districts with very small populations and an exiguous staff.[28] But in the same Parliament, during which the Department of the Environment was doing away with controls over burial-fees and fees charged at local markets, the Government introduced the Housing Finance Act. This measure aroused so much opposition on Labour-controlled authorities that it produced a running fight between the Government and those authorities like Clay Cross and Clydebank which carried defiance of the Government to the ultimate point. In Clay Cross, Merthyr, and Bedwas and Machen, the Government appointed Housing Commissioners to take over the housing functions of the local councils concerned. In these instances, therefore, administration of the Act led to a temporary supersession of the local authority by the central government in this particular service.

The announcement of sweeping cuts in local expenditure in Anthony Barber's mini-budget of December 1973 also highlighted the extent to which local authorities are subject to central control in financial matters. One is therefore entitled to feel a little sceptical about the proposition that the new authorities will be less subject to tutelage from the centre than the old authorities were. The exigencies of economic policy will always result from time to time in significant interventions by the central government into local policy and budgetary planning. Similarly, conflicts in policy between the central government and local authorities over such matters as housing finance, or the introduction of comprehensive education, are bound to recur.

It must also be noted that the Water Act, 1973, took away a number of significant functions from local government. The Act, introduced in February 1973 by Geoffrey Rippon, as Secretary of State for the Environment, set up 10 regional water authorities and a National Water Council. The regional water authorities took over the functions of the former river authorities, and of all the water undertakings and sewerage authorities. Local authorities therefore lost their water supply and sewerage functions. Although local authorities have representation on the new water authorities, roughly one-half of the membership of each water authority consists of nominated members. The object of the reform was laudable, namely to secure better co-ordination and planning in the provision and supply of water and sewerage services.[29] However, it reduced the area of local government, and contributed to the friction over rate increases in 1974.

The Local Government Act, 1972, was only to a small extent concerned with the internal organization of local authorities, but at the same time it was widely recognized that reorganization provided an unprecedented opportunity for improvement. The Act gave scope for innovation by providing that only the education and social services committees of local authorities would be statutory. Apart from this, the new authorities were given a wide degree of freedom in determining their management and committee structures.

The Bains Report

Peter Walker, as Secretary of State for the Environment, had foreseen the need for new thinking on the internal organization of local authorities. Acting in conjunction with the local authority associations, he set up a study group on Local Authority Management Structures in May 1971. This study group was made up of two sections: its Steering Committee consisted of representatives of the local authority associations (the Association of Municipal Corporations, and the County Councils', Rural District Councils' and Urban District Councils' associations), a representative of the Department of the Environment, a financier, and an industrialist. The other section, known as the Working Group, was chaired by M. A. Bains, the Clerk of Kent County Council. It included two town clerks, a county treasurer, the clerk of a rural district council, and the clerk of an urban district council. The seventh member was the Company Secretary of Imperial Chemical Industries. Their report, *The New*

Local Authorities. Management and Structure, published in August 1972 is invariably known as the 'Bains Report'.[30]

This report was to prove highly influential and compares more than favourably with the Maud Committee Report on Management of Local Government (1967). But, as the Bains Report itself acknowledges, the Working Group was able to build upon some of the ideas put forward in the Maud Report, and to benefit from the discussions which followed it. The Bains Report put its finger on one of the major defects in the internal organization of local authorities under the old system, pointing to 'the ingrained departmental approach to management' which still characterized so many authorities.[31] Under the old system, each department in an authority, whether education, social services, health, or highways, was very much a law unto itself. It reported to the relevant committee and the committee's minutes could be challenged in full council. But few authorities had any really satisfactory machinery to co-ordinate the work of these quasi-independent departments. The Town Clerk or County or District Clerk was the leading official, but his principal function was to act as legal adviser to the Council. The Treasurer had a co-ordinating role of a kind but his main function, and that of the Finance Committee, was to prune the estimates put forward by the departments, not to formulate with the departments a coherent system of forward planning of expenditure.

The Bains Report urged upon local authorities the need to adopt a corporate rather than a departmental approach to local affairs. It suggested that each authority should appoint a Policy and Resources Committee 'to provide co-ordinated advice to the Council in the setting of its plans, objectives and priorities'. This Committee 'should also exercise overall control over the major resources of the authority and co-ordinate and control the implementation of the Council's programmes'.[32] The report recommended that each authority should appoint a Chief Executive whose role would be very different from that of the traditional Clerk. He need not necessarily have legal training, and should be appointed on the grounds of his managerial ability and his personality. He should be free of all departmental responsibilities and lead a management team of principal Chief Officers whose tasks would be to prepare 'plans and programmes in connection with the long-term objectives of the Council, and for the general co-ordination of the implementation of those plans'.[33] The Chief Executive would, of course, maintain close contact with the Chairman of the Policy and Resources Committee.

Although the proposals put forward in the Bains Report are in no way binding on the new local authorities, they have been well received, and it seems that a widespread attempt is being made to implement them. For example, in many of the advertisements for principal officers of the new authorities it was emphasized that the principal officer concerned (for example, a Director of Social Services) would take part in the corporate planning of the authority, as a member of the management team. In 1973 the Institute of Local Government Studies of the University of Birmingham made a survey of the new authorities, asking them how far they planned to implement the main proposals of the Bains Report. Twenty-eight of the 31 new counties provided information for this survey. Twenty-six of the counties reported that they were setting up a Policy and Resources Committee, or Policy Committee. Twenty-six counties also reported that they were appointing a Chief Executive Officer, although 4 of them said that he would also be known as County Clerk. Most of the metropolitan counties and more than half of the metropolitan districts also indicated that they were appointing a chief executive, broadly on the lines of the Bains recommendations, although they were less specific about what his role would be.[34]

It remains to be seen how far the new structures recommended by Bains will really be adopted, as distinct from authorities merely deciding to use a new set of labels for their officers and committees. There will also inevitably be problems associated with the Bains ideas. For example, the aim of achieving greater co-ordination by means of a management team of principal officers led by the Chief Executive is obviously laudable. But one immediately asks how busy principal officers are to find the time to be members of such a management team. It may happen that either the management team will be a sham, and will rarely meet, or that it will be so time-consuming that the principal officers will find it difficult to devote enough time to their own departments. The solution to this dilemma may be found in the appointment of an additional senior officer within each main department, in order to take some of the departmental administrative load from the shoulders of the principal officer.

It should not be thought that the Bains Report is only about management structures, important although this aspect is. The report also recommends ways in which channels of information between the authority and the public which it serves can be improved. The report emphasizes the role of the Council as a debating and policy-formulating forum.

Debates on the broad policy options, perhaps on the basis of papers from committees of the sort issued from time to time by central government to stimulate discussion on particular issues, would enable the arguments on each side to be heard before effective decisions are taken. The press and public too would be better informed and, we believe, encouraged to play their part if they felt that important matters were to be debated before the effective decisions were taken.[35]

So the report envisages the Green Paper idea being taken over from central government. One of the strongest features of the report is that it combines ideas for improving management with ideas for improving channels of communication with the public.

We may conclude that reorganization now provides an exceptional opportunity for the improvement of local government. The larger authorities should result in the employment of more specialized staff, a better financial base, and an improvement in the standard of service in such fields as education and the social services. The retention of the district tier and the development of parish, or community, councils should help to prevent decision-making bodies from becoming too remote from the ordinary citizen. The reform of management and committee structures could result in a more unified and coherent approach to the problems of local administration. The opening of all committee meetings to the public, the adoption of general debates on consultative policy documents, the development of public relations, and positive measures to encourage public participation in decision-making, could revolutionize the relationship between local authorities and the public they serve. The opportunities are there: whether they will generally be taken is another matter.

Local Government Finance

One area in which reform was delayed, however, was in the financing of local government. The Heath Government's Green Paper on Local Government Finance discussed various proposals for new sources of local revenue, such as local income tax or sales taxes, and came down in favour of retaining rates as the predominant method of local taxation, backed by central government grants. The disadvantages of this system are, first, that rates on property in the form of buildings are a very inefficient, because inelastic, method of raising revenue, and second, that a heavy dependence on central government grants can make local authorities too subservient to central government and can bring them too much under central control.

The inadequacy of the rating system was dramatically demonstrated in 1974. A combination of circumstances, namely rapid inflation, changes in the method of assessing rate support grants, local government reorganization, and the impact of newly created water and sewerage authorities, resulted in a very big increase in rate demands in many areas. This led to 'rate revolts' and the formation of organizations specifically dedicated to doing away with rates and curbing local expenditure.

The unrest, and the pressure exerted at Westminster by the Opposition Conservative and Liberal Parties, and by Labour backbenchers, led to swift action by the Wilson Government. At the beginning of a Commons debate on rates initiated by the Conservatives on 27 June 1974, Anthony Crosland, Secretary of State for the Environment, announced that the Government had decided to set up a full-scale inquiry. It would be an independent inquiry with wide terms of reference, being instructed 'to review the whole system of local government finance and make recommendations'.[36] He had asked the Committee to report as soon as possible, and in any event before the end of 1975.

The chairman of the Committee, appointed in July 1974, was Frank Layfield, Q.C.[37] Local authority members of the Committee included Dame Kathleen Ollerenshaw, a member of Manchester District Council, Viscount Ridley, the chairman of Northumberland County Council, John Cartwright, a member of Greenwich Borough Council, and George C. Sharp, the Convenor of Fife County Council.[38] Local officials on the Committee were Alexander Bushnell, the County Clerk and Treasurer of Perthshire County Council, and Maurice Stonefrost, the controller of financial services for the Greater London Council. Geoffrey Drain, the General Secretary of the National Association of Local Government Officers, was also a member of the Committee. The three academic members were Professor John Stewart, associate director of the Institute of Local Government Studies at Birmingham University, George Jones, a Senior Lecturer in Political Science at the London School of Economics, and Alan Day, Professor of Economics, also at the L.S.E. Barry Thornton Jones, the Chief Rating Surveyor for

Imperial Chemical Industries, was the one representative of industry on the Committee.

Labour, Conservative, and Liberal leaders were agreed in deciding to await the report of this Committee before introducing legislation for reforming the system of local government finance. But Conservative leaders were sufficiently disenchanted with the rating system to announce at a press conference on 28 August 1974 that the Conservative Party, if returned to power at the forthcoming election, would abolish rates within the lifetime of a Parliament. Mrs. Thatcher, the Shadow Secretary of State for the Environment, said that in the interim a Conservative Government would help ratepayers by transferring to central government the cost of a specified number of teachers' salaries in each local authority. There would also be an increase in central government grants towards police and fire services during this interim period.

One of the associations of local authorities was also considering a radical reform of local finance. In July 1974 the Finance and Rating Sub-Committee of the Association of Metropolitan Authorities reported that in its view the existing system of local government finance was 'outworn and unacceptable to the public'. It favoured a system under which local authorities would be allocated 'a definite proportion of the global total of national taxation, which would thus provide local authorities with a buoyant source of income'. This could be achieved by a 'combination of a block needs element grant distributed on a national formula, with additional grants of a percentage above threshold type, thus providing supplementary help for areas of proved high need and burden'.[39] It seemed that there was a strong possibility of a thoroughgoing reform of local government finance.

Corruption in Local Government

Another cause of continuing concern in local government is the extent to which in recent years court cases and investigations have revealed corruption and favouritism on the part of councillors and officials, particularly in the field of planning applications and contracts. The incidence of corruption is probably very small in relation to the vast number of planning decisions made and contracts awarded each year. However, the Heath Government was sufficiently concerned to set up yet another Maud Committee to consider the problem. In 1973 the Prime Minister announced that a committee, to be chaired by Lord Redcliffe-Maud, would be asked to examine local government law and practice as they related to: (i) 'the conduct of both members and officers in situations where there is or could be a conflict between their position in local government and their private interests, (ii) qualification or disqualification for service as a member of a local authority or any of its committees'. The other members of the Committee were Sir Philip Allen, formerly Permanent Secretary of the Home Office, Stuart Lloyd Jones, Town Clerk of Cardiff, Sir Mark Fleming, a former chairman of the Association of Municipal Corporations, and Leigh Pemberton, Chairman of Kent County Council. David Widdicombe, a London barrister and a member of 'Justice', was also on the Committee.

The Committee's report (*Conduct in Local Government*) appeared in May 1974 and confirmed that the record of convictions for corruption or dishonesty was not high.[40] In the eight years from 1964 to 1972, only 10 elected members and 22 employees were convicted of offences under the Prevention of Corruption Acts, and 16 members were convicted of failure to disclose a pecuniary interest under the Local Government Acts. As the Committee pointed out, these figures were very low compared with the total number of elected members in 1972, around 48,000, and the total of over 2 million employees of local authorities.[41]

The Committee nevertheless recognized that there was widespread disquiet about conduct in local government, and it made a number of recommendations for changes. One important suggestion was that councillors should be required to disclose a pecuniary interest wherever it arose. As things stood, councillors could give a general written notice of interest which, when lodged with the Clerk of the authority, absolved them from making further declarations of interest. The Committee rightly thought that such a written declaration was an insufficient safeguard. They recommended that a councillor who had disclosed a pecuniary interest should be required to withdraw from the meeting unless the Secretary of State had removed his disability from speaking or voting.[42]

Another suggestion was that a compulsory register of pecuniary interests of councillors should be established.[43] This register should be revised annually and should be open to inspection by any elector for the authority. The Committee suggested that local authorities should adopt standing orders prohibiting canvassing for appointments and requiring disclosure of kinship.[44] Finally, the Committee recommended that there should be a national code of local government conduct for all councillors; a suggested text for such a code was included at the end of the report.[45]

One of the best features of the report was the emphasis placed on the need for local authorities to pursue vigorous policies of communication with the public. As the Committee said, 'To secure public confidence the working of the authority should be both visible and intelligible.'[46] This did not mean that no council business should be confidential but that 'the aim should be to keep the total quantity of confidential business as small as possible, and to ensure that initially confidential business which is to become public should do so at the earliest, not the latest, practicable stage'.[47]

A weakness of the report was a certain caution in relation to some of the more radical ideas for change. For example, the Committee turned down the idea that there should be a general inspectorate of local government, in addition to the present specialized inspectorates of schools and constabulary. This was a pity since a national code of conduct in local government would be greatly reinforced by an inspectorate, one of whose tasks would be to see that the code was being adhered to.

The report of the Committee was overtaken by a decision of the Wilson Government to set up a further inquiry into standards of conduct in public life. In the early months of 1974 ramifications of the Poulson affair, which had been one of the main reasons for anxiety about conduct in local government also caused concern about the Civil Service and other parts of the public sector. For example, a Civil Servant at the Scottish Office was sent to prison for accepting a series of favours from Poulson. In April 1974 the Prime Minister announced that a Royal Commission on Standards of Conduct in Public Life would be set up; its terms of reference and part of its composition were announced in July and September 1974. The Commission was instructed 'to inquire into standards of conduct in central and local government and other public bodies in the United Kingdom in relation to the problem of conflict of interest and the risk of corruption involving favourable treatment from a public body', and make recommendations 'as to the further safeguards which may be required to ensure the highest standards of probity in public life'.

The Chairman of the Royal Commission was Lord Salmon, who was appointed a Lord of Appeal in 1972.[48] Other members of the

Commission included two former Labour Ministers, Lord Houghton and Margaret Herbison, Sir Henry Jones, chairman of the Gas Council from 1960 to 1971, Sir Melvyn Rosser, a chartered accountant who had been chairman of the Welsh Council since 1971, Sir Leslie Williams, the Secretary-General of the Staff Side of the Civil Service National Whitley Council, and Sir Hugh Cudlipp, a former editor and editorial director of the *Daily Mirror*. Sir Philip Allen was the one member of the Royal Commission who also served on the Redcliffe-Maud Committee on Local Government Rules of Conduct.

The Royal Commission was empowered by the Government to re-examine points considered by the Redcliffe-Maud Committee, if this was felt to be necessary.[49] The Government made clear that it did not intend to delay in acting on proposals made by the Redcliffe-Maud Committee. A circular sent by the Department of the Environment to all local authorities in the summer of 1974 urged them to give immediate consideration to recommendations of the Committee which could be implemented without a change in legislation. Consultations had already begun on proposals which would require changes in the law.

NOTES

1 See J. B. Cullingworth, *Town and Country Planning in Britain* (Allen and Unwin, 4th ed., 1972), pp. 309–12.

2 Sir Malcolm Trustram Eve was called to the Bar in 1919. During the Second World War he was chairman of the War Damage Commission. He was made 1st Baron Silsoe in 1963.

3 Report of the Local Government Boundary Commission for the year 1947, p. 3, para. 4.

4 Cmnd. 9381, published July 1956.

5 Op. cit., p. 6, para. 19.

6 Cmnd. 1164, Royal Commission on Local Government in Greater London. 1957–60. Report (H.M.S.O., 1960), p. 1.

7 In his preface to G. Rhodes (ed.), *The New Government of London. The First Five Years* (Weidenfeld and Nicolson, 1972), pp. x-xi.

8 Op. cit., pp. 492–6.

9 *Local Government Reorganization. The first years of Camden* (London Borough of Camden, 1972).

10 'The City Region as an Administrative Unit', *Political Quarterly*, 1965, pp. 82–91.

11 Committee on the Management of Local Government: vol. 1, Report of the Committee; vol. 2, The Local Government Councillor; vol. 3, The Local Government Elector; vol. 4, Local Government Administration Abroad (H.M.S.O., 1967).

12 L. J. Sharpe is a Fellow of Nuffield College, and University Lecturer in Public Administration. His publications include *A Metropolis Votes*, 1963, *Research and Local Government*, 1965, and *Voting in Cities* (ed.), 1967.

13 Cmnd. 4040–II, Report of the Royal Commission on Local Government in England 1966–1969, vol. 3, Research Appendices.

14 Cmnd. 4039, Short version of the Report of the Royal Commission on Local Government in England (H.M.S.O., 1969), p. 9.
15 Op. cit., p. 19.
16 Op. cit., p. 21.
17 Cmnd. 4276.
18 Cmnd. 4584, Local Government in England. Government Proposals for Reorganization (H.M.S.O., 1971).
19 Op. cit.
20 Op. cit., p. 10, para. 34.
21 G. W. Jones, 'The Local Government Act 1972 and the Redcliffe-Maud Commission', *Political Quarterly*, 1973, p. 160.
22 In G. Rhodes (ed.) *The New Government of London*, pp. xv-xvii.
23 Local Government Commission for Wales, Report and Proposals for Wales (H.M.S.O., 1963).
24 Welsh Office, The Reform of Local Government in Wales. Consultative Document (H.M.S.O., 1971).
25 See Margaret Cole, *Servant of the County* (Dobson, 1956).
26 H.L. Deb. vol. 844, col. 2040.
27 *Local and Regional Government* (Cassell, 1947).
28 H.C. Deb., vol. 826, col. 233–4.
29 The system set up by the Water Act, 1973, had been proposed by the Central Advisory Water Committee in its report *Future Management of Water in England and Wales* (H.M.S.O., 1971).
30 *The New Local Authorities. Management and Structure* (H.M.S.O., 1972).
31 Op. cit., p. xv, para. 5.
32 Op. cit., p. 124.
33 Op. cit., pp. 125–6.
34 Institute of Local Government Studies, University of Birmingham, *Recommendations to the New Local Authorities, 1973* (mimeographed paper, 1973), pp. 2 and 8–9.
35 Op. cit., p. 21, para. 4. 4.
36 H.C. Deb., vol. 875, col. 1771.
37 He was called to the Bar in 1954. From 1970 to 1973 he was chairman of the Inquiry into the Greater London Development Plan. He is the author (with A. E. Telling) of *Planning Applications and Inquiries*, 1953, and *Applications for Planning Payments*, 1955.
38 John Cartwright left the Committee on being elected Labour M.P. for Greenwich, Woolwich East, at the October 1974 general election.
39 Supplement to *Municipal Review* (August 1974); reports submitted to the meeting of the Association of Metropolitan Authorities on 18 July 1974, p. 45.
40 Cmnd. 5636, Prime Minister's Committee on Local Government Rules of Conduct: Conduct in Local Government, vol. 1: Report of the Committee (H.M.S.O., 1974).
41 Op. cit., p. 3, para. 14.
42 Op. cit., p. 13, para. 51.
43 Op. cit., p. 15, para. 59.
44 Op. cit., p. 18, para 73.
45 Op. cit., pp. 46–9.
46 Op. cit., p. 35, para. 135.
47 Op. cit., p. 36, para. 135.
48 Cyril Barnet Salmon was a Judge of the High Court of Justice, Queen's Bench Division, from 1957 to 1964. He was a Lord Justice of Appeal from 1964 to 1972. In 1966 he was appointed Chairman of the Royal Commission on the Working of the Tribunals of Inquiry Evidence Act, 1921.
49 See H.C. Deb., vol. 875, col. *107*, a written answer by the Prime Minister.

CHAPTER IX

Regional Government Reform

THE Redcliffe-Maud Report advocated an intermediate level of government between the central government and local authorities. It proposed provincial councils for each of the eight economic planning regions into which England had been divided in 1965, although it suggested some changes in the layout of these regions, particularly in the northern part of the country. The principal functions of such councils would be to settle the framework of land use and economic strategy, and to plan the development of education, personal social services, and cultural and recreational services in the region.

The Heath Government announced in February 1971 that it would suspend any action on this aspect of the Redcliffe-Maud recommendations until the Royal Commission on the Constitution had reported.[1] This Royal Commission had been set up in 1969, partly in response to Nationalist successes in by-elections. In 1966 the Plaid Cymru (Welsh Nationalist) Leader, Gwynfor Evans, was elected to the Commons at a by-election in Carmarthen. In 1967 a Scottish Nationalist, Mrs. Winifred Ewing, was successful at a by-election in Hamilton. These were not isolated instances of heavy polling by the Nationalists since they came near to returning Nationalist Members at other by-elections at this time.

To assume, however, that the Royal Commission on the Constitution was set up 'as a sop to the nationalists' would be to underestimate the significance of the trend of opinion which had contributed to Nationalist success. As the Commission's own research findings show, there is a widespread feeling that government has become too remote. Such attitudes are to be found in the English regions as well as in Wales and Scotland, but they were highlighted by the Nationalist victories in 1966 and 1967.

Before we discuss the report of the Royal Commission on the Constitution, which was published late in 1973, it will be helpful to consider the experience of regional government to date in the United Kingdom. This divides naturally into two sections: in

Northern Ireland on the one hand, and in Scotland, Wales, and England on the other. From 1920 to 1972 Northern Ireland had its own government and parliament which enjoyed a wide measure of autonomy in domestic affairs. It would not be accurate to describe the constitutional arrangements which existed at that time with the United Kingdom Parliament as 'federal'. The essence of federalism is that in a federal system the powers both of the general government and of the regional government are limited. The Constitution guarantees the right of the regional government not to be superseded or absorbed by the general government, and normally a supreme court, with power to declare legislation invalid, acts as an arbiter to interpret the Constitution.[2]

The Northern Ireland Government and Parliament at Stormont were always subordinate to the United Kingdom Parliament. Although they enjoyed a wide autonomy in practice, they could at any time be brushed aside by legislation of the United Kingdom Parliament. In fact, in 1972, the Westminster Parliament suspended the Northern Ireland Government and Parliament, and the following year enacted a new constitutional statute for Northern Ireland. The Northern Ireland (Constitution) Act, 1973, made the status of the Northern Ireland Executive clearly subordinate to the Secretary of State for Northern Ireland. The Secretary of State appointed the Chief Executive and departmental heads in the provincial administration, and also had the power to dismiss them. He was able to dissolve the Assembly at any time, if he thought that it was not possible to appoint a provincial Executive likely to be widely accepted throughout the community.

Elections to the Assembly in June 1973 were held under the single transferable vote method of proportional representation, with the express intention of securing increased representation of the Catholic minority. After prolonged negotiation, election of the Assembly was followed by the formation of a 'power-sharing' Executive including the more moderate Unionists, the Social Democratic and Labour Party (a largely Catholic party), and members of the Alliance Party. Talks then took place between the new Executive, the Government of the Irish Republic, and the United Kingdom Government, resulting in the Sunningdale Agreement to set up a Council for Ireland, which was to link, albeit in a tenuous way, the two parts of Ireland which had been separated in 1920.

This was more than the hard-line Unionists were prepared to

tolerate. In the general election of February 1974 an alliance of Unionist groups, who opposed the Sunningdale Agreement, won all except one of the Northern Ireland seats in the United Kingdom Parliament. The alliance had all along followed a policy of non-co-operation with the Executive, and had challenged the legitimacy of the Assembly. In May 1974 a strike by Protestant workers in a number of essential services, including the electricity supply workers, led to the resignation of the Executive and a decision by the United Kingdom Government to revert to direct rule.

The Wilson Government then announced that in due course a constitutional convention would be held in Northern Ireland. The Convention would be asked to examine the various possibilities for constitutional arrangements in Northern Ireland, and to make recommendations. Elections to the Convention in May 1975 produced, as expected, a majority for the 'loyalists'.

The experience in Northern Ireland therefore does not have any clear lessons for the rest of the United Kingdom. The system of devolution set up in Northern Ireland in 1920 had not been requested in the first place by the majority of the population there. It was essentially the pattern of 'Home Rule' which had been proposed by the British Government for Ireland as a whole, but rejected by southern Ireland. It worked quite well in some ways, but the Protestants were always dominant at Stormont, and the Unionists monopolized positions in the Cabinet. Many in the Catholic minority therefore came to regard it as an instrument of Protestant domination. The preference which was apparently given to Protestants in administration, in some trade unions, and even, allegedly, in the allocation of houses by some local authorities, all exacerbated this feeling. In 1969 prolonged disturbances, and street fighting between Catholics and Protestants, led first to British troops being sent in, and then to a period of direct rule by the United Kingdom. There then followed the Northern Ireland Act of 1973, which set up a short-lived Assembly and Executive. The strike by Protestant workers brought a return to direct rule.

It is apparent, then, that the special conditions of Northern Ireland, and in particular the deep divisions between many Protestants and Catholics there, make experience at Stormont an unsure guide to the development of regional government on this side of the Irish Sea. In Britain, Scotland was the pioneer in enjoying a degree of devolution in government. Wales followed along Scottish lines, and since 1965 the English regions have had a shadowy system of regional councils and boards on an appointed basis.

The Scottish Office, set up in 1885, is now responsible for the central administration in Scotland of a great range of services, including health, economic planning, education, new towns and housing, agriculture and fisheries. In fact, it is easier to list those central functions which do not come under the Scottish Office in Scotland. The Department of Employment, the Department of Trade and Industry, the Department of the Environment, and the Social Security side of the Department of Health and Social Security all maintain separate offices in Scotland, but are not part of the Scottish Office. The devolution which Scotland enjoys is merely administrative. The Ministers who control the Scottish Office, namely the Secretary of State for Scotland, the Minister of State, and the three Scottish Under-Secretaries, are responsible to the United Kingdom Parliament at Westminster, and sit in either the House of Commons or the House of Lords.

The Welsh Office was set up as recently as 1964. There had previously been Welsh Departments of some United Kingdom Ministries. For example, the Welsh Board of Health, sited in Cardiff, had the task of applying in Wales the policies on health determined in London at the Ministry of Health. In 1959, during the Macmillan administration, Henry Brooke, a Cabinet Minister at the Department of Housing and Local Government was also given the title of Minister for Welsh Affairs and asked to give particular attention to Wales.

After the 1964 general election the Wilson Government decided to set up a Welsh Office on the lines of the Scottish Office, with a Secretary of State as its head, and a Minister of State to assist him. The functions of the Welsh Office have been progressively widened, and now include health, primary and secondary education, transport, forestry, and agriculture. The Welsh Office is still a much smaller organization than the Scottish Office; in 1973 it had a staff of 990 as compared with a staff of over 6,000 at the Scottish Office.

In 1965 George Brown, as Secretary of State for Economic Affairs, decided to set up a regional organization for economic planning. He appointed economic planning councils for Scotland and Wales, and for eight regions in England. The members of these councils were chosen principally from local government (mostly councillors, but also some officials), from industrialists, businessmen, and trade unionists, and from the staff of universities in the regions. In the English regions economic planning boards were also set up consisting of the senior Civil Servants in each region concerned with such matters as the location of industry, land use, housing, and transport.

Originally, the chairman of each economic planning board was an Under-Secretary in the Department of Economic Affairs. The Department of the Environment now provides the chairmen of these boards. It was intended that the economic planning councils and boards should work in close conjunction. A decision was taken at an early stage to try to bring together into one area the various regional offices of the central departments concerned, if possible in one building, in the de facto capital of the region: Newcastle, Leeds, Birmingham, Bristol, and so on.

The regional economic planning councils and boards have proved useful, and have continued in existence but, on balance, have been somewhat disappointing. For one thing, as the members of the planning councils are bound by the Official Secrets Act they are not able to reveal details of discussion at council meetings, and the Press is not allowed to be present. It is therefore inevitable that little is known about their work. For another thing, the chairmen of the economic planning boards have no executive authority over the other Civil Servants on the board as each is responsible to his own Ministry at the centre. In practice, therefore, the regional board has a rather minor co-ordinating and advisory role.

It was the recognition that these councils and boards were not operating satisfactorily and the awareness of the absence of an elected element in the regional institutions of Scotland, Wales, and England which contributed in part to the appointment of the Royal Commission on the Constitution in 1969. The first chairman of the Commission was Lord Crowther, who held the position up until his death in March 1972. Lord Crowther was at that time chairman of *The Economist*, of Trust Houses Ltd., and of many other companies. He had been editor of *The Economist* from 1938 to 1956, and was one of the best-known writers on economic questions of his generation. After his death, Lord Kilbrandon was appointed chairman, and the Commission's report is generally known as the Kilbrandon Report. Lord Kilbrandon, a Scottish Judge and Lord of Appeal, had been chairman of the Boundary Commission for Scotland in 1963.

Of the other members of the Commission, two were law professors: Professor F. H. Newark was Professor of Civil Law at the

Queen's University, Belfast, from 1963 to 1972; Professor Harry Street is Professor of English Law at Manchester University.[3] Two were former Civil Servants: Sir Ben Bowen Thomas and Mrs. N. K. Trenaman.[4]

One member of the Commission was, when appointed, chairman of one of the economic planning councils for an English region. This was Sir Mark Henig who was chairman of the East Midlands Economic Planning Council from 1968 to 1971. He is chairman of the English Tourist Board. From 1945 to 1970 he was a member of Leicester City Council, and from 1966 to 1967 chairman of the Association of Municipal Corporations

Four other members of the Commission who signed the majority report were Sir James Steel, an industrialist and chairman of Washington Development Corporation, David Basnett, Secretary of the General and Municipal Workers' Union, the Revd. J. B. Longmuir, Moderator of the General Assembly of the Church of Scotland, and Alun Talfan Davies, a Welsh barrister and Queen's Counsel.[5]

There were originally two Members of Parliament on the Royal Commission: Selwyn Lloyd and Douglas Houghton. Selwyn Lloyd resigned when he was elected Speaker of the House of Commons in 1971. He was replaced by Sir David Renton, Conservative Member for Huntingdonshire, who is a barrister, and had been a Minister of State at the Home Office from 1961 to 1962. He was a signatory of the majority report. Douglas Houghton was at this time the chairman of the Parliamentary Labour Party. He had been a Labour Minister from 1964 to 1967. He resigned from the Commission in March 1973, before it had completed its report.

The two authors of the minority report of the Commission, which forms Volume 2 of the Report, were Lord Crowther-Hunt and Professor Alan Peacock. Lord Crowther-Hunt had been a member of the Fulton Committee. As Norman Hunt he had played a major part in drafting the Fulton Report, and was chairman of a Management Consultancy Investigation team for the Fulton Committee.[6] He is a Fellow in Politics at Exeter College, Oxford, and was made a life peer in June 1973. Alan Peacock has been Professor of Economics at York University since 1962. He was appointed to the Commission in November 1970 on the death of D. J. Robertson, Professor of Industrial Relations at Glasgow University.

The terms of reference of the Commission were 'to examine the present functions of the central legislature and government in relation to the several countries, nations and regions of the United Kingdom', and to consider, 'having regard to developments in local government organization' and the administrative and other relationships between the various parts of the United Kingdom, 'Whether any changes are desirable . . . in present constitutional and economic relationships'. The Commission was also to report on whether any changes were desirable in the constitutional and economic relationships between the United Kingdom and the Channel Islands, and the Isle of Man.

The Commission met on 163 days, and on 24 of these held public sessions to hear oral evidence in Scotland, Wales, Northern Ireland, the Isle of Man, and the Channel Islands. The Commission asked Lord Crowther-Hunt to accept special responsibility for the co-ordination of research for the Commission; this included a survey of attitudes to devolution and other aspects of government in the United Kingdom, and was carried out for the Commission by the Office of Population Censuses and Surveys. In addition, research papers were requested and were submitted by Nevil Johnson on Federalism and Decentralization in the Federal Republic of Germany, by Professor M. J. C. Vile on Federalism in the United States, Canada, and Australia, by Neil Elder on Regionalism and the Publicity Principle in Sweden, and by Professor Fred Ridley on the French Prefectoral System. The Study of Parliament Group and a group of members of the Political Studies Association also submitted papers. Three economic papers were prepared: a survey of the Welsh Economy by Professor Graham L. Rees and associates, a study of Revenue and Equalization in Australia, Canada, West Germany, and the U.S.A. by Miss Diane Dawson of the University of Glasgow, and a study of the Financial and Economic Aspects of Regionalism and Separatism by Dr. David N. King, formerly of York University.

Both the majority and the minority reports of the Commission are lengthy: the majority report has 579 pages and the minority report 223 pages. The essential difference between the two reports is as follows. The majority report recommended that both Scotland and Wales should have an elected assembly of about 100 members, chosen by proportional representation. These assemblies would have power to legislate, in the main on those matters which are now the responsibility of the Scottish Office.[7] The Westminster Parliament would retain ultimate sovereignty and would have power to veto egislation passed by the Welsh or Scottish Assembly. The majority report did not advocate elected assemblies for the English regions. It favoured co-ordinating and advisory councils for the eight English regions. Each of these councils would have about 60 members: a fifth nominated by the Minister for Regional Affairs, and the rest elected by local authorities.

Lord Crowther-Hunt and Alan Peacock, the authors of the minority report, favoured treating Scotland, Wales, and the English regions uniformly. They proposed elected assemblies for Scotland, Wales, and five English regions, and argued that England should be divided into five rather than eight regions, as at present. All the elected assemblies would be chosen by proportional representation. The regional assemblies and governments would have responsibility for the administration of services, with the central government retaining an over-all policy-determining function. Therefore, the assemblies proposed in the minority report would not have power to legislate, but would have power to adapt the administration of services decided at the centre to the needs and desires of the region they would serve. All the administrative bodies now existing in the regions, the Scottish and Welsh Offices, and the regional organizations of the central departments in England, would be brought under the control of the elected regional assemblies.

The authors of the minority report geared their recommendations to some of the principal findings of the survey made for the Commission of attitudes to the system of government. Lord Crowther-Hunt and Alan Peacock pointed out that the survey showed that over half the sample interviewed was dissatisfied with the way things were run at the time, well over half felt that 'the views of people like themselves were ignored', and an even larger percentage favoured devolution of power to directly elected Scottish and Welsh assemblies, and to similarly elected bodies in the English regions.[8] They also pointed out that people in Scotland were only marginally more in favour of devolution than people in England, and that people in Wales were less interested in devolution than people in certain English regions. They concluded that there was as great a need and demand for regional elected assemblies in England as there was in Scotland and Wales. Whether this was as true for the active political elites as for the ordinary citizen is open to question. But the underlying attitude that government was felt by a large proportion of ordinary people to be too remote, was clearly there.

Another point on which the minority report showed perhaps a

better grasp of practical politics than did the majority report was in relation to representation at Westminster. The majority report argued that once elected assemblies for Scotland and Wales had been established, the representation of both countries at Westminster could be substantially reduced. The minority report, since it advocated administrative devolution to the English regions, as well as to Wales and Scotland, could reasonably argue that Welsh and Scottish representation at Westminster should remain unchanged.

The fact is that Scotland and Wales are at present overrepresented in relation to their populations. If they were to have representation on a strictly equal basis with England, the Scottish seats at Westminster would have to be reduced from 71 to 57, and the Welsh seats from 36 to 31. The political difficulties about such a change are, first, that this would quite considerably reduce Labour representation at Westminster, and second, that it would reduce Scottish and Welsh influence in national decision-making. At present, Scotland and Wales have a minority voice in the Westminster Parliament, but the fact that the Welsh and Scottish minorities are generously represented there helps to ensure that they are minorities which will not be ignored.

We have emphasized the differences between the majority and minority reports of the Kilbrandon Commission, but we must also note those aspects on which they were agreed. Both reports rejected a federal solution on the grounds that a federal system, or any looser form of confederation, would have considerable economic disadvantages for Britain. They also concurred in their opposition to a transfer of power from local government to regional authorities, and both suggested that assemblies for Scotland and Wales should be elected by proportional representation.

The two reports met in recognizing the sense of remoteness from the decision-making centres of government experienced by many people. The widespread feeling of a need for better methods for redress of grievances for the citizen against government authorities was another point which was highlighted in both reports.

When the reports were published towards the end of 1973, many commentators thought that both the weighty main report and the only slightly less voluminous memorandum of dissent would be left to gather dust on the shelves. But the general election in February 1974 brought about a dramatic change, and aroused new interest in the subject. The fact that the Liberals, the Scottish Nationalists, and

Plaid Cymru together held the balance of power in the Commons, and that all three parties were in favour of implementing the recommendations in the main Kilbrandon Report, meant that the minority Wilson Government had to take these recommendations seriously. Harold Wilson appointed Lord Crowther-Hunt as a special adviser to the Government on constitutional questions. Lord Crowther-Hunt began a series of discussions with Party leaders and, early in April, Harold Wilson told the Commons that the Government would publish a White Paper setting out its proposals for constitutional reform.

The White Paper was published in September 1974 under the title *Democracy and Devolution—Proposals for Scotland and Wales*;[9] in it, the Government announced some firm proposals for Scotland and Wales while indicating that consultation was still taking place regarding England.[10] The firm proposals were as follows: first, directly elected assemblies should be set up for Scotland and Wales. Second, the Scottish Assembly should have legislative powers within those fields in which there was already separate Scottish legislation, for example in housing, health, and education. Third, the Welsh Assembly should not have legislative powers on the lines of the Scottish Assembly, but powers in relation to delegated legislation, by inference in those areas where the Welsh Assembly took over executive functions from the Welsh Office. Fourth, there should continue to be Secretaries of State for Scotland and Wales who 'would act as full members of the United Kingdom Government in forming United Kingdom policies'. Finally, the existing number of Members of Parliament from Scotland and Wales should not be reduced. These last two decisions were justified on the grounds that the United Kingdom Parliament and Government would remain responsible for the distribution of resources between Scotland, Wales, and the regions of England, and for the over-all determination of United Kingdom policies.[11]

There were also aspects of the membership and functions of the Scottish and Welsh assemblies for which the Government made provisional proposals, noting that they would need detailed study and consideration. As regards membership of the assemblies it was proposed that this should be on the same system as in the United Kingdom Parliament, with single-member constituencies; the possibility of proportional representation was therefore not considered. As regards functions, the White Paper said that the assemblies should assume some of the executive functions of the Scottish and Welsh Offices, and of the nominated authorities now operating in Scotland and Wales. The assemblies should not take over any of the existing powers of local authorities.[12]

The provisional proposals which were made in relation to finance were interesting. The suggestion was that the financial allocation to the Scottish and Welsh assemblies should be 'in the form of a block grant voted by the United Kingdom Parliament under arrangements which will take account of both local needs and the desirability of some uniformity of standards of services and of contributions in all parts of the United Kingdom'.[13] It would then be a matter for the assemblies in Scotland and Wales to decide how to allocate resources from the block grant, judging their own priorities in the light of their own assessment of the needs of their communities, choosing, for example, between hospitals and roads, or schools and houses.

A great deal of work will need to be done in order to translate these proposals into legislation. The Wilson Government's aim at the end of 1974 was to introduce legislation setting up Scottish and Welsh assemblies in the session 1975–76. This meant that within a year discussions would have to be completed about the arrangements for setting up the new assemblies, about the functions of the assemblies, about the transfer of functions from the Scottish and Welsh Offices, and from the appointed bodies in Scotland and Wales, and, perhaps most complicated of all, about the relationships, financial, legal, and administrative, which the assemblies would have with the United Kingdom Government.

Discussions would be continuing at the same time about the regions of England. The economic planning councils and boards in the English regions were principally involved in these discussions. During the summer of 1974, the economic planning councils had been asked to comment on the Government's White Paper which set out various alternative methods of devolution, derived from the majority and minority reports of the Kilbrandon Commission.[14] Three alternatives were put forward and were listed in the White Paper as schemes B, F, and G. Scheme B was the proposal put forward by Lord Crowther-Hunt and Professor Peacock in Volume 2 of the Kilbrandon Report which envisaged directly elected assemblies for the English regions, taking over the administration of some central government services for which the central departments would retain a degree of over-all policy control. Scheme F was the proposal put forward by eight members of the Commission who signed the majority report for co-ordinating and advisory councils for the English regions. Four-fifths of the members of these councils would be elected by local authorities, and one-fifth would be nominated by the central government 'to secure representation from industry and commerce, trade unions, education and other interests'.[15] Each council would have about 60 members in all. The councils would take over the functions of the present nominated regional economic planning councils. In addition they would advise on government spending in the regions, advise and make representation to the central government about government policies in the regions, and about the operations of nationalized industries, and have a co-ordinating function in local government.

Finally, scheme G recommended, by one signatory of the majority report, proposed a system of co-ordinating committees of local authorities. This scheme was based on the view that the best way of devolving power from the centre in England was to concentrate on strengthening the power of the new larger local authorities set up under the 1972 Local Government Act. It proposed a formal system of regional committees to co-ordinate the planning activities of local authorities. All the members of these committees would be representatives of local authorities. It would be mandatory for local authorities to submit their plans to these regional committees, and to obtain their comments, before submitting them for Ministerial approval.[16]

The associations of local authorities in England were also asked to comment on these three alternatives. In September 1974 the Policy Committee of the Association of Metropolitan Authorities considered the White Paper and put forward its views to the Department of the Environment. Of the three alternatives given, the Committee preferred scheme G. But its overriding view was that the most suitable way of devolving power from the central government was to strengthen the powers of the new larger local authorities and give them greater autonomy, rather than creating an intermediate tier of government at the regional level. If, however, it was decided to create elected regional assemblies to administer health and water functions, and other functions of government such as regional economic planning, the members of such assemblies should be chosen by the local authorities in the region.[17]

It is likely that any legislative proposals for new institutions of government in the English regional areas will take even longer to formulate than those for Scotland and Wales, if only because there is much less pressure for new regional machinery in England among M.P.s and councillors, than there is in Scotland and Wales for national assemblies. If any changes are made eventually they could affect the regional organization in England for administration of the National Health Service. A major reorganization had taken place in the health services in 1974, and it is to this area of reform that we turn in the next chapter.

NOTES

1 Cmnd. 4584, Local Government in England. Government Proposals for Reorganization, p. 11, para. 35–7.

2 K. C. Wheare (*Federal Government*, Clarendon Press, 4th edn., 1963) has the clearest discussion of the essential features of a federal system.

3 Professor Street's best-known books on constitutional questions are *Freedom, the Individual and the Law* (3rd ed., 1972), and *Justice in the Welfare State* (1968).

4 Sir Ben Bowen Thomas had been Permanent Secretary to the Welsh Department of the Ministry of Education from 1945 to 1963; Mrs. Trenaman had been an Under-Secretary at the Board of Trade, and since 1966 had been Principal of St. Anne's College, Oxford.

5 There were a number of reasons why Davies was chosen to serve on the Commission as he was a graduate of University College, Aberystwyth, former Recorder of Cardiff, former Liberal candidate in Carmarthen and Denbigh, and vice-chairman of Harlech Television. He is also Judge of the Courts of Appeal for Jersey and Guernsey.

6 See chap. VII, p. 98.

7 Two members of the majority were in favour of a legislative assembly for Scotland only.

8 Royal Commission on the Constitution 1969–1973, volume 2, Memorandum of Dissent (H.M.S.O., 1973), pp. 25–6.

9 Cmnd. 5732, Democracy and Devolution. Proposals for Scotland and Wales (H.M.S.O., 1974).

10 Op. cit., p. 8, para. 26.

11 For details of these proposals see op. cit., pp. 8–9, paras. 27, 29, 30, 32, and 33.

12 Op. cit., p. 9, para. 31.

13 Op. cit., p. 9, para. 31, sub-para. (c).

14 Office of the Lord President of the Council: Devolution within the United Kingdom. Some Alternatives for Discussion (H.M.S.O., 1974).

15 Op. cit., p. 15, para. 46.

16 Op. cit., pp. 15–17, para. 51.

17 Supplement to *Municipal Review*, November 1974, p. 105.

CHAPTER X

Health Service Reform

THE administrative structure of the National Health Service had remained virtually unchanged since it was set up in 1948 under the National Health Service Act, 1946. The 1946 Act provided for a tripartite structure. Hospitals were administered by appointed boards responsible to the Minister. The general practitioner services were run by Executive Councils responsible to the Minister, but only partly appointed by him. Many members of these Councils were chosen by the doctors, dentists, pharmacists, and opticians practising in the area, and a further section of members was nominated by the local authority. The third arm of the Service was provided by the local authorities who had responsibility for a variety of clinics, particularly in the field of maternal and infant health, for midwifery services, and for the ambulance service. These services were administered by the local Medical Officers of Health and their departments, who were responsible to Health Committees consisting of locally elected councillors (and aldermen in some cases).[1]

We must first question the need for a modification of the tripartite system as, despite its faults, the Health Service was internationally recognized as probably the best nationally provided system. Of course, some of its admitted defects were not a product of the tripartite structure. For example, there was a general need for more finance, much dissatisfaction with the length of waiting-lists for non-urgent surgery (for operations for hernias and prolapses, for example), and widespread agreement that there had been a neglect of the long-stay patient in hospitals, particularly of the elderly, and of the long-stay mental patient. All these faults could have been remedied without altering the tripartite system.

We should look first at the reasons given in 1968 by Kenneth Robinson, as Minister of Health, for starting on reorganization. He argued that the system established in 1948 was well-suited to the needs of the time, and 'in particular to the reorganization of hospital and specialist services. That phase, however, is past. It seems that the organization of medical and related services, in the community and in the hospitals, has now progressed almost as far as is possible within the present divided administrative structure.'[2] That statement on its own does not take us very far in explaining the decision to embark on reorganization. We can, however, point to a combination of factors which were providing a strong impetus at that time.

A number of people with experience in the Health Service argued that some of the strains to which it was subject were aggravated by the tripartite structure. Patients and field-workers sometimes experienced lack of co-ordination in the Service. As Michael Ryan has shown, co-ordination can be achieved across administrative boundaries where there is sufficient goodwill and enthusiasm.[3] By contrast there can be lack of co-ordination within a single authority. But the presumption is that a unified service must make co-ordination easier.

Some of the committees which advised the Ministry on specific problems of the Service supported continuation of the tripartite system, but envisaged the possibility of a unified structure being achieved in time. This view was taken by the Cranbrook Report on Maternity Services in 1959, and the Gillie Report on the Field of Work of the Family Doctor in 1963.[4] The medical profession as a whole had been opposed to unification of the Service. But in 1962 the Porritt Committee, which was widely representative of the profession, produced a report advocating a unified service administered by area health boards.[5] The British Medical Association approved the report at a Representative Meeting in 1963, and instructed the Council of the B.M.A. 'to support the setting up of Area Health Boards as this would increase co-ordination and co-operation between the three parts of the service'. Opinion in the profession was therefore moving towards the concept of a unified service.

A further factor which in 1968 gave greater immediacy to the idea from the point of view of the Ministry of Health was the impending reorganization of local government. The Redcliffe-Maud Royal Commission on Local Government had been set up in 1966, and was to publish its report in 1969. The larger local authorities which would result from local government reorganization would mean that the Executive Council areas which with few exceptions had always been coterminous with county borough and county council areas would have to be redrawn. It seemed a great opportunity, and in keeping with the reforming spirit of the time, to go further and bring in a unified health system.

Influenced by all these factors, Kenneth Robinson decided in 1967 to set up a small high-powered team in his Ministry which would give all its time to planning reorganization of the Health Service. This team remained in continuous existence until the passage of the National Health Service Act in 1973. It fluctuated in size during its five-year life. At its largest it numbered 19, including 1 Under-Secretary, 2 Assistant Secretaries, and 3 Principals. The supporting members of the team, made up of Executive and Clerical Officers, numbered only 8 at this time. The team was assisted by 5 typists. It was, in a sense, a multi-disciplinary team, bringing together people in the Ministry who had experience of the main sectors of the Health Service, including some special aspects such as the problem of hospital administration in the London region, which had always been a special headache for the planners. A doctor, one of the Minister's medical advisers, was always attached to the team.

The first of the Green Papers was issued by Kenneth Robinson in 1968. He emphasized in his introduction that he was putting forward 'some tentative proposals for England and Wales as a basis for wide public discussion and consultation with representative bodies'.[6] The Green Paper pointed to the problems involved in co-ordinating the work of local authorities, Executive Councils, and hospital authorities. It emphasized the large number and variety of authorities concerned with health; for example, there were at that time, counting all the Regional Hospital Boards and Hospital Management Committees, 350 employing authorities in the national hospital service. There were also 134 Executive Councils, and 175 local health authorities.[7]

The Green Paper proposed a single tier of administration for the unified service, and suggested that between 40 and 50 Area Health Boards be set up in England and Wales. These would take over all the functions of the Regional Hospital Boards, and of the Executive Councils, and many of the health functions of local authorities, including, it was suggested, clinics, health centres, health-visiting, midwifery, and the ambulance service. There was to be no regional tier above the Area Boards, which would be directly responsible to the Ministry of Health, and no district authorities.

The Green Paper said that the new health areas could be made the responsibility of committees of the new local authorities which might be established following the recommendations of the Royal Commission on Local Government.[8] No conclusion had yet been reached on this question, and the Paper went on to elaborate proposals for appointed Area Boards, if the local government alternative was not taken up. The members of the Boards would be appointed by the Minister. Some members would be appointed for their 'broad professional knowledge of medical and related services', but it would not be desirable for them 'to be nominated to represent special interests'. The interests of local authorities would be taken into account, but again the implication was that the Minister would himself choose whom to appoint to the Boards. In areas containing medical schools 'the Minister might appoint on the nomination of universities one or two additional members'.[9]

As regards internal organization of the Boards, the Green Paper stated that in order to promote integration, 'There would be a clean break from the present divisions: committees would not for instance be set up to deal with particular services in the area such as "hospital services" or "general practitioner services". Any standing committees appointed by the Area Board should cover all parts of the service.'[10] The Paper recommended that each Board should set up four or five major departments concerned respectively with Planning and Operation of Services, Staff, Logistics, Finance, and Secretariat.[11] The directors of these departments would together make up a small Executive which 'would meet frequently and be collectively responsible to the Board for advising it on its objectives and policies'.[12] Each area would be divided into 'operational districts', but there would be no district authorities subordinate to the Area Boards.

The Green Paper was widely distributed throughout the Health Service. Sufficient copies were sent out to supply one for each member of every Executive Council, all the members of each Hospital Management Committee and Regional Board, and of the Health Committees of local authorities. It was distributed to staff associations and voluntary bodies connected with the Health Service, and was put on sale to the public. The Paper was widely discussed by all these bodies as well as by local medical committees, local dental committees, local pharmaceutical committees, committees of hospital doctors, and so on. Resolutions were then sent either direct to the Minister or through the national associations of Executive Councils, of Hospital Management Committees, through the B.M.A., the British Dental Association, and through the associations of local authorities.

The main burden of the resolutions which reached the Minister can be briefly summarized as follows. First, virtually no one except the local authority associations was in favour of the Health Service being brought under local authority control. The Medical Officers of Health within the B.M.A. argued that the larger authorities which would result from local government reorganization would be better run than the old authorities, and that local authority control was acceptable. But theirs was a minority voice in the B.M.A., and they did not press this view. There has been long-standing opposition to local authority control in the B.M.A. What was perhaps surprising was that the other professions, including the nurses and the administrators, took a similar view.

Second, there was a widespread feeling that the Area Boards would be too remote from the patient and from people working in the Service, and that there should be district authorities below the Area tier. Third, there was much criticism of the recommended composition of the proposed Area Boards. The Associations of Executive Councils, in particular, thought that the Boards should include representatives of the health professions. The B.M.A. agreed, but were ploughing their own particular furrow. A special Representative Meeting of the B.M.A. on 30 January 1969 resolved that there should be '(1) active and effective elected representation of doctors by doctors at the appropriate levels in all planning and administrative units; and (2) adequate participation by the community in the administrative units'. The second point was obviously much vaguer than the first. The B.M.A. was, as we have seen, opposed to local authority control. Indeed the resolution stated: 'The Association is opposed to the transfer of the administration or financing of the Health Service to local authorities, either in their present form or in any modified form under which the Health Service would be subject to the fluctuating and conflicting pressures of local government.' What the B.M.A. proposed, therefore, was that there should be some representatives of the local community on the Area Boards, and at district level, but that the local authorities should not have control.

Fourth there was much criticism of the absence of a regional tier in the proposed unified Service. The hospital doctors especially argued that there were many things which could not be adequately organized on an area basis, for example, the rarer specialities such as neurology and neurosurgery, and the deployment of senior hospital medical staff. Fifth, the general practitioners, as well as the dentists, pharmacists, and opticians, were very concerned that they would lose the opportunity to participate in the running of the Service which they had always enjoyed through the Executive Councils. They therefore pressed for the perpetuation of bodies of the Executive Council type within the new machinery.

The resolutions were received by a new Minister and a new Ministry. The Wilson administration decided in 1968 to merge the Ministry of Health and the Department of Social Security, creating the first of the new 'giant' departments, the Department of Health and Social Security. Richard Crossman became its first Ministerial head with the title of Secretary of State for the Social Services. In February 1970 he published a Green Paper which announced that the Government had made three firm decisions about the future of the Health Service. First, it would not be administered by local authorities but by Area Health Authorities directly responsible to the Secretary of State. He gave two reasons for this decision: first, that the professions 'believe that only a service administered by special bodies on which the professions are represented can provide a proper assurance of clinical freedom', and second, that 'the independent financial resources available to local authorities are not sufficient to enable them to take over responsibility for the whole health service'.[13]

The second decision was that an administrative boundary would be drawn between the new National Health Service and the local authority health and personal social services. In general, the services to be transferred from local government were those envisaged in the Robinson Green Paper with the addition of the school health service. The third decision was that the new Area Health Authorities would in general be coterminous with the new local authorities.

Crossman emphasized that, these decisions apart, everything else proposed in the Green Paper was open to discussion, and commented on the vigorous debate that had been sparked off by the previous Paper. He said three strong criticisms had been expressed from many quarters, first, the '40 to 50 area boards with no participation of local people below this level would have made the day to day running of the health service too remote from the people it serves'; second, 'many feared that the boards would be dominated by the hospital service'; third, 'there was concern that no provision had been made for regional planning'.[14]

Taking account of these criticisms, he now proposed that there should be many more Area Health Authorities than had been envisaged by Robinson. He suggested 97 Area Health Authorities for England and Wales, as against the 40 to 50 proposed in the earlier Green Paper. He also accepted the idea that the Area Authorities should in part be representative of the professions and of the local authorities, and suggested a membership of from 20 to 25. One-third of these members would be chosen by the health professions, one-third by the local authorities, and one-third, plus the chairman, appointed by the Secretary of State.

He accepted the proposal for a tier of administration below the Area Health Authorities. In most areas he envisaged that the Area Authorities would establish district committees whose functions would be to supervise the running of services in the district, and to act as channels of communication with local people. These functions would not be delegated to them by statute but would be arranged with the Area Health Authorities. One-half of the members of the district committees would be appointed by and drawn from the Area Health Authorities, as would the chairman of the district committee. The other half would be drawn from people living and working in the district who must not be members of the Area Health Authority.

To meet the criticism of the absence of a regional tier, Crossman proposed that there should be 14 or more regional health councils for England, covering areas similar to those of the Regional Hospital Boards. Each of the Area Health Authorities in the region would appoint one member of the regional health council, the professions would appoint several members, and the chairman and some members would be appointed by the Secretary of State. The functions of the regional councils would be the over-all planning of the hospital and specialist services, the organization of facilities for post-graduate medical and dental education, the deployment of senior hospital medical, dental and scientific staff, and the regional organization of staff training, blood transfusion services, and the ambulance services.[15]

Finally, the Green Paper proposed that each Area Health Authority should be required by statute to set up a family-practitioner committee. This committee would be responsible for the provision of services formerly administered by the Executive Councils. The composition of the committee would resemble that of the existing

Executive Councils, including members appointed by the local professional committees (medical, dental, pharmaceutical, etc.). There would be some common membership of the Area Health Authority and the family-practitioner committee, and both bodies would be served by a common staff. This proposal went a long way towards meeting the case put forward by the Executive Councils, but it did not detract from the unity of the Service, although some hospital doctors and administrators maintained that it did.

The Crossman Green Paper was generally well received. The Associations of Executive Councils were in favour of the main lines of the scheme but asked for some detailed changes. For example, the Welsh Association of Executive Councils wanted the Area Health Authorities to have more members, to permit a wider and more equitable representation of the health professions, and to provide more members for manning committees of the Authorities. The Special Representative Meeting of the B.M.A., on 6 and 7 May 1970, took a broadly favourable view of the Green Paper and welcomed the introduction of a regional tier. The meeting pressed that one-third of the members of the Area Health Authorities should be elected by members of the medical profession. (The Crossman Green Paper suggested that one-third of the members of the Area Authorities should be elected by the *health* professions.) The B.M.A. also had a number of other recommendations for detailed changes, and in particular was dissatisfied with what it considered were the 'perfunctory references' in the Green Paper 'to the essential part which the N.H.S. must play in teaching and research'. It considered that the disappearance of the Boards of Governors of teaching hospitals would mean a dilution of the voice of university medical men in the running of the Service.

Finally, the local authority associations maintained their view that the unified Service should come under local control. But consumer organizations in the Health Service welcomed the proposals on the whole. The idea of district authorities with executive functions with half their members drawn from people living and working in the district was felt to be a great improvement. Quite what this would mean in practice, however, remained to be defined. A number of ideas were put forward for direct or indirect election of representatives of patients on these district authorities, but they were not considered a serious possibility by the Department of Health and Social Security.

In June 1970 the planning group in the Department had already prepared the first draft of a White Paper outlining the Government's proposals for legislation unifying the Health Service on the lines of the Crossman Green Paper. If Labour had won the general election, the Bill would probably have had a high priority. The Conservative victory at the polls for the time being placed a brake on plans for reorganization. Whereas the Conservative Party in Opposition had taken a great deal of interest in local government reorganization and espoused the cause of the districts, it had shown little interest in administrative reorganization of the Health Service. There had been ideas in the Party for enlarging the area of private medicine and for providing an injection of private funds into the health sector. But when the Conservatives gained office, Ministers soon appreciated that the size of public expenditure on health was so great that private finance would make only a tiny dent in it. In the take-over period, Sir Keith Joseph, as Secretary of State for the Social Services, had the task of reviewing the whole of the responsibilities of the D.H.S.S. About four months after the general election he decided that reorganization of the Health Service should go through. The planning group, which had continued in being in the Department, was asked to draft proposals on lines in keeping with the new administration's over-all attitude to government reorganization. The new direction, with its commitment to a managerial approach, was very much the Minister's own contribution rather than coming from the Civil Service, or from management consultants who were brought in at a later stage.

On 4 May 1971 Sir Keith Joseph issued a Consultative Document on National Health Service Reorganization. This was not a Green Paper. It was not on sale to the public, and many bodies who were consulted were sent only one copy of the document. Executive Councils, for example, received only one copy, and had to reproduce the text in order to circulate copies to their members. The tone of the document was only partly consultative. For example, the Minister said, 'We are perhaps in danger of a surfeit of plans and prospectuses; there must be early decisions, so that enthusiasm for reform does not wither away.'[16]

We can summarize first those features of the Joseph proposals which were the same as in the Crossman proposals, and then consider what was changed. Two of the Crossman ideas were taken over unchanged, first, the decision that Area Health Authority boundaries should be the same as those of the top-tier local authorities, and second, the proposal for family-practitioner committees of the Area Health Authorities with a statutory basis, and a composition and role similar to that of the Executive Councils. The main differences in the Joseph Document were threefold. First, the regional tier in England was strengthened. The regional councils became regional health authorities with broader functions than were proposed by Crossman. The Joseph Document said that the regional authorities would be responsible for the general planning of the National Health Service, for allocating resources to the Area Health Authorities, for co-ordinating their activities, and for monitoring their performances. In addition they would themselves provide some services, and would be the building authorities for all major projects.

Second, the Area Health Authorities would be appointed bodies. They would have a small membership, perhaps 14 members in addition to the chairman. The Secretary of State would choose the chairman. Some members would be appointed by the local authority, one member would be chosen by 'the university providing medical and dental teaching facilities'. The remaining members would be chosen by the regional authorities. They would include at least two doctors, and a nurse or midwife, appointed after consultation with the professions (but not chosen by the relevant professional bodies). Management ability would be the main criterion for the selection of members of the Area Health Authorities.

Third, any question of a district tier, as proposed in the Crossman Green Paper, was ruled out. At the district level there would be only Community Health Councils without executive functions. The members of these councils would be appointed by the area authorities 'after consultation with a wide range of interested local organizations'. They would have to be consulted by the area authorities on the development and operation of services in the district. Their members would have the right to visit hospitals and other institutions.

The Minister himself explained the difference in his approach from that in the Crossman Green Paper:

The previous Government sought to secure increased local participation in the administration of the health services not only by giving the area authorities a representational character, but also through the establishment of district committees, composed as to half their membership, of people living or working in the district. In the present Government's view, these proposals would have led to a dangerous confusion between management on the one hand and the community's reaction to management on the other.[17]

The Secretary of State's argument prompts the comment that this 'dangerous confusion' is the principle upon which local government services are based, since the heads of local departments are directly responsible to representatives of the community. His argument ran directly counter to the Crossman Green Paper, and was deplored by those who had welcomed the Crossman proposals. But the Minister was so strongly wedded to his ideas that the possibility of influencing him in the consultative process seemed remote. As before, all the representative bodies met and passed their resolutions, but the Minister's proposals showed no change of any significance when the English White Paper appeared in 1972.[18]

As we have seen already, the Minister's position, which was widely dubbed 'managerial', did not seem to have originated from the management consultants who advised on Health Service reorganization. McKinsey's were brought in to assist the study groups on Management Arrangements for the Reorganized Health Service which were set up for England and Wales.[19] But McKinsey's were not brought in until after Sir Keith Joseph had issued his Consultative Document. The English Study Group was also assisted by the Health Services Organization Research Unit of Brunel University under Professor Jaques.

Although the B.M.A. had welcomed the Crossman Green Paper in general, its attitude to the Joseph proposals was not so critical as that voiced by the Association of Executive Councils and the Association of Hospital Management Committees. There was in fact much in the Government's scheme of which the B.M.A. approved. Although the representative idea had been rejected, and the B.M.A. had lost its proposal that one-third of the membership of the Area Authorities be chosen by doctors, the following gains had been made. First, in England the regional authorities were strengthened and, as we have seen, the B.M.A. had throughout been in favour of this. Second, a concession was made to the B.M.A.'s view that the medical faculties of universities should be given a greater say in running the Service. Under the scheme which was to be adopted each area which had a teaching hospital within its boundaries was designated an Area Health Authority (Teaching), and was given at least two additional members with teaching experience. A third gain for the B.M.A. was that although the Government refused to concede a representative element to the doctors (except in the family-practitioner committee), it agreed to an extensive professional advisory machinery in which the doctors would play a big part. Thus although there would be no district authorities, there would be District Management Teams with a major part in the running of the Service. These would consist of the district community physician, the district nursing officer, the district finance officer, the district administrator, a consultant elected by the Area Medical Committee, and a general practitioner elected by the Area Medical Committee.[20] In this way the doctors would have 3 members out of 6 on the District Management Teams, which naturally gave satisfaction to the B.M.A. Finally, the B.M.A. was pleased that the National Health Service Reorganization Act gave a statutory basis to regional and area professional committees. Whereas the 1946 Act gave statutory recognition to the local medical committees to which all general practitioners in the Health Service were entitled to belong, the Act did not recognize the representative bodies formed by hospital doctors. Now G.P.s and hospital doctors would be represented on area and regional committees which would have a statutory basis.

There was one major respect, however, in which the B.M.A. was critical of the scheme. It was strongly opposed to what the Council of the B.M.A. called 'the tragic decision to separate the control of the social services from the Health Authorities'. In its view, all social workers concerned with health questions, from medical and psychiatric social workers to home helps, should have been employed by the Area Health Authorities.

Before going on to discuss the passage of the National Health Service Reorganization Bill it is appropriate that we examine one feature of reorganization which, for the sake of clarity, has so far been omitted from discussion, and that is, the absence of a regional tier in Wales and Scotland. The Crossman Green Paper proposed a regional tier for England which had been absent in the Robinson proposals. But the Wilson Government decided not to introduce a regional tier for Wales, and a similar decision was made for Scotland. The Welsh Association of Executive Councils did not oppose this decision when it met to discuss the Crossman proposals in 1970. This was largely because members were hoping that the Commission on the Constitution would recommend the creation of an elected Welsh Assembly, and that health planning, and the control of health authorities, would be one of its functions.

The Heath Government maintained the decision not to have a regional tier, and this came in for much more criticism than it did at the time of the Crossman Green Paper. The special conference of the Welsh Association of Executive Councils, for example, voted in 1972 for the introduction of a regional tier in Wales. There were a number of reasons for this change of front. One was that, with the Kilbrandon Commission taking so long to report, and the somewhat equivocal attitude towards devolution apparently being adopted at that time by the Heath Government, the possibility of an elected Welsh Assembly which would be given responsibility for health administration in Wales became more remote. The second reason was that the prospect of the Welsh Office taking over from the Welsh Hospital Board was viewed with concern in many quarters.

The Welsh Hospital Board was not popular, but Civil Servants in the Welsh Office were viewed with even more suspicion, (and concern) particularly as the critics of the new model unified Health Service felt that it would be dominated by 'managers and bureaucrats'. Two questions in particular were often asked. Would the Welsh Office be competent to plan, and monitor, the Health Service in Wales in view of its wide-ranging responsibilities in economic and industrial affairs, physical planning, housing, and many other fields? Would the interested public be adequately informed about key decisions in health planning when they were made behind closed doors by Civil Servants in the Welsh Office, instead of in the freer atmosphere of the Welsh Hospital Board where debates on allocation of resources between different sectors of the service, and between different geographic areas in Wales, were freely reported in the Press? It was not without significance that the hospital consultants in Wales were divided over the question. The consultants from the Cardiff area were in favour of control by the Welsh Office, the consultants from other parts of Wales were in favour of having a Welsh Health Authority.[21] Administrators in the Welsh Office had, it was claimed, long favoured the large teaching hospital in Cardiff to the detriment of other parts of Wales. The Welsh Office is of course subject to political control. But the channel of control is long and tortuous. The Secretary of State for Wales, and the Minister of State, are normally to be found in that part of the Welsh Office which is located in London, and not in the Cardiff part. The debates at Westminster, at which they are held accountable on health matters in Wales, are infrequent, as are occasions when they answer questions on health from Welsh Members.

Although the Welsh Hospital Board disappeared in April 1974, not all its functions were taken over by the Welsh Office. A body known as the Welsh Health Technical Services Organization, irreverently known in Wales as 'WOTSO', was set up to concern itself with the design and construction of major capital works, with certain specialized management functions such as the computer, with the central supply function, and with printing, and prescription pricing.[22] The Welsh Management Arrangements Document said that the board of WHTSO would 'combine its membership, business and organizational experience with knowledge of health affairs'.[23]

Scotland also does not have a regional tier in its reorganized Health Service but, surprisingly, this did not seem to give rise to much criticism in Scotland. There is an equivalent in Scotland of WHTSO, called the Common Services Agency which, like WHTSO, is concerned with the execution of major building projects, and the provision of certain common services to the Area Boards. The management committee of this Agency consists partly of representatives of the Boards, and partly of Civil Servants from the Scottish Home and Health Department.[24]

The National Health Service Reorganization Bill was first introduced in the Lords. This was in response to a plea from leading peers at the end of the 1971–72 session which had had to be greatly prolonged in order to allow the Lords to complete the Local Government Bill. Peers suggested that one of the major government measures of the new session should begin its consideration in the Lords, and the Health Service Bill was chosen. This proved to be a good arrangement in many ways. Some of the best speeches on the Bill were made in the Lords, and some of the most important amendments originated there.

As soon as printed copies of the Bill were available, after its introduction in the Lords, the B.M.A. went into action, lobbying for the amendments it favoured. Lords Brock, Platt, Amulree, and Rosenheim were sent lists of the B.M.A.'s suggested amendments, and officers of the B.M.A. held discussions with them. The B.M.A. also sent copies of its amendments to Lady Serota, a leading Labour spokesman on the Bill.

When the Bill reached the Commons, the B.M.A. sent its suggestions for amendments to selected M.P.s of both major parties, and discussions took place between B.M.A. officers and M.P.s. During the whole legislative stage the B.M.A. had frequent meetings with Ministers and senior Civil Servants, either pressing for its amendments, or asking for clarification of amendments the Government was proposing. The extent of this activity may come as a surprise to those who consider that legislation is agreed between the government department and pressure groups before it reaches Parliament. In this case, the B.M.A. had been able, in common with other professional associations and interested groups, to give its views to the D.H.S.S. during discussion of the Department's proposals. Certain features of the Bill were, in the B.M.A.'s opinion, a result of the firm position it had taken up; for example, the provision in the Bill that the Health Service Commissioner would be excluded from clinical matters. Yet when the Bill reached Parliament there was still a great deal in it which the B.M.A. wanted to change, and the B.M.A. had a fair amount of success in getting amendments accepted which suited its point of view.

The Labour Party in both Houses took a strongly critical attitude to the character of the Bill. Whereas Health Service reorganization had not been an issue between the parties before 1970, the Crossman Green Paper had been warmly welcomed in the Labour Party, and the abandonment of the representative principle in the Joseph proposals was just as strongly deplored. This is not to say that all Conservative M.P.s approved the changes which Sir Keith Joseph introduced. Dr. Thomas Stuttaford, for example, Conservative Member for Norwich South, said on Third Reading that he had difficulty in supporting the Bill as he felt that there would now be bureaucracy in the Health Service, not democracy. But Conservative critics were not numerous enough, or determined enough, to induce the Government to make any real concessions towards the representative principle. One of the few concessions which was won was an amendment which provided that each Area Health Authority should have four members appointed by the relevant local authority. The Bill, as introduced, had not specified how many members would be chosen by the local authority.

Labour spokesmen were scornful of the proposal for Community Health Councils without executive powers. For example, Elystan Morgan described the Community Health Councils, in Standing Committee, as 'little more than soft toys for the public to play with, toys which will do them, and certainly their bureaucratic masters, no harm'.[25] At Third Reading, John Silkin claimed that the Bill was a disaster but fortunately not a disaster that would go on for ever. It would be swept away and forgotten in a short time, and the real reorganization of the Health Service would be done by a Labour Government.

At the February 1974 general election the Labour Party was committed to democratizing the Health Service. The Labour Manifesto said that a Labour Government would 'transform the area health authorities into democratic bodies'.[26] But on taking office after the general election, on 4 March 1974, Labour was faced with a situation in which there was less than a month to go before the reorganized system would come into operation concurrently with the new local government system, on 1 April. Furthermore, the transition to the pattern of the new Health Service had been less thoroughly prepared than that of local government, and to a tighter schedule. Whereas, for example, shadow county authorities had been elected in April 1973 and had nearly a year to prepare for taking over on 1 April 1974, the Area Health Authorities were nominated less than seven months before reorganization day.

The incoming Secretary of State for Social Services, Barbara Castle, did not therefore attempt a wholesale and immediate modification of the new reorganized health system. It was not until the end of May 1974 that she published a White Paper setting out the Government's intentions. The Paper, entitled Democracy in the National Health Service. Membership of Health Authorities, was, in the jargon of the time, a 'white paper with green edges'.[27] That is, it announced some firm decisions taken by the Government, but in other areas put forward proposals on which the Department was prepared to make modifications of detail.

The firm decisions were that the Community Health Councils were to be strengthened in a number of ways. The Government had decided firstly that the Secretaries of Community Health Councils should be chosen by open competition 'to give the greatest possible scope for attracting suitable candidates'.[28] Second, District Medical Teams were being instructed that one or more spokesmen of the team should attend Community Health Council Meetings, to answer questions in public session.[29] Third, Regional Health Authorities were instructed to consult Community Health Councils before making appointments to the Area Health Authorities, and the Government suggested that in making appointments weight should be given to prior service on a Community Health Council.[30] Fourth, the Department said that appointing bodies should not feel inhibited from inviting N.H.S. employees, or family practitioners, from serving on Community Health Councils, providing they were not members of District Management Teams or of Regional or Area Teams of Officers.[31] Fifth, Community Health Councils were to have a special responsibility in relation to hospital closures. They would be consulted about all projected closures and, where they objected, would be expected to make detailed and constructive counter-proposals.[32] In addition the Department stated that the Government considered there should be a National Council, with a budget drawn from central government funds, to advise and assist the Community Health Councils.[33]

These decisions should help to make the Community Health Councils more effective. The Act already provides that the members of each Area Health Authority are required to meet its relevant Community Health Council (or Councils) at least once a year, that the Councils are to make annual reports to the Regional Authorities, and that the Area Authorities must comment on these reports. As we shall see in Chapter XI, Community Health Councils also have a role in assisting dissatisfied patients to complain to the Area Authorities or to the Health Service Commissioner.[34]

The sector in which the Department's Paper made tentative proposals related to the composition of the Area and Regional Health Authorities. The principles which the Department enunciated were first, that a third of the members of each Regional Health Authority should be members of local authorities. Second, that as a general rule each Community Health Council should elect two of its members to serve on the Area Health Authority. Third, the medical and nursing members of the Area Health Authorities, and of the Regional Authorities, should be chosen by the medical and nursing profession, instead of being nominated, respectively, by the Area Authority or the Minister. Fourth, there should also be representatives of N.H.S. staff, other than doctors and nurses, on the Area and Regional Authorities.

It was on the detailed application of these principles that the Government invited comment. The Department suggested that each Community Health Council, in electing two members to the Area Health Authorities, should always choose at least one district councillor. Where an Area Authority still did not have one-third of its members chosen from local authorities, the relevant local authorities should be asked to make further nominations. Since, under the 1973 Act, an overlapping of the representative and management functions was precluded, the members elected by the Community Health Councils would have to resign from those Councils. The Department suggested that they should then be reappointed to the Community Health Councils. They also welcomed comment on whether there should be legislation to allow concurrent membership.[35] On the question of election of medical, nursing, and other staff representatives to the Area and Regional Authorities, the Department invited the views of the medical and nursing professions, and of the N.H.S. General Whitley Council.[36]

If all these proposals are accepted, a great deal will have been done to bring the reorganized system nearer to the pattern proposed in the Crossman Green Paper. The main difference will be in the absence of a representative district authority with executive powers. But the strengthening of Community Health Councils may do something to fill this gap.

NOTES

1 Parts of this chapter have been updated from an article by the author, 'The Reorganization of the National Health Service', *Public Administration Bulletin*, no. 15 (December 1973). They have been incorporated in the chapter with the kind permission of the editor of the *Bulletin*.

2 Ministry of Health, National Health Service. The Administrative Structure of the Medical and Related Services in England and Wales (H.M.S.O., 1968), p. 5.

3 See Michael Ryan, 'Reform of the Health Service Structure', *Public Administration*, 1968, pp. 315–30, and the same author, 'The Tripartite Administrative Structure of the National Health Service—its Genesis and Reform', *Social and Economic Administration*, 1972, pp. 218–31.

4 Ministry of Health, Report of the Maternity Services Committee 1959 (The Cranbrook Report); see, for example, p. 83, para. 29. Ministry of Health, Central Health Services Council, The Field of Work of the Family Doctor 1963 (The Gillie Committee); see p. 57, para. 206.

5 Social Assay, *A Review of the Medical Services in Great Britain 1963* (The Porritt Report).

6 Ministry of Health, National Health Service. The Administrative Structure, p. 5.

7 Op. cit., pp. 7 and 9.

8 Op. cit., p. 19, para. 53.

9 Op. cit., p. 20, para. 59.

10 Op. cit., p. 21, para. 61.

11 Op. cit., p. 21, para. 63.

12 Op. cit., p. 21, para. 65.

13 Department of Health and Social Security: National Health Service. The Future Structure of the National Health Service (H.M.S.O., 1970), p. 7, para. 19.

14 Op. cit., p. 5.

15 Op. cit., p. 23, paras. 83 and 84.

16 National Health Service Reorganization, Consultative Document (H.M.S.O., 1971), p. 1.

17 Op. cit., p. 20.
18 Cmnd. 5055, National Health Service Reorganization: England (H.M.S.O., 1972).
19 Department of Health and Social Security: Management Arrangements for the Reorganized National Health Service (H.M.S.O., 1972); Welsh Office: Management Arrangements for the Reorganized National Health Service in Wales (H.M.S.O., 1972).
20 Department of Health and Social Security: Management Arrangements for the Reorganized National Health Service, p. 29.
21 See report in the *Western Mail*, 28 March 1973.
22 Welsh Office: Management Arrangements for the Reorganized National Health Service in Wales, pp. 40–1.
23 Ibid.
24 Cmnd. 4734, Scottish Home and Health Department: Reorganization of the Scottish Health Service (H.M.S.O., 1971), pp. 12–13.
25 Official Report of Standing Committee G.: National Health Service Reorganization Bill (Lords), thirteenth sitting, col. 680.
26 The Labour Party, *Let us Work Together*, Labour Manifesto for the 1974 General Election.
27 Department of Health and Social Security: Democracy in the Health Service. Membership of Health Authorities (H.M.S.O., 1974).
28 Op. cit., p. 10, para. 23(a).
29 Ibid., para 23(b).
30 Ibid., para 23(c).
31 Op. cit., p. 11, para. 23(d).
32 Ibid., para. 23(e).
33 Ibid., para. 24.
34 See p. 197.
35 Op. cit. p. 9, para. 19.
36 Op. cit., p. 10, paras. 21 and 22.

CHAPTER XI

Reforms in the Redress of Grievances

THIS has been a period in which there has been a great deal of interest in reforms designed to provide improved methods of redress against central and local government. The most significant developments have been made in providing for institutions of the Ombudsman type for investigating complaints against central government departments (in 1967), against Health Service authorities (in 1973), and against local authorities (in 1974).

Administrative Tribunals

As concerns redress against public authorities through administrative tribunals and the ordinary courts, there have been developments of lesser importance. But useful reforms in this field had been initiated in 1958, and their adequacy was being tested in this period. In a number of ways, increasing criticism was being directed against aspects of the administrative tribunal system, as we shall describe.

The 1958 Tribunals and Inquiries Act implemented some of the recommendations made in the report of the Committee on Administrative Tribunals and Inquiries which sat under the chairmanship of Sir Oliver Franks and reported in 1957.[1] Its most important single recommendation was that two permanent Councils on Tribunals should be set up, one for England and Wales, and one for Scotland, to keep the operation of administrative tribunals under continuous review. The 1958 Act set up one Council of Tribunals, with a Scottish Committee, and this Council has proved an active body issuing useful annual reports.

Originally, the 1958 Act empowered the Council on Tribunals to investigate 55 types of statutory tribunals, and all statutory inquiries.[2] This left outside its jurisdiction a great many non-statutory inquiries which are set up by Ministers at their own discretion. The 1966 Tribunals and Inquiries Act did something to fill this gap. It gave the Lord Chancellor power to bring discretionary inquiries within the jurisdiction of the Council on Tribunals. In 1967, Lord Gardiner, as Lord Chancellor, made an Order bringing 65 classes of inquiry of this type within the Council's purview. This was an important development since some inquiries on the most far-reaching topics are of the discretionary type, such as, for example, the Roskill Commission inquiry on the siting of the third London Airport.

There remains a more significant gap in the powers of the Council on Tribunals as it does not have power to recommend the creation of new tribunals. The Whyatt Committee recommended in 1961 that it should have this power but nothing has been done to implement this recommendation. This is quite a serious failing, since the provision of administrative tribunals in Britain is somewhat haphazard. There are areas in which there has been a conspicuous lack of statutory tribunals, for example, in the investigation of complaints against hospital personnel, and against the police.

There are two further main defects in the Council on Tribunals. The first is that, apart from the chairman of the Council, none of its members receive a salary, and all give their services voluntarily. The Council has a small permanent staff, but the important function of visiting tribunals, and observing them in operation, falls to the Council members which inevitably means that they cannot visit many tribunal hearings in a year. For example, between 1 August 1972 and 31 July 1973, members of the Council visited twenty-five tribunal hearings in all. In 1972, 32,437 cases were dealt with by National Insurance Local Tribunals alone.[3] There is a strong case for providing more funds for the Council on Tribunals to enable it to appoint a full-time inspectorate of tribunals. In this way a much better coverage of tribunal hearings could be secured, and the inspectors' reports could do a great deal to help remedy anomalies and defects in tribunal procedures.

The other great failing with the Council on Tribunals is that it is relatively unknown to the general public. It receives an average of about 40 complaints in a year.[4] This should not be held to indicate general satisfaction with the working of tribunals, but rather is a reflection of the fact that very few people who appeal to tribunals have ever heard of the Council on Tribunals. The Council does little to publicize its activities, and no statutory duty is placed upon tribunals to inform appellants that, if they are not satisfied with the conduct of a tribunal, they can complain to the Council on Tribunals.

Partly, perhaps, because of these two defects in the Council on Tribunals there remain many respects in which some administrative tribunals are very much open to criticism, in both their constitution and procedures. The Franks Committee recommended that in order to enhance the independence of administrative tribunals all chairmen of tribunals should be appointed by the Lord Chancellor, and all members of tribunals by the Council on Tribunals. In 1973 Wraith and Hutchesson pointed out that the latter recommendation had not been acted upon while, although some progress had been made towards the former recommendation, about one-third of the chairmen of statutory tribunals were still not appointed either by the Lord Chancellor, or from a panel selected by the Lord Chancellor.[5] It seems particularly inappropriate that the Chief Immigration Adjudicator, and his fellow adjudicants, are appointed by the Minister and not by the Lord Chancellor.

Defects in some kinds of tribunal remain unremedied despite calls for their improvement. The author has pointed to a number of defects in the procedures of the Service Committees which examine complaints against doctors, dentists, pharmacists, and opticians providing treatment under contract to the National Health Service.[6] These Committees, which have existed since the introduction of the National Health Service in 1948 and had their predecessors in the Medical Service Sub-Committees of the local Insurance Committees, set up under the 1911 National Insurance Act, work reasonably well. But they are little known or understood by users of the Service. Their procedures are by and large not fully explained to complainants, nor to the professional men against whom the complaints are levelled. Nor are the procedures always properly adhered to. For example, a doctor's legal adviser may sometimes address the Committee although he is not allowed to do so under the regulations. Since these Committees, probably rightly, meet in private, the extent of such irregularities is impossible to determine.

No provision is made for representing and assisting patients at Service Committees, and consequently they may find themselves baffled and bewildered by the arguments put forward on the professional side. Finally, provision for appeal is defective. Although patients can appeal to the Secretary of State against the decisions of the Family Practitioner Committees of the Area Health Authorities, they are told that the Minister can award costs on appeal.[7] This effectively deters many appeals since complainants are aware that the professional man can be represented by a barrister at the appeal committee, and the award of costs, when it involves payment of the barrister's fees, can be a serious matter.

Nothing has been done, however, to remedy these defects. One change which was introduced in 1968, in response to suggestions from the British Medical Association, was the introduction of the informal procedure. Under this procedure, a complaint can be investigated by a lay member of a Family Practitioner Committee (formerly Executive Council), assisted by a professional member. This small committee of two interviews the complainant, and the doctor who is the object of complaint, and attempts to conciliate between the two parties. If conciliation is not possible, the case can go to the Service Committee.

It was made clear when the system was introduced that it would be a matter for each Executive Council to decide whether to make use of the informal procedure. Some Executive Councils, for example, the Inner London Executive Council, decided to make use of the procedure only for the less serious complaints. Other Executive Councils have used it extensively, for example, the Swansea Executive Council, of which the author was a member from 1965 to 1974, which used it for a high proportion of complaints against doctors. It was perhaps not surprising that this coincided with a considerable decline in the number of cases going to the Medical Service Committee. Whether this was a matter for congratulation was not altogether clear, since it is possible that some of the cases dealt with by conciliation should have been considered by the Service Committee.

In 1973 Rudolf Klein published his study *Complaints against Doctors* which concluded that the Service Committee system leaves much to be desired as a machinery for complaints.[8] That there is a need for representation of patients at Service Committees is something with which we would emphatically agree. But whether the whole system should be replaced by another method of securing accountability by general practitioners is more doubtful. Undoubtedly doctors do not like the system. They have come to accept it, but resist ideas for improving it in the interest of patients. There is nevertheless a clear need for looking again at this aspect of the tribunal system. The machinery for complaints against staff in the hospitals also needs review. A committee chaired by Sir Michael Davis reported to the Secretary of State for Social Services in 1973, making extensive proposals for improving complaints procedures in the hospitals. In March 1975 the committee's recommendations were still being discussed with representatives of the medical profession. Since this question interlocks with the functions of the Health Service Commissioner it is appropriate to consider the Davies Committee Report later in this chapter, after looking at the Commissioner's role in investigating complaints.[9]

Another kind of administrative tribunal which has come in for much criticism recently is the Supplementary Benefit Appeal Tribunal. These tribunals also meet in private. The case for excluding the public from their proceedings is less strong than that of the Medical Service Committees. Whereas in the latter case the reputation of a professional man might be jeopardized, in the case of Supplementary Benefit Appeal Tribunals, it should surely be a matter for the appellant to say whether he or she wishes the public to be excluded. This is the practice with National Insurance Local Tribunals. Another defect of these tribunals is that there is no appeal system, apart from appeal on restricted grounds to the ordinary courts. Wide variations can therefore arise in decisions made by the 151 Supplementary Benefit Appeal Tribunals in the whole of Great Britain. Other defective procedures include the practice whereby, for example, benefit is withdrawn from a woman who is said to be cohabiting prior to any appeal to a tribunal, whereas the fair procedure would seem to be only to withdraw benefit after a tribunal had considered the case.

Finally, the absence of any system for providing representation and aid to claimants is particularly damaging. After the Child Poverty Action Group and similar organizations began to provide voluntary helpers to assist claimants at these tribunals, it soon became clear how much the unrepresented claimant was at a disadvantage. Tony Lynes, for example, writing in ,*New Society*, estimated that of 10 claimants of whom he had personal knowledge, more than half would have lost their benefit if they had not had access to expert advice and assistance, including representation at tribunal hearings where necessary.[10] We have argued that there is a need for a nationwide system to provide advice and assistance to people using administrative tribunals.[11]

The closer one looks at administrative tribunals in their various forms, the more convinced one becomes that there is a need for a new committee to look into administrative tribunals, but with broader terms of reference than the Franks Committee of 1955–7 was given. The committee would also need to have a research staff so that the actual operation of each type of tribunal could be studied. The Franks Committee did not have any such staff, nor did the Committee itself attend tribunal hearings.

The committee should also look at the operation of inquiries. The Town and Country Planning Act of 1968 has made some major changes in the planning system, and it is still early to evaluate their full impact. What is clear, however, is that there are major delays in hearing planning appeals. In January 1974 Mr. George Dobry Q.C. published his interim report on the operation of the development control system. He reported that the number of appeals had risen by 123 per cent in the preceding 3 years. At that time, the interval between the fixing of an inquiry and the earliest date for which an inspector would be available was on average 6 months. One suggestion which he discussed was that instead of appeals being heard individually by inspectors they should be grouped together in regular regional 'assizes'.

During this period there has been much discussion about improving the remedies which the ordinary courts provide for citizens seeking redress against public authorities. These are, briefly, that the courts can provide remedies against public authorities who are exceeding their powers, are not exercising powers which they are statutorily required to do, or are behaving in ways which are contrary to natural justice. Critics of this situation, such as Professor J. D. B. Mitchell, have argued that there is a need in Britain for an administrative court on the lines of the French *Conseil d'État*. Such a court, in his opinion, should have jurisdiction over administrative tribunals, should review the legality of administrative acts, and have jurisdiction in public contracts and in reparation for administrative fault.[12] Similarly, in 1966 a group of Conservative lawyers prepared a scheme for providing a British version of the *Conseil d'État* by creating Judicial and Investigating Divisions of the Privy Council.[13]

In response to proposals of this kind, the Law Commission circulated a discussion document to judges, public officials, and practising and academic lawyers, asking their opinion on whether there was a need for a major reform of administrative justice. When it had digested the replies, the Law Commission reported to the Lord Chancellor in May 1969, recommending that a Royal Commission be set up to consider the citizen's rights and remedies against the State.[14] This recommendation was not taken up, and in 1971 the Law Commission published its own *Working Paper on Remedies in Administrative Law*. This made the modest but useful proposal that the ancient prerogative orders by which citizens can seek redress against government departments or local authorities should be replaced by a new procedure of 'application for review' by the High Court. Even this mild proposal has not yet been acted upon. In this area of reform, therefore, there has been much talk but little action.

The Parliamentary Commissioner for Administration

The most rapid growth area, as we have seen, has been in the development of institutions of the Ombudsman type. Neither the Parliamentary Commissioner for Administration, the Health Service Commissioner, nor the Local Commissioners for Administration are officially known as Ombudsmen. But, in practice, they are most commonly referred to as 'the Ombudsman', 'the Health Service Ombudsman' and 'the Local Ombudsmen'. All are modelled to some extent on the pattern of the Danish Ombudsman, but there are major differences which make the British Ombudsmen, for good or ill, unique. They are still, however, sufficiently close to the classic style of Ombudsman to merit the name.

The author has described in some detail the process by which the proposals for a British Ombudsman were first developed in this country, the translation of these proposals into legislation through the passage of the Parliamentary Commissioner Act, 1967, and the operation of the Parliamentary Commissioner's Office in the years 1967–71.[15] The background to the reform can be summarized as follows. The initial proposal for an Ombudsman was formulated by a committee of the organization known as 'Justice' which is the British section of the International Committee of Jurists, and is an inter-party group of lawyers with its office in the City of London. The research for this committee was carried out by Sir John Whyatt, and its report, *The Citizen and the Administration. The Redress of Grievances*, was published in 1961.

The Whyatt Committee's proposals were to prove very influential, and played a major part in shaping the lines on which the Ombudsman institution would develop in its British form. It is important first to recall the political circumstances at the time when the report was prepared. The Macmillan Government was then in office.

Members of the Committee forecast rightly that the Government would be reluctant to introduce a thoroughgoing Ombudsman system. They were also aware that many M.P.s were jealous of their position as 'grievance-men' for their constituents, and might look upon a powerful Ombudsman as an unnecessary and unwelcome competitor.

The Whyatt Committee therefore put forward a scheme which was very cautious in a number of respects. The Committee proposed that a Parliamentary Commissioner for Investigations should be appointed who would for the first five years only investigate complaints forwarded to him by M.P.s and peers. He would not be able to examine all the documents in the case, but only the ingoing and outgoing correspondence from the Ministry. Each Minister would be given the right to veto an investigation by the Commissioner. Finally, the Commissioner would be empowered to investigate alleged maladministration in government departments but would not have power to examine complaints against the discretionary actions of Ministers where maladministration was not alleged. The Committee considered that consideration of such complaints should be the concern of a much expanded administrative tribunal system.

Some, but not all, of this caution was carried over into the Parliamentary Commissioner Act, 1967. But before we make a comparison here, it is necessary to look at the reception given to the Whyatt Report by the Macmillan Government. The Government waited for over a year, and then turned down the Whyatt Committee's recommendations altogether. In a statement issued in November 1962 the Government said that it rejected the suggestion for a Parliamentary Commissioner because he would 'seriously interfere with the prompt and efficient despatch of public business'. The statement added that, in the Government's view, there was already adequate provision for redress of grievances 'by means of the citizen's right of access to Members of Parliament'. As regards the Committee's proposals for extending the system of administrative tribunals, the Government turned these down on the grounds that they 'would lead to inflexibility and delays in administration'.[16]

The Labour Opposition soon after took up the idea with some enthusiasm, and Harold Wilson, as Leader of the Labour Party, gave considerable emphasis to appointment of a Parliamentary Commissioner in his campaign for the 1964 general election. This proposal attracted so much interest that when Labour came to power in the autumn of 1964 there was a sufficient head of steam within the Government and the Parliamentary Labour Party to ensure not only that the necessary legislation would be passed to set up a Parliamentary Commissioner, but also that improvements would be made to some of the Whyatt Committee's proposals. Thus the Committee's suggestion that the Commissioner should only look at the ingoing and outgoing correspondence was abandoned, and under the 1967 Act the Parliamentary Commissioner has access to all internal files. The Minister can instruct him not to publish all the information to which he has access, but no departmental files may be withheld from him. In practice, the Minister's power to instruct the Parliamentary Commissioner not to publish information which he has seen was used on only one occasion between 1967 and 1973.

The second major improvement in the Act, over the Whyatt Committee's proposals, is that no power is given to a Minister to veto an investigation by the Commissioner. Apart from this, the caution which characterizes the Whyatt Committee's recommendations is retained in the Act. In fact, access to the Commissioner is even more restricted than in the Whyatt Committee's proposals. Under the Act, all complaints to the Parliamentary Commissioner must be channelled through M.P.s. Peers are not given any part to play, and there is no mention of limitation of access being for a defined period. Exclusion of peers was partly a result of feeling which existed in the Parliamentary Labour Party at that time against giving a significant role to the Upper House. Making limitation of access a permanent feature of the Act reflects the feeling dominant among M.P.s at the time that the Parliamentary Commissioner should complement their role, rather than being a rival channel for complaints from members of the public.

Finally, the Whyatt Committee's cautious proposal that the Parliamentary Commissioner should be confined to investigating allegations of maladministration was embodied in the Act. The crucial section in the Act (Section 5) states that the Parliamentary Commissioner may investigate a written complaint made to an M.P. by a member of the public who claims 'to have sustained injustice in consequence of maladministration'. The Act also provides, at Section 12, that the Commissioner is not required 'to question the merits of a decision taken without maladministration by a government department or other authority in the exercise of a discretion vested in that department or authority'.

Limiting the Parliamentary Commissioner to maladministration has all along been one of the most controversial features of the reform. The Whyatt Report, in proposing that he should be so limited, argued that this was following Danish practice. In fact this is not altogether accurate. The Danish Ombudsman can investigate complaints against discretionary decisions which do not involve maladministration, but he is restrained about using his powers in this area.[17] The Swedish Ombusdmen have no such inhibitions, and the New Zealand Ombudsman is expressly empowered by the 1962 Act to report on any administrative decision which is, in his opinion, 'unreasonable, unjust or improperly discriminatory'.[18]

To be fair to the Whyatt Committee, the New Zealand Act had not been passed when it was drawing up its report, although it printed the text of the Act as an appendix to the report. When the Labour Party made it clear in 1964 that it intended to set up a Parliamentary Commissioner, if returned to power, 'Justice' set up a new committee to make recommendations about the form legislation might take. The memorandum which this Committee sent to Lord Gardiner, who became Lord Chancellor in the Wilson Government, suggested that Britain should follow New Zealand's example, and empower the Parliamentary Commissioner to report on 'unreasonable' decisions by government departments.[19] But the Treasury, which had been put in charge of the Parliamentary Commissioner Bill, proved inflexible, both when the Bill was being drafted, and during its passage through Parliament. In effect, the Treasury had been persuaded to adopt the Whyatt formula, but was not prepared to go any further.

The House of Commons Select Committee on the Parliamentary Commissioner for Administration has from time to time attempted to persuade him to interpret the word 'maladministration' in the Act in a broad sense. During the first phase of the Select Committee's work, from 1967 to 1970, it suggested that the Parliamentary Commissioner should consider the quality of a decision. In other words, if a decision was bad—for example, clearly unfair—that could be considered maladministration even though the manner of taking the decision was correct. Sir Edmund Compton, the first Parliamentary Commissioner to be appointed, accepted the Committee's recommendation, but this seemed in practice to have little effect on his reports. There was little discernible widening of his jurisdiction.

After the second Parliamentary Commissioner, Sir Alan Marre, was appointed in 1971 much less was heard about the need for the Parliamentary Commissioner to consider the quality of decisions. In fact, in an interview with the author in May 1973, Sir Alan voiced some scepticism about the advantages of considering the quality of a decision. Nevertheless, Sir Alan Marre is, in the author's view, giving a wider interpretation to the word in the following way. He distinguishes two broad types of maladministration. The first is procedural: if there has been a fault in procedure, and this has led to an error of judgement, it is maladministration. This has been the case ever since the office of Parliamentary Commissioner began to operate in 1967. The second main category of maladministration which Sir Alan distinguishes is when the decision, although procedurally correct, is one which no reasonable person could have made on the evidence. This, in the author's opinion, is moving closer to the concept of an unreasonable decision, as in the New Zealand Act.

It is perhaps significant that Sir Alan Marre has found a higher proportion of cases in which there is an element of maladministration than his predecessor did. In 1970 Sir Edmund Compton found maladministration in 23 per cent of the cases he investigated. This was his highest score. In 1968 he found 10 per cent, and in 1969 the proportion was 16 per cent. In 1971 Sir Alan Marre found maladministration in 37 per cent of the cases he investigated, in 1972 in 30 per cent, and in 1973 in 37 per cent.

It would still be desirable, in the author's view, to amend the Act, and give the Parliamentary Commissioner power to report on decisions which are unreasonable. This is the position in New Zealand and in the five Canadian provinces which have well-established Ombudsmen systems: Quebec, Alberta, Manitoba, New Brunswick, and Nova Scotia. Neither in New Zealand, nor in the Canadian provinces, does the power to report on unreasonable decisions create special problems in the relationship between Ombudsmen and Ministers, as the Treasury spokesman, during passage of the Parliamentary Commissioner Act in Britain, alleged that it would.[20] But Sir Alan Marre's interpretation of 'maladministration' should help to make the provisions of the Act less restrictive.

In general, the British Parliamentary Commissioner has achieved some modest success, but his achievements have gone largely unnoticed because he works behind the scenes, out of the glare of publicity. The exception was his investigation into the Sachsenhausen case. Here he managed to win redress for four men to whom the Foreign Office had denied compensation from the funds provided by the West German Government for victims of Nazi persecution held in concentration camps during the Second World War The M.P.s who had taken up the case had exhausted all possibilities, and had been turned down by three Ministers at the Foreign Office, including the Foreign Secretary himself, and by the Prime Minister. Sir Edmund Compton's achievement in uncovering documents which showed the unreliability of the original decision was a considerable one. This report was debated in the Commons, and received good publicity in the Press.[21]

No subsequent cases investigated by the Parliamentary Commissioner have achieved so much publicity. It is true that none of them has been so spectacular, but in many instances the Commissioner has secured redress for individuals which would otherwise have been denied them. For example, in 1971 Sir Alan Marre succeeded in convincing the Department of Health and Social Security that they should backdate payment of a disability pension for a retired Army officer, Captain R. C. Horsley, which it had previously refused to do. The Department not only paid the disputed arrears to Captain Horsley but also reconsidered its policy in other comparable cases.[22]

Many similar instances could be given from the Parliamentary Commissioner's reports over the years, but the impact he makes is not fully appreciated because of the little publicity given to his reports. This lack of publicity is partly due to the institutional arrangements, and partly to the reticence shown by the two Parliamentary Commissioners who have held office since 1967. The Parliamentary Commissioner's results reports are sent to the M.P. who forwarded the complaint, to the person complained against, and to the principal officer of the department concerned. It is, then, normally a matter for the M.P. concerned, and for the complainant, to decide whether to give publicity to the Parliamentary Commissioner's findings. Many M.P.s do not inform the Press about these results reports, or send information to the local newspaper only, and not to the national Press.

The Parliamentary Commissioner only gives full information about his results reports in relatively rare cases. He is empowered by the Act (under Section 10(4)) to publish special reports of investigations which throw light on the performance of his functions. Sir Edmund Compton only published three such reports, on Sachsenhausen, on a complaint about aircraft noise, and on the Duccio painting case.[23]

Sir Alan Marre has been similarly sparing in publishing special reports. But he has introduced a change of policy in relation to his other reports. Sir Edmund Compton used to give a selection from the other reports in an appendix to his annual report. The selected reports were all in an 'anonymised' form, that is the names of complainants were not given, neither were the names of the M.P.s forwarding the complaints. Sir Alan Marre decided that it would be better for him to publish all his results reports, but still in an 'anonymised' form. From August 1972 onwards he has therefore published quarterly reports giving in an anonymous form the results of all the cases he has investigated.

This change has resulted in very little discernible improvement in publicity. There are two main reasons for this. The first is that an 'anonymised' report has much less intrinsic interest than a report in which the name of the complainant is given. The second is that Sir Edmund Compton steadfastly refused to single out or in any way emphasize the reports of the cases in which he found maladministration. He told the Select Committee that he thought that to do this would be unfair to departments. Sir Alan Marre has followed his example. This means that the reports are now published by department in chronological order, without even an index or any method of reference to guide the reader to those reports which throw most light on the activities of the Commissioner. Certainly they are all there, but the journalist or scholar has to burrow through a mass of less important reports in order to find the most interesting ones. Even when he finds these, they are harder to appreciate owing to their anonymous form which makes assessment of the full circumstances of the case impossible.[24]

It is true that many other Ombudsmen do not mention names in the cases which they describe in their annual reports. But, in the first place, the cases which they select for illustration are cases of particular interest because of the light they throw on the Ombudsman's activities and on his effectiveness in securing redress of grievances. In the second place, in almost every country which has an Ombudsman journalists have much readier access to the Ombudsman's results reports than in Britain. In Sweden, under the law which gives free access to official information, journalists must be allowed to see the full text of all the Ombudsman's results reports, as well as the texts of the original complaints. In Denmark and Norway, journalists regularly call at the Ombudsman's office, and are allowed to read the files of cases upon which the Ombudsman has just reported. The law in Denmark and Norway does not require the Ombudsman to open his files in this way. He does so at his discretion, and with full appreciation that he is likely to be much more effective if the Press and public have a clear idea of what he can achieve.

The author has suggested that the British Parliamentary Commissioner has much more discretion in this kind of way than he in fact allows himself. There is nothing in the Act which, in the author's opinion, would prevent the Commissioner when he has completed a results report from telling the M.P. in every case that he proposed to give the Press a copy of the full text of the report unless the M.P. and the complainant did not wish him to do so. The reason why the Parliamentary Commissioner does not adopt this practice is because he considers that it is a matter for the M.P. to decide whether the report should be published. Making M.P.s the only channel for complaints has the effect therefore of reducing the amount of publicity which the Parliamentary Commissioner's work achieves.

The British Parliamentary Commissioner investigates far fewer cases in relation to the population of Britain than the Scandinavian Ombudsmen do. In 1971 in Sweden, which has a population of around 8 million, the Ombudsmen investigated 1,973 cases, in Denmark, with a population of about 5 million, the Ombudsman investigated 396 cases, and in Norway, population around 4 million, the Civil Ombudsman (Norway has a separate Military Ombudsman) investigated 354 cases. In comparison, in the same year the British Parliamentary Commissioner investigated 182 cases;[25] Great Britain has a population of around 53 million.

The relatively small impact which the Parliamentary Commissioner is making in Britain can be attributed to four factors in particular. First, he has a narrower jurisdiction than the Scandinavian Ombudsmen have. He cannot, for example, investigate complaints by Civil Servants about their pay and conditions. Second, he is limited to maladministration. As we have seen, the Swedish Ombudsmen are not excluded, and the Danish and Norwegian Ombudsmen are not wholly excluded from looking at discretionary decisions which do not involve maladministration. Third, his activities receive much less publicity than those of the Swedish, Danish, and Norwegian Ombudsmen. We have examined the reasons for this. Finally, limiting access to him through M.P.s means that he is relatively inaccessible to the public. Many M.P.s make little use of the Parliamentary Commissioner.[26] Many members of the public clearly do not know how to get a case to him even when they know of his existence. In the Scandinavian countries where all that is necessary is a letter to the Ombudsman, or a call at his office, access is much easier.

This has been a somewhat dismal record of the limitations which surround the Parliamentary Commissioner and his effectiveness. But the Parliamentary Commissioner has scored one major success in that he has been accepted by the Civil Service. The Macmillan Government's fear that the activities of a Parliamentary Commissioner 'would seriously interfere with the prompt and efficient despatch of public business' has proved to be unfounded.[27] This has had the important consequence that the cautious attitude which prevailed in the higher ranks of the Civil Service, at the time of the inauguration of the Parliamentary Commissioner's Office in 1967, has been a little modified. In particular, some of the areas which were initially excluded from consideration by an Ombudsman are now being brought in.

The Health Service Commissioner

The principal exclusions from the Parliamentary Commissioner's jurisdiction, under the 1967 Act, were local government, National Health Service Hospitals, personnel matters in the Civil Service and the armed forces, the nationalized industries, and the police. There were advocates for including all these areas when the Bill was being discussed in Parliament, but the Wilson Government was adamant. Although the Standing Committee which considered the Bill in the Commons carried an amendment which would have brought in the National Health Service hospitals, the Government insisted on having this amendment reversed at Report stage in the Commons.

It was understood, however, that the last word had not been said on the matter and that the excluded areas would be looked at again. The Select Committee on the Parliamentary Commissioner took upon itself to see that this was carried out. It published a series of reports advocating that personnel matters in the Civil Service and the armed forces be included, and supporting extension of the Ombudsman principle to the hospitals and local government.[28]

Governments since 1967 have not accepted the first of these recommendations. Successive government memoranda have argued that the Whitley Council system in the Civil Service is an adequate channel for complaints on personnel matters. But the Heath Government introduced legislation to set up a Health Service Commissioner, and Local Commissioners for Administration. Power to appoint Health Service Commissioners was included in the National Health Service Reorganization Act, 1973 (and in the National Health Service, Scotland, Act, 1972), and to appoint Local Commissioners in the Local Government Act, 1974.

Kenneth Robinson's Green Paper suggested in 1968 that in the reorganized Health Service either the Area Health Boards should be brought within the ambit of the Parliamentary Commissioner, or that special Health Service Commissioners should be set up to examine complaints from the Area Boards.[29] The Crossman Green Paper in 1970 announced that discussions were going on with professional and other interests on the proposal to set up a Health Service Commissioner. While the British Medical Association was critical of the idea the voluntary organizations concerned with the Health Service were very much in favour of some kind of Health Ombudsman. This was not surprising. In 1967 the association called Aid for the Elderly in Government Institutions (AEGIS) had published its indictment of the treatment of geriatric patients in many hospitals. Its book *Sans Everything* was rounded off by a powerful plea from Brian Abel-Smith for establishing a Hospital Commissioner.[30]

When the Heath Government produced its Consultative Document on reorganization of the Health Service in May 1971, it contained no reference to a Health Service Commissioner. But pressures were building up in favour of the reform. The main impetus was given by the publication of a series of reports of inquiries into scandals in psychiatric hospitals; at Ely Hospital in

1969, and at Farleigh and Whittingham Hospitals in 1971 and 1972. For example, the report of the inquiry into Farleigh Hospital recommended that 'A Health Commissioner, given the widest possible powers, should be appointed urgently to meet public anxiety about the investigation of complaints in the health service'.[31] In February 1972 the Heath Government announced its proposals for Health Service Commissioners for England, Wales, and Scotland. These proposals were embodied in the National Health Service, Scotland, Act, 1972, and in the National Health Service Reorganization Act, 1973.

It cannot be said that the legislation confers the 'widest possible powers' on the Health Service Commissioners. It does, however, constitute a real advance on the powers given to the Parliamentary Commissioner in that members of the public have been given direct access to the Health Service Commissioner. They do not have to go through an M.P., or other intermediary, although the Acts require that they must first of all have complained to the relevant health authority.

The grounds on which the Commissioner can investigate are a little wider than is the case with the Parliamentary Commissioner. The Health Service Commissioner can investigate complaints that individuals have sustained injustice, or hardship, as a result of failure in a service provided by a Health Service authority, failure to provide a service which it was its duty to provide, or any other action by a Health Service authority which involved maladministration. The provisions in the 1973 National Health Service Reorganization Act echo the 1967 Parliamentary Commissioner Act by saying, at Clause 39(2), that 'nothing in this Part of this Act authorizes or requires a Commissioner to question the merits of a decision taken without maladministration by a relevant body in the exercise of a discretion vested in that body'. The emphasis on maladministration is therefore retained but the power to report on 'failure of the service' or 'failure to provide a service' is a power which the Parliamentary Commissioner does not possess.

The cautious features of the reform are principally two. First, the Commissioner is not allowed to look at complaints, or aspects of complaints, in which the clinical judgement of Health Service staff is in question. This was written in at the insistence of the British Medical Association. It is a limitation which is hard to justify, particularly since the Health Service Commissioner could receive expert advice on the clinical aspects of a case. This, in fact, is what the Parliamentary Commissioner has done in investigating complaints with clinical aspects which have come to him from Broadmoor and Rampton hospitals. These are high-security mental hospitals which come within his jurisdiction since they are the direct responsibility of the Minister. In investigating these complaints the Parliamentary Commissioner has taken the advice of a medically qualified assessor.[32]

Second, the Health Service Commissioner is expressly excluded from looking at the operation of Medical Service Committees, or of the Dental and other Service Committees of Family Practitioner Committees. The Health Service Commissioner is not, however, excluded from investigating complaints about the administration of the general practitioner service. The Health Service Commissioner's first annual report, published in June 1974, gave examples of complaints he had investigated about the closure of a doctor's surgery, and the assignment, against her wish, of a patient to another doctor's list.[33]

The provisions in the National Health Service Reorganization Bill were strengthened in one important respect by an amendment inserted in the Lords as a result of pressure from Opposition and cross-bench peers. The Bill, as introduced, provided that the Health Service Commissioner would only investigate complaints which had already been considered by the relevant health authority. The amendment provides that he can, at his discretion, investigate complaints made by members of staff which have not already been put to the relevant authority where a member of staff is complaining on behalf of a patient who is not able to complain for himself. This allows a nurse, for example, to complain directly to the Commissioner where complaint to the relevant authority might result in victimization, or blocking of the complaint.

The National Health Service Reorganization Act refers to 'Health Service Commissioners for England and Wales', and the National Health Service (Scotland) Act refers to the 'Health Service Commissioner for Scotland'. The Heath Government decided, however, that it would be better in the first instance at any rate for all three posts to be taken on by the Parliamentary Commissioner. Since October 1973, therefore, Sir Alan Marre has worn one hat as Parliamentary Commissioner, and three separate hats as Health Service Commissioner for England, Wales, and Scotland. His position might seem anomalous, particularly since, as Parliamentary Commissioner, he can receive complaints only through M.P.s, and, as Health Service Commissioner, can be approached directly by members of the public.

In fact, the system has worked well. There are several reasons for this. The first is that, as Parliamentary Commissioner, Sir Alan investigates complaints against administration of the Health Service by the Department of Health and Social Security. When he investigates a complaint in which both the Department and a health authority are involved, there is therefore no problem of overlapping. He can, acting in his two capacitites, investigate both aspects of the case. Second, as Parliamentary Commissioner, he had more than sufficient staff to investigate the cases which M.P.s were sending to him. In fact, he had considerable spare capacity. When Sir Edmund Compton inaugurated the office as Parliamentary Commissioner in April 1967, he anticipated receiving 6,000 to 7,000 complaints a year. The size of his staff was planned to cope with this kind of flow of complaints. In fact, in 1973, Sir Alan Marre, as Parliamentary Commissioner, received only 571 complaints through M.P.s.

Third, the experience which the Parliamentary Commissioner and his staff had already gained in investigating complaints was highly relevant to their new role in looking at Health Service cases. One of the advantages of having such a large staff in relation to the number of complaints (in 1973 the Parliamentary Commissioner had 31 full-time investigating staff), is that in a high proportion of cases the investigator can interview the complainant as well as the Civil Servants of the Department against which a complaint is made. Such interviews are especially useful in Health Service cases. The investigator normally interviews the complainant in his or her home and tries to establish the facts of the case as seen by the complainant. The investigator then interviews members of staff complained against, and can call for all relevant files and records. The same powers to inspect the files are given to the Health Service Commissioner as to the Parliamentary Commissioner.

Finally, Sir Alan Marre is particularly well-fitted by experience and temperament to the post of Health Service Commissioner. Before being appointed Parliamentary Commissioner in 1971 he was a senior Civil Servant, Second Permanent Secretary, in the Department of Health and Social Security. He had had numerous contacts as a Civil Servant with voluntary organizations, and had a reputation for thoroughgoing and sympathetic concern with the interests of the consumer.

Sir Alan Marre's first report as Health Service Commissioner appeared in June 1974.[34] He sub-titled it 'Annual Report for 1973–4', but since he began work in October 1973 it only relates to his first six months of operation from 1 October 1973 to 31 March 1974. The report deals with his activities in England, Wales, and Scotland. During his first six months, he completed investigation of 23 cases. A further 52 investigations were at that time in progress, but had not been completed.

As with his work as Parliamentary Commissioner, Sir Alan Marre has to turn down a large number of cases because of lack of jurisdiction. He rejected 203 such cases in his first six months. He says in the report that there are three main grounds on which he has to decline to investigate. They are that the action complained of is in the exempted area of general practice, that it is an action taken solely in the exercise of clinical judgement, or that it is an action taken by local authorities. The last category should become less significant as on 1 April 1974 the personal health services, formally administered by local authorities, were taken over by the Area Health Authorities in the reorganized system. Complaints against the personal health services have therefore come within his jurisdiction. The other two categories will still be excluded, unless the statutes governing the work of the Commissioner are amended.

The fourth main category of cases which the Health Service Commissioner has to decline are those cases in which the complainant has not already stated his case to the health authority. Sir Alan Marre says in his first report that he has sometimes found it necessary to get in touch with the health authority to establish whether the complaint had already been made to the authority. On occasion, this has itself resulted in the matter being put right. This happened, for example, when two patients complained to him of a long waiting-period for admission to hospital. When the Commissioner asked the authority if a complaint had been made, the patients concerned were admitted for treatment. 'In other cases,' Sir Alan Marre says, 'I have advised the complainant himself to approach the authority, and to bring his complaint to me again if he is dissatisfied with the outcome; and some have already done so.'[35] The provision that complaint must first of all be made to the relevant authority is therefore not as negative as it might appear as the Commissioner's inquiry to verify the situation may itself produce remedying action. When he decides instead to tell the complainant to take his case first to the relevant authority, he indicates that he is poised to follow up the complaint if satisfaction is not obtained by taking it to the health authority.

Sir Alan Marre's first report, as Health Service Commissioner, was much more informative than his reports as Parliamentary Commissioner have been. After discussing the scope of his activities, he provided summaries of certain of the cases he had investigated in chronological order. Although they were anonymized, the important points in each case were clearly brought out. Some of the cases showed what an effect his investigations can have. Perhaps the most interesting was a case where a man requiring nose surgery complained to him that he had been waiting 18 months for treatment, and that the hospital failed to make an appointment for the consultant to review his condition when he told them that this was deteriorating. When the consultant heard that the Commissioner was looking into the case, he arranged for the patient to be examined, reclassified his case as urgent, and the operation was carried out without any further delay.

More important, however, than the immediate remedy provided for the individual were the Commissioner's recommendations in the case. His investigator called for the admission records in ear, nose, and throat cases at the hospital, and discovered that some patients had been waiting over six years for admission. The Commissioner found that the major cause of these delays was the refusal by the Regional Hospital Board to agree to appointment of an additional consultant, on the grounds that other specialities needed to be given higher priority in the region. He said in his summary that he hoped 'that the Board would keep under review the clearly unsatisfactory situation revealed by my investigation'. He also criticized the unsatisfactory admission arrangements in the hospital. He reported that the Hospital Management Committee concerned had submitted a revised scheme to the Board for the necessary supporting funds. Finally, he recommended that more information should be given by the hospital to patients about the length of time they might be kept waiting for admission, and what action they should take to get urgent treatment if their condition deteriorated.[36]

In this case, therefore, we see the Commissioner not only suggesting improved procedures, in the interest of the patient, but also making policy recommendations about the need for a review of priorities for the development of the various specialities in a hospital region. The case well illustrated the impact which the Health Service Commissioner can make if he interprets his function imaginatively.

There are several other aspects of the first report by the Health Service Commissioner which are worthy of note. We have seen that a complaint must be made to the Commissioner by the individual who claims to be suffering injustice or hardship, or by someone acting on his behalf if he is unable to make the complaint himself. This does not preclude organizations from bringing complaints on behalf of patients. The Commissioner says in his report 'Sometimes the complaint has come from an organization which I have looked upon as representing, collectively, the views of particular individuals who were aggrieved.' He points out that from 1 April 1974 the Community Health Councils, set up under the National Health Service Reorganisation Act, may play a similar role. He says that he will accept from them 'a complaint forwarded at the request and on behalf of a patient or other individual against a service in which the Council are interested, where the complaint has not been resolved locally to the complainant's satisfaction'.[37]

The other points of interest in his report are his comments on the recommendations of the Davies Committee on hospital complaints procedures. He welcomes the emphasis given in the Committee's Report to the need for external checks on the hospital service, such as are provided by the operation of the Health Service Commissioner.[38] He also says that he is hopeful that, when the Secretary of State for the Social Services and the Secretary of State for Wales have 'reached their conclusions on the Davies Committee's recommendations on hospital complaints procedures, the comprehensive guidance which no doubt will follow will help also in making it clear how my own responsibilities are related to those of the health service authorities themselves'.[39] This should help to make his functions as Health Service Commissioner more widely known and understood.

The Davies Committee on Hospital Complaints Procedure

In June 1975 the Wilson Government had still not announced a decision on the recommendations of the Davies Committee. As with the negotiations over setting up a Health Service Commissioner, it was the doctors' organizations which were reluctant to agree. This was despite the fact that the Davies Committee included a leading consultant among its membership. This was Sir John Richardson, a consultant physician and since 1974 chairman of the General Medical Council. Other medical members of the Committee were Dr. John Revans, Senior Administrative Medical Officer of the Wessex Regional Hospital Board, and Dr. R. M. Mayon-White, a consultant paediatrician and vice-chairman of the Joint Consultants Committee. The other members of the Committee included three academics, Kathleen Bell, Professor of Social Studies at Newcastle University, Maurice Kogan, Professor of Government and Social Administration at Brunel University, and Margaret Stacey, at that time Director of the Medical Sociology Research Centre at University College, Swansea. The Committee also included two representatives of voluntary associations, Miss Mary Appleby, then Director of MIND (the National Association for Mental Health), and Miss Olive Williams, Secretary of the National Association of Leagues of Hospital Friends. There were two hospital administrators on the Committee, and a member of the board of governors of a hospital, as well as a chief nursing officer, and the Staff Side Secretary of the Health Services Whitley Council. There were also two journalists on the Committee: Barry Askew, editor of the *Lancashire Evening Post*, and Ann Shearer, at that time a social services correspondent for the *Guardian*. The chairman of the Committee, Sir Michael Davies, was in January 1973 appointed a Judge of the High Court.

The Davies Committee's report, which was completed in October 1973, is long and complex, but its main recommendations can be summarized as follows.[40] The Committee recommended that a national Code of Practice for dealing with suggestions and complaints about hospital services should be uniformly applied by all health authorities, and in all hospitals. On admission to hospital, all patients should be given a booklet including information about how to make a complaint. (The Committee made a survey to ascertain how many hospitals already did this, and found that only a small proportion provided information about complaints procedure to patients.) It also recommended that this information should be sent to the relatives of patients when the patients were too young, or too infirm, to speak for themselves.

The Committee proposed that there should be standardized procedures for investigating complaints, both on an informal basis and where an independent inquiry was necessary. Some of the suggestions made about inquiries are of special interest. It was recommended that anyone appearing before a formal inquiry should be allowed legal representation. Where the inquiry was informal he should be permitted to bring a friend to help or represent him. The Committee also suggested that all essential witnesses at a formal inquiry should have the costs of legal representation met from public funds. It recommended that all formal inquiries established by health authorities should be brought within the jurisdiction of the Council on Tribunals. This is an extremely important recommendation. One of the chief weaknesses about the procedures for investigation of complaints in the hospitals had been not only that procedures were not standardized, but that investigating inquiry panels were not subject to scrutiny by the Council on Tribunals.

As regards the Health Service Commissioner, the Committee suggested that he 'should interpret his own powers liberally and widely, extending his jurisdiction to its statutory limit'.[41] As we have seen, Sir Alan Marre can reasonably be said to be doing this in his role as Health Service Commissioner. A further suggestion was that 'If the Commissioner's powers do not enable him to receive and investigate a complaint from a member of staff who alleges that he has been victimized because he made complaints on behalf of patients, they should be amended accordingly as soon as practicable.'[42] Sir Alan Marre has replied to this point in his first report as Health Service Commissioner. He says that, although personnel matters in the Health Service are specified in the statute as being outside his jurisdiction, he would not regard this as necessarily preventing him 'in the course of an investigation of a complaint submitted by a member of an authority's staff, from looking into an allegation that the submission of the complaint had led to victimization'.[43]

The Committee also emphasized the importance of Community Health Councils and of the Hospital Advisory Service as external checks on the operation of the Health Service. The Hospital Advisory Service was set up early in 1970 by Richard Crossman, as Secretary of State for the Social Services. Its creation was prompted by the series of scandals in long-stay hospitals to which we have already referred. The Service consists of teams of doctors, nurses, and other professional people, mostly on secondment, who visit long-stay hospitals to give advice on hospital organization. These teams try, by discussion with staff in the hospitals, to identify defects in organization and encourage procedures which will 'allow complaints to surface', and remedy unhappy situations. They do not investigate individual complaints. The teams themselves decide which hospitals to visit, and they have already done very valuable work. They report to the hospital concerned, to the Area Health Authority, and to the Department of Health and Social Security.

The Davies Committee was concerned that in 1973 there was a degree of curtailment of the work of the Hospital Advisory Service. It regretted the decision to reduce the scale of operations of this Service during the period of reorganization and urged not only that the period of run-down should be kept to a minimum, but that the Service should be expanded as soon as possible.[44] David Owen, the Minister of State for Health, announced in July 1974 that the team for visiting hospitals for the mentally handicapped, which had been disbanded in 1972, had not yet been re-formed, although it was the Department's intention to set up a newly constituted team. He also announced that the Advisory Service was to be extended to cover community health facilities (including residential and rehabilitation centres) which were provided by local authorities.[45] Some action, although rather belated, was therefore being taken on the Davies Committee's proposal for extension of the Advisory Service.

The Local Commissioners for Administration

When we survey developments in relation to redress of grievances in the Health Service we can therefore see some improvements. In particular, the 'Health Service Ombudsman' is an improvement on the Parliamentary Commissioner. Similarly, the Local Ombudsmen may prove to be somewhat less limited in their manner of operation than the Parliamentary Commissioner. The Local Commissioners for England and Wales were created following the passage of the Local Government Act, 1974; parts I and II of that Act are concerned with Grants and Rating, part III is concerned with the Local Commissioners for Administration.

It was very much a bipartisan reform. Both Conservative and Labour governments helped on the reform, and there was considerable back-bench opinion in its favour. When the Parliamentary Commissioner Bill was being discussed in the Commons, many members argued that there was an even greater need for an Ombudsman for local government than for central government. Spokesmen for the Wilson Government, however, successfully resisted attempts to empower the Parliamentary Commissioner to investigate complaints against local authorities, on the grounds that the central government did not have direct responsibility for local government. They did not dispute that there was a need for local Ombudsmen, but argued that they should be kept separate from the Parliamentary Commissioner.

Early in 1970, the Wilson Government put forward in consultative form a scheme for ten or more 'Local Commissioners of Administration' who would examine complaints against local authorities. On the model of the Parliamentary Commissioner, all complaints to the Local Commissioners would have to be made through councillors. After the Heath Government came to power in July 1970, it took up this scheme, and presented it in a modified form in a Consultative Document in May 1972. The document proposed that there should be 10 Commissioners for Local Administration: 9 for England, and 1 for Wales. The Commissioners would investigate complaints from members of the public which would normally be referred to them by councillors, but if a member of the public took his complaint to two councillors both of whom declined to refer the case to a Commissioner, the Commissioner could investigate the complaint. The Commissioners would be answerable to a specially constituted representative body of local authorities and water authorities, and their operation would be financed by the authorities. The reports of the Commissioners on investigations they had made would normally be made public. The Commissioners would be limited, like the Parliamentary Commissioner, to investigating complaints of alleged maladministration.

Copies of the Consultative Document were sent by the Minister to the associations of local authorities, and to the National Association of Local Government Officers, and their comments were invited. The proposals were then put into legislative form by the Department of the Environment, and incorporated, as we have seen, in the Local Government Bill, 1974. The Bill was rushed through its final stages in the Lords on the last day of the 1973–74 session of Parliament before the general election in February 1974.[46]

Part III of the Local Government Act, 1974, provides that there shall be a body of Commissioners known as the Commission for Local Administration in England, and a body of two or more Commissioners known as the Commission for Local Administration in Wales. The Parliamentary Commissioner is a member of each Commission, his function being not to investigate complaints against local authorities and water authorities, but to advise generally, and to work with Local Commissioners on the investigation of complaints which involve both local authorities and a central government department (as well as those which overlap with his functions as Health Service Commissioner). The Act does not specify the number of Commissioners to be appointed. It states that they may be either part-time or full-time. Commissioners are appointed by the Queen on the recommendation of the Secretary of State for the Environment, after consultation with the representative body of local authorities. Commissioners hold office during good behaviour, and retire at the age of 65. In practice, formal consultation with the representative body for the first appointment of Commissioners for England in 1974 meant little more than the representative body being informed of the Secretary of State's choice and of his recommendations to the Queen.

Three Commissioners of Local Administration were appointed for England in June 1974. They were Baroness Serota, who was designated chairman of the Commission, Denis Harrison, and Patrick Cook. Baroness Serota had been a member of Hampstead Borough Council from 1945 to 1949, a member of London County Council from 1954 to 1965, and served on the Greater London Council from 1964 to 1967. She was Minister of State for Health at the Department of Health and Social Security from 1969 to 1970. Denis Harrison was Town Clerk of Sheffield until local government reorganization in April 1974. Patrick Cook had been chief executive of the English Tourist Board since 1970, and before that Principal of the British Transport Staff College.

The Act provides that the English Commission shall divide England into areas and shall provide for one or more of the Commissioners to be responsible for each area. As only three Commissioners were appointed at the outset they had to be responsible for very large areas. But it was anticipated that, as the system became known, and the work-load of the Commissioners increased, more Commissioners would be appointed. The Local Commissioner for Wales, also appointed in 1974, is Dafydd Jones-Williams. He was

Clerk to Merionethshire County Council, and after local government reorganization was appointed Circuit Administrator for Wales for the Crown Courts. He is Welsh-speaking.

Although the representative body of local authorities had only a passive role in the appointment of the first Commissioners for England, it is meant to play an important part since it receives the annual report of the Commission, as well as the annual reports of the individual Commissioners. The representative body then publishes the reports, and sends them to all local authorities and water authorities. It can, if it wishes, comment on the conclusions and recommendations in the Commission's report. This arrangement underlines the status of the Local Commissioners. They are not appointed by, or responsible to, specific local authorities. They are, therefore, independent investigators of complaints about local administration; this would not be the case with Ombudsmen who were appointed by, and were responsible to, individual authorities. At the same time, they are accountable to the whole body of local authorities as a collectivity, and the central government has only a limited supervisory role, mainly through its powers of appointment.

The representative body for England consists of 3 representatives of the Association of Metropolitan Authorities, 3 representatives of the Association of County Councils, 3 representatives of the Association of District Councils, 1 representative of the Greater London Council, and 1 representative of the Water Authorities. The Greater London Council might seem to be accorded dual representation since it is also a member of the Association of Metropolitan Authorities. Care was taken, however, to see that the representatives of the Metropolitan Authorities did not include a representative of the G.L.C. The Water Authorities have a representative because complaints against them can be investigated by the Local Commissioners. The Local Councils Association is not included because the Commissioners are not empowered to consider complaints against parish councils or community councils, except when they are acting as agents for the district councils.

We have seen that the 1972 Consultative Document suggested that a direct approach could be made to a Local Commissioner by a member of the public if two councillors declined to refer his complaint. During discussion of the document in the Department of the Environment, it was decided that it would be sufficient if one councillor had been approached before the Commissioner could investigate, and this was put into the Act. This is therefore not far from permitting direct access to the Commissioners. The Act provides that before the Commissioner investigates a complaint he must satisfy himself that the authority concerned has been given a reasonable opportunity to investigate, and to reply to the complaint. This is comparable to the provision in the statutes governing the work of the Health Service Commissioner under which he only investigates complaints which have been first taken to the relevant health authority (except in the case of complaints made to him by a member of staff where a patient is not able to complain for himself).[47]

The provisions relating to publicity are a big improvement both on the Parliamentary Commissioner Act and on the statutes dealing with the powers of the Health Service Commissioner. When a Local Commissioner has completed investigation of a complaint, he is required by the Act to send his report to the person, if any, who referred the complaint, to the complainant, and to the authority complained against. The local authority (or police, or water authority) complained against is then required to make copies available at one or more of their offices for inspection by the public for a period of three weeks. An officer of the authority is also required by the Act to 'give public notice, by advertisement in newspapers and such other ways as appear to him appropriate, that the report will be available for inspection'.[48]

A Local Commissioner may direct that one of his reports be withheld from publication. The Act does not state on what grounds he may do this other than saying that he shall take into account 'the public interest as well as the interests of the complainant and of persons other than the complainant'.[49] The understanding is that the majority of a Commissioner's reports will be published. Only when a report would be likely to be embarrassing to individuals would a Commissioner direct that it be not published.

Furthermore, the Act provides that if, in the opinion of a Commissioner, 'injustice has been caused to the person aggrieved in consequence of maladministration', the Commissioner's report must be laid before the authority concerned, 'and it shall be the duty of that authority to consider the report and to notify the Local Commissioner of the action which the authority have taken, or propose to take'.[50] If the Commissioner does not receive any such notification within a reasonable time, or if he is not satisfied with the action which the authority concerned has taken, he is instructed by the Act to make a further report, and this report too must be published by the local authority.

Some such provisions as these were no doubt necessary in order to ensure that adverse publicity would be the sanction which would make a recalcitrant authority sit up and take notice of the Commissioner's reports. It is still true that the completeness of the provisions relating to publicity of the reports should make the operation of the Local Commissioners much more open, and intelligible to the public, than are the activities of the Parliamentary Commissioner. In addition, the Local Government Act, 1974, provides that publication of the Commissioners' reports, and publication of communications between members of the authority and the Commissioner, are absolutely privileged. No suit for defamation can therefore succeed against them on account of matters published in this way. This is an important safeguard which should enable the Local Commissioners to make their reports on investigations properly informative and intelligible.

The powers which the Local Commissioners have to examine documents are as extensive as those of the Parliamentary Commissioner. The Act states that 'a Local Commissioner may require any member or officer of the authority concerned, or any other person who in his opinion is able to furnish information or produce documents relevant to the investigation, to furnish any such information or produce any such documents'.[51] This includes information in the possession of a government department. As with the Parliamentary Commissioner, a Minister may not deny access by a Local Commissioner to such information, but he can require the Commissioner not to publish departmental documents which he sees. In order to make this provision effective, the Act requires that a Local Commissioner must give a government department at least one month's notice that he intends to publish a document, and must obtain written consent to publication from an officer of the department concerned.

Local Commissioners are empowered by the Act to obtain expert advice in the conduct of an investigation and to pay fees to such advisers at rates to be determined by the Minister for the Civil Service.[52] If anyone obstructs a Local Commissioner in carrying out an investigation this is equivalent to contempt of court and proceedings may be taken against such a person in the High Court. The Local Commissioners are therefore effectively armed to require that documents be produced, to employ expert advisers, and to overcome obstructive tactics.

As with the Parliamentary Commissioner, Local Commissioners are instructed not to investigate matters which could be taken to a tribunal or a court, but are given discretion to make investigations in such cases where they think it is not reasonable for the person concerned to use these avenues of redress. The same applies to matters where there is a right of appeal to a Minister.[53]

There is provision in the Act for cases in which there is an overlap between the jurisdiction of the Local Commissioners and that of the Parliamentary Commissioner, or the Health Service Commissioner. In such cases, the relevant Commissioners are instructed to consult about investigation of the complaint and about the form, content, and publication of any results report.[54]

The Local Government Act, 1974 also follows the Parliamentary Commissioner Act in specifying in a Schedule those aspects of local government which are not subject to investigation by Local Commissioners. As with the Parliamentary Commissioner Act, these exempted aspects may be taken out by Order in Council, so enlargement of the Commissioner's powers is easier than if a new statute had to be enacted. The exempted aspects are: the commencement or conduct of criminal proceedings in a court, action taken in conjunction with the investigation or prevention of crime, the commercial and contractual transactions of any authority, the operation of transport, docks or harbour undertakings, entertainment, industrial establishments and markets, personnel matters, and some aspects of education.

On this rather formidable list of exclusions the following comments may be made. First, it is clear that the Commissioners will not be able to investigate complaints about police behaviour, but Roy Jenkins, the Home Secretary, announced in July 1974 that an independent element was to be grafted on to the system of investigating complaints against the police. He told the Commons in a written answer on 30 July 1974 that legislation would be introduced to establish an independent statutory commission to consider appeals against the findings of internal investigations carried out by the police themselves. In certain circumstances Chief Constables would also send the papers on complaints to the commission at an early stage.[55]

Second, the exclusion of commercial and contractual transactions lops off an area in which some of the greatest disquiet with local administration has been expressed. But malpractices in this area can be exposed by the district auditors and, if exposed, can result in prosecution in the courts. Third, the exclusion of personnel matters is regrettable but follows on from the similar exclusion from investigation by the Parliamentary Commissioner into personnel matters in the Civil Service.

Finally, the exempted areas in education concern secular or religious instruction, the curriculum, and internal management and organization of schools and colleges. Aspects of educational administration which will be subject to investigation by the Commissioners include choice of school, provision of school meals, school transport, student awards, and the availability of playgrounds and sports fields. The decision to exclude matters of internal organization, discipline, and curricula in schools follows from the long-standing tradition that head teachers should have a high degree of autonomy in these matters. Whether or not this is altogether a sound principle is open to question. There can be instances of arbitrariness and high-handed behaviour in the running of schools, as in other forms of administration.

We have seen that the Local Commissioners are limited to investigating complaints of maladministration. The Act closely follows the Parliamentary Commissioner Act by stating that a Commissioner may investigate 'a written complaint made by or on behalf of a member of the public who claims to have sustained injustice in consequence of maladministration'.[56] Section 34 of the Act also states (at sub-section (3)) that 'It is hereby declared that nothing in this part of this Act authorizes or requires a Local Commissioner to question the merits of a decision taken without maladministration by an authority in the exercise of a discretion vested in that authority.' This exactly reproduces Section 12-(3) of the Parliamentary Commissioner Act, merely substituting the words 'an authority' for reference to 'a government department' in the Parliamentary Commissioner Act.

All the objections to limiting the Parliamentary Commissioner to investigating maladministration which we have discussed earlier apply to the identical limitation on the Local Commissioners. But the provisions for access to the Commissioners, and for securing publicity for their reports, all constitute a major advance on the system under which the Parliamentary Commissioner operates.

Whether, in fact, the Local Commissioners will come to be better understood by the public, and more frequently used than the Parliamentary Commissioner is, remains to be seen. There was disappointingly little interest taken by the Press in the appointment of the first three Local Commissioners for England. Although a handout was provided on the subject by the Department of the Environment, and sent to all national newspapers, it was ignored by most of them. The *Guardian* was one of the few papers to give the news, and it printed only two short paragraphs setting out the names of the Commissioners and a brief note of their qualifications. Much will depend therefore on how imaginative and courageous the Commissioners are in interpreting their powers, if the new system of local Ombudsmen is to become effective.

NOTES

1 Cmnd. 218, Report of the Committee on Administrative Tribunals and Inquiries (H.M.S.O., 1957).
2 The 1971 Tribunals and Inquiries Act increased the number of types of tribunal covered to 74.
3 Annual Report of the Council on Tribunals for 1972–73 (H.M.S.O., 1974), pp. 2 and 37.
4 See R. E. Wraith and P. G. Hutchesson, *Administrative Tribunals* (Allen and Unwin, 1973), p. 218.
5 Op. cit., p. 97.
6 See F. Stacey, 'The Machinery for Complaints in the National Health Service', *Public Administration* (Spring 1965), pp. 59–70, and F. Stacey, *A New Bill of Rights for Britain*, pp. 57–9.
7 The Family Practitioner Committees, like the National Health Service Executive Councils which they replaced in April 1974, receive reports of Service Committee hearings. They cannot dissent from the findings of Service Committees but can vary the penalties imposed.
8 Charles Knight, 1973.
9 See pp. 197–200.
10 *New Society*, 20 January 1972, p. 111.
11 See F. Stacey, *A New Bill of Rights for Britain*, pp. 65 and 87.
12 J. D. B. Mitchell, 'Administrative Law and Parliamentary Control', *Political Quarterly*, 1967, pp. 360–74.
13 Inns of Court Conservative and Unionist Society, *Let Right Be Done* (Conservative Political Centre, 1966).
14 Cmnd. 4059, (H.M.S.O., 1971).
15 F. Stacey, *The British Ombudsman* (Clarendon Press, 1971).
16 H.C. Deb., vol. 666, col. 1124.
17 See Stacey, *The British Ombudsman*, pp. 24–5.
18 New Zealand, Parliamentary Commissioner (Ombudsman) Act, 1962, section 19.
19 Stacey, *The British Ombudsman*, pp. 43–6.
20 Op. cit., p. 92, and pp. 103–5.
21 For an account of the Sachsenhausen case, see Stacey, op. cit., pp. 248–58.

22 H.C. 587 of 1970–71, Second Report of the Parliamentary Commissioner for Administration.
23 H.C. 54 of 1967–68 (Sachsenhausen); H.C. 47 of 1967–68 (Aircraft noise); H.C. 316 of 1968–69 (Duccio painting).
24 In his annual report for 1973 Sir Alan Marre provided a few pages of summarized cases to illustrate his activities. They were still in anonymized form, and were grouped by department. They were not very informative. See H.C. 106 of 1973–74, Second Report of the Parliamentary Commissioner for Administration: Annual Report for 1973, pp. 6–15.
25 In 1972 the Parliamentary Commissioner investigated 261 cases, and in 1973 only 239 cases.
26 From a sample of 77 M.P.s surveyed in 1970 only 8·3 per cent said that they often, or very often, sent cases to the Parliamentary Commissioner; 10·9 per cent said they never used him. See R. Gregory and A. Alexander, '"Our Parliamentary Ombudsman" Part II: Development and the Problem of Identity', *Public Administration*, 1973, p. 48.
27 See the evidence given by senior Civil Servants from several departments to the Select Committee on the Parliamentary Commissioner, discussed in Stacey, *The British Ombudsman*, pp. 284–8.
28 See for example, H.C. 127 of 1969–70, Second Report from the Select Committee on the P.C.A.; H.C. 215 of 1971–72, First Report from the Select Committee on the P.C.A.; H.C. 334 of 1971–72, Second Report from the Select Committee on the P.C.A.
29 Ministry of Health: National Health Service. The Administrative Structure of the Medical and Related Services in England and Wales, pp. 24–5.
30 Barbara Robb, *Sans Everything* (Nelson, 1967), pp. 128–35.
31 Cmnd. 4557, Report of the Farleigh Hospital Committee of Inquiry, p. 29, recommendation 12.
32 See Stacey, *The British Ombudsman*, p. 294.
33 H.C. 161 of 1974, First Report of the Health Service Commissioner. Annual Report for 1973–74, pp. 13–14, and 22–3.
34 H.C. 161 of session 1974.
35 H.C. 161 of 1973–74, pp. 8–9.
36 H.C. 161 of session 1974, pp. 14–15.
37 Op. cit., p. 7.
38 Op. cit., p. 4, para. 9.
39 Op. cit., p. 10, para. 41.
40 Department of Health and Social Security, The Welsh Office: Report of the Committee on Hospital Complaints Procedure (H.M.S.O., 1973).
41 Op. cit., p. 103.
42 Ibid.
43 H.C. 161 of session 1974, p. 8, para. 27.
44 Report of the Committee on Hospital Complaints Procedure, pp. 82–3, paras. 10.44–10.46.
45 Report in the *Guardian*, 1 August 1974.
46 Provision for regional and local Ombudsmen in Northern Ireland to some extent anticipated developments in England and Wales. In 1969 a Parliamentary Commissioner for Northern Ireland was appointed; a Commissioner for Complaints who investigates complaints against local authorities and other public bodies, including hospitals and health authorities, was appointed the same year.
47 See pp. 192–3.
48 Local Government Act, 1974, section 30–(5).
49 Ibid., section 30–(7).

50 Ibid., section 31–(1).
51 Ibid., section 29–(1).
52 Ibid., section 29–(6).
53 Ibid., section 26–(6).
54 Ibid., clause 33–(1) and (2).
55 H.C. Deb., vol. 877, col. 144–6.
56 Ibid., section 26–(1).

CHAPTER XII

Conclusion

WE may ask, in conclusion, what it was that initiated the main reforms in this period. In the case of Civil Service reform it was clearly the Fulton Committee. As for local government reform, although the Redcliffe-Maud Commission propounded different solutions from those which in fact followed in the 1972 Act, the Redcliffe-Maud Report made reform possible, indeed perhaps inevitable, and ideas in the majority and minority reports were used in shaping the reorganized local government system.

National Health Service reform was in one sense an adjunct of local government reform but was also generated by re-thinking in the central government department concerned, and by the doctors' own examination of the question in the report of the Porritt Committee. The unification of local authority personal social services in the Social Services Departments, established under the Local Authority Social Services Act of 1970, was a main recommendation of the Seebohm Committee which reported in July 1968.

The reforms in the structure of central government, for example the giant departments and the Central Policy Review Staff, were brought about by re-thinking within the government machine and the two main political parties. Both Harold Wilson and Edward Heath were concerned to improve the machinery for advising the Prime Minister. The idea of a Central Policy Review Staff had been foreshadowed by a Conservative study group of which Ernest Marples was the chairman and David Howell a principal spokesman. The same group played a part in the introduction of Programme Analysis Review in 1970, but other reforms in the Treasury were partly the outcome of re-thinking in the Department which was focused by the Plowden Committee Report of 1961; this had itself been prompted by an Estimates Committee report in 1958.

Reform in the House of Commons was, as we have seen, brought about largely by the Commons' own machinery for reviewing procedure. But this was influenced not only by celebrated *francs-tireurs* like Bernard Crick, but also by the Study of Parliament Group which includes both academic specialists on Commons reform and members of the House of Commons' own staff of Clerks and advisers.

The introduction of an Ombudsman was also stimulated by a body outside government, namely the Committee of 'Justice'. However, once the reform had been taken up by the Labour Party, and implemented by the Wilson Government, internal pressures in the Commons and the departments played their part. The strength of opinion, expressed in the Standing Committee and at Report Stage on the Parliamentary Commissioner Bill in 1966–67, in favour of the inclusion of the hospital service helped to pave the way for a Health Service Commissioner. The campaign was continued by the Select Committee on the Parliamentary Commissioner, and helped on by pressure groups such as Aid for the Elderly in Government Institutions (AEGIS). 'Justice' came in once again to recommend Ombudsmen for local government. But the impetus for reform here was largely maintained within the central government department concerned, the Department of the Environment.

Since Royal Commissions and Committees set up by governments have played such a large part in stimulating reform in this period it is useful to see how far we can generalize about their role and composition. We can say firstly that in these years Commissions and Committees were not set up in order to stave off reform. The popular belief that Commissions are set up in order to provide an excuse for not changing anything has certainly proved to be a fallacy in this period. The Fulton, Redcliffe-Maud, and Seebohm Reports have, as we have seen, already produced results. As regards Redcliffe-Maud on Conduct in Local Government, the Kilbrandon and Salmon Commissions, and the Davies and Layfield Committees, we can confidently predict that time will show that all of them have made some impact on the shape of administration in Britain.

An analysis of the composition of these Commissions and Committees is of considerable interest. Of the seven chairmen, one, Lord Fulton, was an academic with Civil Service experience. One, Lord Redcliffe-Maud, was a Civil Servant with academic experience. Three have been judges: Kilbrandon, Salmon, and Davies. Layfield is a senior barrister. Seebohm is a businessman. The judges therefore predominate as chairmen, although academic/Civil Servants chaired two of the most important investigations.

There would seem to be a kind of rough formula for choosing

some of the members of these Commissions or Committees. If the Committee (we will for brevity use this word to include Commissions) is concerned with central government, then it should have two M.P.s among its members. Thus, the Fulton Committee included a Conservative and a Labour M.P., as did the Kilbrandon Commission. Such committees should normally also include at least one serving or retired Civil Servant. The Fulton Committee, because of its subject-matter, had a high proportion of Civil Servants, including 2 Permanent Secretaries, 1 senior scientific Civil Servant, and 1 senior Civil Service economist. The Kilbrandon Commission included 1 retired Civil Servant, the former Permanent Secretary of the Welsh Department of Education, and 1 academic/Civil Servant, the Principal of St. Anne's College, Oxford.

In a similar way, committees which are concerned with local government should include several members with local government experience, some with experience on the elected, and some on the official side of local government. Thus the Redcliffe-Maud Commission included 3 members with experience of the representative side, a Director of Education, and an academic who had formerly been a City Treasurer. The Layfield Committee includes 4 members with experience as councillors, and 3 local officials. The Redcliffe-Maud Committee on Conduct included 1 member with experience of the elected side, and 2 local officials. A committee concerned with local government may or may not include a former Civil Servant among its membership. Thus Dame Evelyn Sharp was a member of the Redcliffe-Maud Commission, and Sir Philip Allen a member of the Committee on Conduct in Local Government. But the Layfield Committee includes neither a serving nor a retired Civil Servant.

Both types of Committee normally include a businessman or industrialist among their membership. Thus the Fulton Committee included a former head of the Federation of British Industries and the Managing Director of a large industrial company. The Redcliffe-Maud Commission included a company chairman who was also Vice-President of the British Institute of Management. The Layfield Committee includes the chief rating surveyor for Imperial Chemical Industries.

Such committees also normally include a prominent trade unionist. The General Secretary of the National Association of Local Government Officers was a member of the Fulton Committee, and his successor is on the Layfield Committee. Victor Feather, at that time Secretary of the Trades Union Council, was a member of the Redcliffe-Maud Commission. David Basnett, the Secretary of the General and Municipal Workers' Union, was on the Kilbrandon Commission. The Redcliffe-Maud Committee on Conduct included neither a trade unionist nor an industrialist. This was a small committee with rather specialized terms of reference. It did include a London barrister who is also a member of 'Justice'.

Most of these committees included one or more academic members. Norman Hunt, later Lord Crowther-Hunt, a political scientist, was a member of both the Fulton and Kilbrandon inquiries. The Kilbrandon Commission also included two Professors of Law and a Professor of Economics, as well as an Oxford College Principal. The Redcliffe-Maud Committee included Hedley Marshall, who was a Senior Research Fellow at the Institute of Local Government Studies at that time (and formerly City Treasurer of Coventry). L. J. Sharpe, although not a member of the Commission, was its Director of Intelligence, and gave continuing advice. The Layfield Committee includes 2 academic specialists in Public Administration among its membership, George Jones and Professor John Stewart. A Professor of Economics, Alan Day, is also on the Committee. The Redcliffe-Maud Committee on Conduct did not include an academic member.

These committees have therefore included more academic members than academics themselves often suppose. Political scientists in Britain are apt to complain that their research has relatively little impact on the machinery of government. When we consider, however, that Lords Redcliffe-Maud and Fulton were both formerly university teachers of politics, that Lord Crowther-Hunt was a prominent member of the Fulton and Kilbrandon Commissions, and that Hedley Marshall, L. J. Sharpe, John Stewart, and George Jones have been associated with the Redcliffe-Maud and Layfield inquiries, the picture does not look quite so bleak. We should also bear in mind that Richard Chapman was commissioned to carry out research for the Fulton Committee, as were Nevil Johnson, Professor Maurice Vile, Professor F. W. Ridley, and Neil Elder for the Kilbrandon Commission. Many other political scientists have also submitted memoranda to these committees. Their contributions can be read in the published volumes of evidence, and may to some extent have influenced conclusions of the committees.

To sum up at this stage, we may say that the composition of these committees permits a certain amount of interpenetration between the world of practical politics, the official side of politics, the universities, and both sides of industry. The criticism that can be, and is, made is that the people chosen from each sector are not necessarily representative, and that some tend to be invited to take part over and over again. There is a certain 'cosiness' about these committees. Or, to put it another way, their members tend to be, in Margaret Cole's phrase, the 'stage army of the good'. Thus Redcliffe-Maud is asked to head 3 major committees. Sir Philip Allen appears on 3 committees, and Lord Crowther-Hunt on 2. It must be remembered, however, that it is difficult to find public-spirited people who will give sufficient time to these committees while at the same time having the necessary experience and talent for sifting evidence and helping draft reports. When the member of a committee shows these qualities, he is likely to be used again.

Having thus defined a kind of formula for these committees, we must note that special considerations may require that certain committees be constituted in a rather different way. Thus the Kilbrandon Commission also had some members with particular experience or standing in Scotland, Wales, or a region of England. The Davies and Seebohm Committees, and the Salmon Commission are, each in a different sense, special cases; it is to these committees that we now turn. Since the Davies Committee was concerned with hospital complaints procedures, it was important that it should include representatives of the medical and nursing professions, hospital administrators, and a member of a hospital board, as well as academics with special knowledge of administration, medical sociology, and the redress of grievances. The addition of representatives of voluntary associations in the Health Service, and two journalists interested in social questions, was an imaginative touch.

The Salmon Commission is another kind of special case since it is concerned with 'public life', including both central government and the nationalized industries. Its membership therefore includes 2 former M.P.s, both of whom had been Ministers, the Chairman of the Gas Council, and the Secretary General of the Staff Side of the Civil Service National Whitley Council. A former journalist and newspaper executive, Sir Hugh Cudlipp, is on the Commission, as is a former Civil Servant, Sir Philip Allen. There is a particular advantage in having him on this Commission, as well as on the Committee on Conduct in Local Government, in that it helps the Commission to complement the work of the Committee on Conduct in Local Government, rather than duplicating it.

Finally, the Seebohm Committee was another kind of special case since not only did it deal with a specialized area but was set up in a way which was both likely and, it would seem, intended, to produce a certain result. The predominant influence on the Committee was that of the National Institute of Social Work Training which has been described as 'the staff college of the social work profession'.[1] Frederic Seebohm himself was not only a banker but, more significantly, Chairman of the Institute. A key member of the Committee, Robin Huws Jones, was Director of the Institute, and another member of the Committee, Roy Parker, joined the Institute while the inquiry was in progress. Most of the Committee's meetings were held at the premises of the Institute in London.[2]

Other members of the Seebohm Committee included a County Clerk and the Clerk of a County Borough, and Mrs. Bee Serota, formerly Labour chairman of London County Council's Children's Committee (and later, as Lady Serota, to become the first Chairman of the Commissioners for Local Administration for England). The voluntary body representative was M. R. F. Simpson who was the Secretary of the National Corporation for the Care of Old People. There were two other academics on the Committee in addition to Huws Jones and Parker. One was Professor J. N. Morris who was also a member of the Royal Commission on the Penal System; the other, Peter Leonard, was at that time a teacher of social work at Liverpool University. Finally, Lady James had experience as a magistrate in a juvenile court. Her husband, Lord James of Rusholme, was President of the National Institute of Social Work Training.

The Seebohm Committee was, therefore, very much hand-picked, in the sense that a large section of its membership consisted of people committed to raising the status of the social work profession, and to providing a more efficiently co-ordinated system of local social services. This characteristic prompts the question, when is it good tactics to form a committee in order to produce a recommendation in favour of a particular kind of reform and when is it better to have a more representative committee? As compared with the Seebohm Committee, the Redcliffe-Maud Commission had to be more broadly representative since it was necessary to convince the local authority associations of the need for reform. Although Crossman put Derek Senior on the Commission to advocate the city region solution, he could not have stacked the Commission with people who shared Senior's point of view since this would have seriously weakened its influence on opinion in the local authorities.

Even if the composition of a committee is 'stacked' it will not achieve the end in view unless there is a strong body of opinion outside the committee which supports the reform. Thus the Seebohm reforms were supported by an influential element in the social work profession. After the report was published a Seebohm Implementation Group was formed and lobbied energetically for legislative action.[3] When Mrs. Serota became a life peer she entered the Wilson Government as a Baroness-in-Waiting. She was then able to advise from within the Government on implementation of the reform, and was ably assisted by Brian Abel-Smith, Professor of Social Administration at the London School of Economics, and a personal adviser to Richard Crossman, then Secretary of State for Social Services.

A major role of a Royal Commission or Committee is to provide a forum for intensified debate on an issue. The invitation to interested people and organizations to produce memoranda, and the publication of the memoranda, give an opportunity for public examination of the various possibilities for reform. The role of such Committees in making open debate possible is most valuable. They can act as catalysts, enabling such ideas as are already current or immanent to be brought into the open and react upon each other. The views put forward by members of the Committees themselves can only be influential if they are in tune with ideas already burgeoning in the minds of the wider public which is interested in Civil Service reform, reorganization of local government, reform of local finance, and so on.

This brings us, finally, to the questions which we advanced in the Introduction to this book: what have been the main themes of reform in this period? What has been the climate of reform? We suggested then that the main themes have been the attempt to achieve greater efficiency in government, and the attempt to make government more responsive, to enhance democratic control. We suggested that while there can be conflicts between these objectives these need not necessarily arise.

These years have certainly seen conflict between the two themes in reorganization of the Health Service. The managerial model chosen by Sir Keith Joseph came in for strong criticism. The controversy over local government reform was fought to some extent in terms of efficiency versus participation, but the controversy here was not clear-cut, if only because there was dispute on the one hand about which kind of system was more efficient, and on the other hand about how greater participation could be stimulated.

It is not necessary that these objectives should conflict. As we have seen, the Bains Report has provided the most influential blueprint for corporate planning in local government, but also advocated better communication between local authorities and their electors, and more open government at local level. If, indeed, one of the objectives of better management in government is to improve the quality of decisions made, then manifestly the quality of decisions will be enhanced if the decision-making process is as open as possible, and if all interested persons and organizations have an opportunity to influence the decision.

We may say that the dominant theme of reform in this period has indeed been the thrust towards more open government. This is seen in the Fulton Report, and in the use of Green Papers by central government. The opening of select committees of the Commons to the public, initiated by Crossman and since maintained, was a move in the same direction. The attempt to involve the public in decision-making in planning, advocated by the Skeffington Report, and the opening of local authority committee meetings to the public, under the Local Government Act, 1972, have done something to encourage more open government at local level. The setting-up of the Central Policy Review Staff has brought more outside advice into the centre of government, and key members of this staff have not always felt conscience-bound not to reveal some of the advice they are giving. A revision of the Official Secrets Act has been urged by the Franks Committee, and action on its report can hardly be long-delayed. If there is a clear trend towards more open government, and towards encouraging greater participation, it is still important not to overlook the difficulties involved. For example, the Skeffington Report on People and Planning, which appeared in 1969, recommended that local authorities should set up community forums which would bring voluntary associations, like Civic Societies and residents' associations, into a more or less continuous dialogue with the local authority on planning matters. Further, recognizing that this would still leave the vast majority of ordinary people uninformed and unconsulted, the Report suggested that local authorities should appoint community development officers to 'secure the involvement of those who do not join' voluntary associations.[4] This is the phraseology used in the summary of recommendations at the end of the Report. The bald language of the summary seems to indicate a greater naïvety than is found in the developed argument of the Report, but it still implies an immense optimism about the extent to which ordinary people will be prepared to interest themselves in planning proposals.

Similarly, there are problems about the move towards more open government. Objections will certainly be raised, from time to time, on the grounds that the quality of administration will suffer if we have really open government. That such objections have any substance is by no means clear. In Sweden, every member of the public has long had the right of access to government information unless the Civil Servant can show that there are overriding considerations of national security etc., which preclude access. Any citizen may inspect the files of government departments and can only be denied this right by a decision of the Civil Servant. Such a decision can only be made on strictly limited grounds, and can be challenged in the courts.

It would not seem that this high degree of openness in government has proved inconsistent with efficient and humane administration in Sweden. Its success is attested by the fact that Denmark and Norway have recently passed similar legislation giving the citizen the right of access to information in the hands of public authorities. Further moves towards open government in Britain will, of course, require a modification at numerous points of the conventions under which government operates. The conventions of individual and collective ministerial responsibility, for example, will need to be redefined. But it has always been recognized that one of the advantages of a system of government which is based largely on convention is that it permits flexibility and a ready adaptation of institutions to the changing needs and aspirations of the people.

NOTES

1 A. Sinfield, 'Which Way for Social Work?' in *The Fifth Social Services* (Fabian Society, 1970), p. 41.
2 See N. M. Thomas, 'The Seebohm Committee on Personal Social Services' in R. A. Chapman (ed.), *The Role of Commissions in Policy Making*, p. 153.
3 N. M. Thomas, op. cit., p. 165.
4 Ministry of Housing and Local Government: People and Planning: Report of the Committee on Public Participation in Planning (H.M.S.O., 1969), p. 47, recommendation vi.

TIME SCALE OF REFORMS AND EVENTS OF CONSTITUTIONAL SIGNIFICANCE

1966

February: Fulton Committee on the Civil Service appointed.
March: *General Election.* Wilson Government confirmed in power with increased majority.
May: Royal Commission on Local Government in England appointed (Redcliffe-Maud Commission).
December: Commons Select Committees on Agriculture and on Science and Technology set up.
Report from Commons Procedure Committee on Urgent and Topical Debates.
Tribunals and Inquiries Act (enabled non-statutory inquiries to be made subject to the Council on Tribunals).

1967

February: Ministry of Aviation merged with the Ministry of Technology.
March: Report of Maud Committee on Management in Local Government.
Iron and Steel Act (set up British Steel Corporation to run renationalized steel industry).
Parliamentary Commissioner for Administration Act.
April: Parliamentary Commissioner began investigating complaints.
July: Sexual Offences Act (legalized homosexual practices, in private, between consenting adults in England and Wales. A private Member's measure introduced by Leo Abse).
Experiment with morning sittings in the Commons proved unpopular and was abandoned.
October: Abortion Act (a private Member's measure introduced by David Steel).
December: Commons Select Committee on Education and Science set up.

1968

February: Parliamentary Labour Party approved a more relaxed Code of Conduct.
May: Finance Bill was taken in Standing Committee at Committee stage.
June: Report of the Fulton Committee on the Civil Service.
July: Theatres Act (ended censorship of plays in London. A private Member's measure introduced by George Strauss).
Report of Seebohm Committee on Local Authority and Allied Personal Social Services.
Robinson Green Paper on the Structure of the National Health Service.

October: Foreign Office and Commonwealth Office were combined.
November: Department of Health and Social Security set up.
White Paper on House of Lords Reform.
Commons Select Committee on Race Relations and Immigration first appointed.
Civil Service Department set up.
December: Commons Select Committee on Agriculture terminated.

1969

March: Commons Select Committee on Scottish Affairs set up.
April: Representation of the People Act (lowered voting age to 18. Provided for description of candidates' party affiliations on the ballot paper).
Royal Commission on the Constitution appointed.
Parliament (No. 2) Bill (reforming the House of Lords) abandoned by the Wilson Government.
May: Finance Bill split at Committee stage: part taken in whole House, part in Standing Committee.
June: White Paper 'In Place of Strife' abandoned by Wilson Government.
Report of the Redcliffe-Maud Royal Commission on Local Government in England.
July: Commons Procedure Committee Report on Scrutiny of Public Expenditure and Administration.
Post Office Act (converted the Post Office from a government department to a public corporation).
October: Department of Economic Affairs abolished (its staff was distributed among the Ministry of Technology, the Treasury, and the Economic Section of the Cabinet Secretariat).

1970

February: Wilson Government's proposals for reorganization of local government in England.
Crossman Green Paper on the Future Structure of the National Health Service.
May: Local Authority Social Services Act (implemented Seebohm Report).
June: *General Election.* Majority for Conservatives and Heath Government formed.
October: White Paper on the Re-organization of Central Government.
Commons Select Committee on Education wound up.
November: Department of the Environment set up, merging the Ministries of Housing and Local Government, Transport, and Public Building and Works.
Ministry of Trade and Industry established combining the Board of Trade and the Ministry of Technology.
Central Policy Review Staff set up.

1971

January: Administrative, Executive, and Clerical Classes of the Civil Service were merged into one Administration Group.

February: Heath Government's proposals for reorganization of local government in England.

First meeting of the newly created Expenditure Committee of the Commons.

May: Sir Keith Joseph's Consultative Document on National Health Service Re-organization.

July: Commons Procedure Committee Report on the Process of Legislation.

Tribunals and Inquiries Act (increased the number of tribunals subject to investigation by the Council on Tribunals).

August: Industrial Relations Act.

1972

August: White Paper on National Health Service Re-organization

National Health Service, Scotland, Act (reorganized Health Service in Scotland. Provided for Health Service Commissioner for Scotland).

Report of the Joint Lords and Commons Committee on Delegated Legislation.

Report on Management and Structure of the New Local Authorities (The Bains Report).

September: Franks Committee Report on the Official Secrets Acts.

October: European Communities Act (gave legislative effect to adherence to the E.E.C.).

Local Government Act (reorganized local government in England and Wales).

National Health Service (Family Planning) Amendment Act (provided for vasectomy operations under the N.H.S. A private Member's measure introduced by Philip Whitehead).

1973

February: Joint Lords and Commons Committee on Delegated legislation first set up.

July: National Health Service Re-organization Act (reorganized Health Service in England and Wales. Provided for Health Service Commissioners for England and Wales).

Employment and Training Act (reorganized the Department of Employment and Productivity).

October: Report of the Davies Committee on Hospital Complaints Procedure.

Report of the Royal Commission on the Constitution (Kilbrandon Commission).

Local Government (Scotland) Act (reorganized local government in Scotland).

December: Department of Energy set up (from parts of the Department of Trade and Industry).

1974

February: Local Government Act (made new provisions for rate support grant and rating. Set up Local Commissions for Administration for England and Wales).

February: *General Election.*

March: Wilson minority Government formed.

Department of Trade and Industry split into separate Departments of Trade and Industry.

Department of Prices and Consumer Protection set up.

April: Reorganized local government system for England and Wales came into operation.

Reorganized structure for the National Health Service came into operation.

House of Lords European Communities Committee first set up.

May: Commons Committee on European Secondary Legislation first set up.

Report of the Committee on Local Government Rules of Conduct.

White Paper on Democracy in the National Health Service.

June: Chairman of Local Commissioners for England and two other Local Commissioners appointed.

July: Local Commissioner for Wales appointed.

Layfield Committee on Local Government Finance appointed.

Trade Union and Labour Relations Act (repealed Industrial Relations Act 1971).

September: Royal Commission on Standards of Conduct in Public Life appointed (Salmon Commission).

White Paper on Democracy and Devolution. Proposals for Scotland and Wales.

October: *General Election.* Wilson Government gained small over-all majority.

1975

May: Report of the Committee on the Preparation of Legislation (Renton Committee).

May: Northern Ireland Convention elected.

May: Local Government (Scotland) Act (set up Local Commissioners for Administration for Scotland).

May: Referendum Act (provided for referendum on continued Membership of the E.E.C.).

June: Referendum on Membership of the E.E.C.

BIBLIOGRAPHY

Except for Chapter I, only books and articles which appeared in, or since, 1966 are included in this bibliography.

CHAPTER I

B. Chapman, *British Government Observed* (Allen and Unwin, 1963).
B. Crick, *Reform of the Commons* (Fabian Society, 1959).
B. Crick, *The Reform of Parliament* (Weidenfeld and Nicolson, 1964).
B. Crick (ed.), *Essays on Reform, 1967. A Centenary Tribute* (O.U.P., 1967).
Fabian Society, *The Administrators. The Reform of the Civil Service* (Fabian Tract No. 355, 1964).
A. Hill and A. Whichelow, *What's Wrong with Parliament?* (Penguin, 1964).
J. Robertson, *Reform of British Central Government* (Chatto and Windus/Charles Knight, 1971).
T. Smith, *Anti-Politics: Consensus, Reform and Protest in Britain* (Charles Knight, 1972).
F. Stacey, *The Government of Modern Britain* (Clarendon Press, 1968).
H. Thomas (ed.), *The Establishment* (Anthony Blond, 1959).

CHAPTER II

D. Butler and A. King, *The British General Election of 1966* (Macmillan, 1966).
D. Butler and M. Pinto-Duschinsky, *The British General Election of 1970* (Macmillan, 1971).
D. Butler and D. Kavanagh, *The British General Election of February 1974* (Macmillan, 1974).
R. Hodder-Williams, *Public Opinion Polls and British Politics* (Routledge, 1970),
G. C. Moodie and G. Studdert-Kennedy, *Opinions, Publics and Pressure Groups* (Allen and Unwin, 1970).
P. Pulzer, *Political Representation and Elections in Britain* (Allen and Unwin, 3rd edn., 1975).
P. M. Williams, 'The Politics of Redistribution', *Political Quarterly*, 1968. pp. 234–54.

Northern Ireland Office, the Future of Northern Ireland, a paper for discussion (H.M.S.O., 1972).
Representation of the People Act, 1969.

CHAPTER III

P. Byrne, 'The Expenditure Committee: A Preliminary Assessment' in *Parliamentary Affairs*, 1974, pp. 273–86.
R. Clarke, 'Parliament and Public Expenditure', *Political Quarterly*, 1973, pp. 137–53.
B. Crick, *The Reform of Parliament* (Weidenfeld and Nicolson, 2nd edn., 1968).
A. H. Hanson and B. Crick (eds.), *The Commons in Transition* (Fontana, 1970).

A. King and A. Sloman, *Westminster and Beyond* (Macmillan, 1973).
J. M. Lee, 'Select Committees and the Constitution', *Political Quarterly*, 1970, pp. 182–94.
D. Leonard and V. Herman, *The Backbencher and Parliament* (Macmillan, 1972).
A. Morris (ed.), *The Growth of Parliamentary Scrutiny by Committee* (Pergamon, 1970).
M. Partington, 'Parliamentary Committees: Recent Developments', *Parliamentary Affairs*, 1970, pp. 366–79.
G. T. Popham and D. Greengrass, 'The Role and Functions of the Select Committee on Agriculture', *Public Administration*, 1970, pp. 137–51.
P. G. Richards, *The Backbenchers* (Faber, 1972).
D. R. Shell, 'Specialist Select Committees', *Parliamentary Affairs*, 1970, pp. 380–404.
A. Silkin, 'The Expenditure Committee: A New Development', *Public Administration*, 1975, pp. 45–66.

H.C. 410 of 1968–69, First Report from the Select Committee on Procedure: Scrutiny of Public Expenditure and Administration.
H.C. 475 of 1968–69, Sixth Report of the Select Committee on Estimates: Motorways and Trunk Roads.
H.C. 172 of 1971–72, Fourth Report from the Expenditure Committee: National Health Service Facilities for Private Patients.
H.C. 57–I of 1972–73, Second Report from the Expenditure Committee: Urban Transport Planning.
H.C. 148 of 1972–73, Fourth Report from the Expenditure Committee: Youth Employment Services.

CHAPTER IV

A. P. Barker and M. Rush, *The Member of Parliament and his Information* (Allen and Unwin, 1970).
M. J. Barnett, *The Politics of Legislation: The Rent Act 1957* (Weidenfeld and Nicolson, 1969).
I. Burton and G. Drewry, 'Public Legislation: A Survey of the Session 1971–2', *Parliamentary Affairs*, 1973, pp. 145–85.
I. Burton and G. Drewry, 'Public Legislation: A Survey of the Session 1972–3', *Parliamentary Affairs*, 1974, pp. 120–58.
R. Butt, *The Power of Parliament* (Constable, 2nd edn., 1969).
G. Drewry, 'Reform of the Legislative Process: Some Neglected Questions', *Parliamentary Affairs*, 1972, pp. 286–302.
P. Goodhart, *Referendum* (Tom Stacey, 1971).
J. A. G. Griffith, *Parliamentary Scrutiny of Government Bills* (Allen and Unwin, 1974).
K. Hindell and M. Simms, 'How the Abortion Lobby Worked', *Political Quarterly*, 1968, pp. 269–82.
K. Hindell and M. Simms, *Abortion Law Reformed* (Peter Owen, 1971).
R. Kimber and J. J. Richardson, 'Specialization and Standing Committees', *Political Studies*, 1968, pp. 97–101.

M. Niblock, *The E.E.C: National Parliaments in Community Decision Making* (Chatham House, 1971).
P. G. Richards, *Parliament and Conscience* (Allen and Unwin, 1970).
M. Rush and M. Shaw, *The House of Commons, Services and Facilities* (Allen and Unwin, 1974).
Study of Parliament Group, 'Parliament and Legislation', *Parliamentary Affairs*, 1969, pp. 210–15.
S. A. Walkland, *The Legislative Process in Great Britain* (Allen and Unwin, 1968).

H.C. 282 of 1966–67, Second Report from the Select Committee on Procedure. Standing Order No. 9: Urgent and Topical Debates.
H.C. 538 of 1970–71, Second Report from the Select Committee on Procedure: The Process of Legislation.
H.L. 184 and H.C. 475 of 1971–72, Report from the Joint Committee on Delegated Legislation.
H.C. 185–vi of 1972–73, Sixth Report from the Select Committee on Statutory Instruments.
H.C. 143 of 1972–73, First Report from the Select Committee on European Community Secondary Legislation.
H.C. 463–I of 1972–73, Second Report from the Select Committee on European Community Secondary Legislation.
H.L. 139 of 1974, Special Report of the House of Lords European Communities Committee.

CHAPTER V

P. Bromhead and D. Shell, 'The Lords and their House', *Parliamentary Affairs*, 1967, pp. 337–49.
G. Drewry and J. Morgan, 'Law Lords as Legislators', *Parliamentary Affairs*, 1969, pp. 226–39.
J. P. Morgan, *The House of Lords and the Labour Government 1964–70* (Clarendon Press, 1975).
J. R. Vincent, 'The House of Lords', *Parliamentary Affairs*, 1966, pp. 475–85.

Cmnd. 3799, House of Lords Reform (H.M.S.O., 1968).

CHAPTER VI

R. Clarke, *New Trends in Government* (Civil Service Department and H.M.S.O., 1971).
R. Crossman, *Inside View* (Jonathan Cape, 1972).
G. George-Brown, *In My Way* (Penguin, 1972).
S. Goldman, *The Developing System of Public Expenditure Management and Control* (Civil Service College Studies No. 1, H.M.S.O., 1971).
H. Heclo and A. Wildavsky, *The Private Government of Public Money* (Macmillan, 1974).
C. Pollitt, 'The Central Policy Review Staff, 1970–1974', *Public Administration*, 1974, pp. 375–92.
P. G. Walker, *The Cabinet* (Jonathan Cape, 1970).

M. Williams, *Inside Number 10* (Weidenfeld and Nicolson, 1972).
H. Wilson, *The Labour Government 1964–70. A Personal Record* (Weidenfeld and Nicolson, 1971).

Cmnd. 4506, The Reorganization of Central Government (H.M.S.O., 1970).

CHAPTER VII

R. G. S. Brown, *The Administrative Process in Britain* (Methuen, 1970).
R. A. Chapman, *The Higher Civil Service in Britain* (Constable, 1970).
R. A. Chapman (ed.), *The Role of Commissions in Policy Making* (Allen and Unwin, 1973).
J. Garrett, *The Management of Government* (Penguin, 1972).
H. Parris, *Constitutional Bureaucracy* (Allen and Unwin, 1969).
H. Parris, *Staff Relations in the Civil Service: Fifty Years of Whitleyism* (Allen and Unwin, 1973).
F. F. Ridley (ed.), *Specialists and Generalists* (Allen and Unwin, 1968).
A. Silkin, 'Green Papers and Changing Methods of Consultation in British Government', *Public Administration*, 1973, pp. 427–48.
P. Self, *Administrative Theories and Politics* (Allen and Unwin, 1969).
G. Stuttard (ed.), *Teaching Industrial Relations: Industrial Democracy and Industrial Relations. A Report* (Society of Industrial Tutors, 1972).
H. Thomas (ed.), *The Crisis in the Civil Service* (Anthony Blond, 1968).

H.C. 308 of 1964–65, Sixth Report from the Estimates Committee: Recruitment to the Civil Service.
Cmnd. 3638, The Civil Service, vol. 1: Report of the Committee 1966–68 (H.M.S.O., 1968).
The Civil Service College 1970–71. First Annual Report by the Principal to the Civil Service College Advisory Council (H.M.S.O., 1972).
The Civil Service College 1971–72. Second Annual Report by the Principal to the Civil Service College Advisory Council (H.M.S.O., 1973).
The Civil Service College 1972–73. Third Annual Report by the Principal (H.M.S.O., 1974).
Civil Service Department, First Report of the Civil Service Department (H.M.S.O., 1970).
Civil Service Department, Second Report of the Civil Service Department (H.M.S.O., 1971).
Civil Service Department, Third Report of the Civil Service Department (H.M.S.O., 1974).
Department of Economic Affairs and H.M. Treasury, the Development Areas. A Proposal for a Regional Employment Premium (H.M.S.O., 1967).
Iron and Steel Act, 1967.
Employment and Training Act, 1973.

CHAPTER VIII

J. Brand, *Local Government Reform in England* (Croom Helm, 1974).
R. Buxton, *Local Government* (Penguin, 2nd edn., 1973).
J. B. Cullingworth, *Town and Country Planning in Britain* (Allen and Unwin, 4th edn., 1972).

D. L. Foley, *Governing the London Region. Reorganization and Planning in the 1960s* (University of California Press, 1972).
R. Greenwood and J. D. Stewart, *Corporate Planning in English Local Government* (Charles Knight, 1974).
J. A. G. Griffith, *Central Departments and Local Authorities* (Allen and Unwin, 1966).
W. Hampton, *Democracy and Community. A Study of Politics in Sheffield* (O.U.P., 1970).
N. P. Hepworth, *The Finance of Local Government* (Allen and Unwin, 2nd edn., 1971).
D. M. Hill, *Democratic Theory and Local Government* (Allen and Unwin, 1974).
D. M. Hill, *Participating in Local Affairs* (Penguin, 1970).
G. W. Jones, 'The Local Government Act 1972 and the Redcliffe-Maud Commission', *Political Quarterly*, 1973, pp. 154–66.
G. W. Jones, 'The Functions and Organization of Councillors', *Public Administration*, 1973, pp. 135–46.
J. M. Lee and others, *The Scope of Local Initiative: a Study of Cheshire County Council 1961–74* (Martin Robertson, 1974).
Local Government Chronicle, *Corporate Management in Action* (Brown, Knight and Truscott, 1974).
Redcliffe-Maud and B. Wood, *English Local Government Reformed* (O.U.P., 1974).
G. Rhodes (ed.), *The New Government of London. The First Five Years* (Weidenfeld and Nicolson, 1972).
R. A. W. Rhodes, 'Local Government Reform: Three Questions', *Social and Economic Administration*, 1974, pp. 6–21.
P. G. Richards, *The Reformed Local Government System* (Allen and Unwin, 1973).
W. A. Robson, *Local Government in Crisis* (Allen and Unwin, 1966).
L. J. Sharpe (ed.), *Voting in Cities* (Macmillan, 1967).
J. Stanyer, *County Government in England and Wales* (Routledge, 1967).
W. Thornhill, *The Growth and Reform of English Local Government* (Weidenfeld and Nicolson, 1971).
E. Wistrich, *Local Government Reorganisation. The first years of Camden* (London Borough of Camden, 1972).

Committee on the Management of Local Government (The Maud Committee):
vol. 1, Report of the Committee.
vol. 2, The Local Government Councillor.
vol. 3, The Local Government Elector.
vol. 4, Local Government Administration Abroad.
(H.M.S.O., 1967.)
Cmnd. 4040–II, Report of the Royal Commission on Local Government in England 1966–1969 (Redcliffe-Maud Commission):
vol. 1, Report.
vol. 2, Memorandum of Dissent by Mr. D. Senior.
vol. 3, Research Appendices.
(H.M.S.O., 1969.)
Cmnd. 4276, Reform of Local Government in England (H.M.S.O., 1970).

Cmnd. 4584, Local Government in England. Government Proposals for Reorganization (H.M.S.O., 1971).
Welsh Office: The Reform of Local Government in Wales. Consultative Document (H.M.S.O., 1971).
Local Government Act, 1972.
The New Local Authorities. Management and Structure. (H.M.S.O., 1972—'The Bains Report').
Cmnd. 5636, Prime Minister's Committee on Local Government Rules of Conduct: Conduct in Local Government, vol. 1: Report of the Committee (H.M.S.O., 1974).
Cmnd. 4039, Short version of the Report of the Royal Commission on Local Government in England (H.M.S.O., 1969).

CHAPTER IX

J. G. Kellas, *The Scottish Political System* (C.U.P., 1973).
D. G. Kermode, 'Regional Self-Government: A Case Study of the Isle of Man', *Public Administration*, 1974, pp. 161–77.
J. P. Mackintosh, *The Devolution of Power* (Penguin, 1968).
E. Rowlands, 'The Politics of Regional Administration: The Establishment of the Welsh Office', *Public Administration* 1972, pp. 333–51.
B. C. Smith, *Advising Ministers. A Case Study of the South West Economic Planning Council* (Routledge, 1969).
J. Stanyer, 'Nationalism, Regionalism and the British System of Government—The Report of the Royal Commission on the Constitution 1969–73', *Social and Economic Administration*, 1974, pp. 136–57.

Cmnd. 5460, Royal Commission on the Constitution 1969–1973 (The Kilbrandon Commission):
vol. 1, Report.
vol. 2, Memorandum of Dissent by Lord Crowther-Hunt and Professor A. T. Peacock (H.M.S.O., 1973).
Office of the Lord President of the Council: Devolution within the United Kingdom. Some Alternatives for Discussion (H.M.S.O., 1974).
Cmnd. 5732, Democracy and Devolution. Proposals for Scotland and Wales (H.M.S.O., 1974).

CHAPTER X

R. G. S. Brown, *The Changing National Health Service* (Routledge, 1973).
M. Ryan, 'Reform of the Health Service Structure', *Public Administration*, 1968, pp. 315–30.
M. Ryan, 'The Tripartite Administrative Structure of the National Health Service—its Genesis and Reform', *Social and Economic Administration*, 1972, pp. 218–31.
A. J. Willcocks, *The Creation of the National Health Service* (Routledge, 1967).

Ministry of Health: National Health Service. The Administrative Structure of the Medical and Releated Services in England and Wales (H.M.S.O., 1968) (The Robinson Green Paper).

Department of Health and Social Security: National Health Service. The Future Structure of the National Health Service (H.M.S.O., 1970) (The Crossman Green Paper).

National Health Service Reorganization, Consultative Document (H.M.S.O., 1971).

Cmnd. 5055, National Health Service Reorganization: England (H.M.S.O., 1972).

Department of Health and Social Security: Management Arrangements for the Reorganized National Health Service (H.M.S.O., 1972).

Welsh Office: Management Arrangements for the Reorganized National Health Service in Wales (H.M.S.O., 1972).

Department of Health and Social Security: Democracy in the Health Service. Membership of Health Authorities (H.M.S.O., 1974).

Cmnd. 4734, Scottish Home and Health Department: Reorganization of the Scottish Health Service (H.M.S.O., 1971).

National Health Service, Scotland, Act, 1972.

National Health Service Reorganization Act, 1973.

CHAPTER XI

K. Bell, *Tribunals in the Social Services* (Routledge, 1969).

L. H. Cohen, 'Local Government Complaints: The M.P.'s Viewpoint', *Public Administration*, 1973, pp. 175–83.

C. D. Drake, 'Ombudsmen for Local Government', *Public Administration*, 1970, pp. 179–89.

H. J. Elcock, *Administrative Justice* (Longmans, 1969).

H. J. Elcock, 'Opportunity for Ombudsman: The Northern Ireland Commissioner for Complaints', *Public Administration*, 1972, pp. 87–93.

R. Gregory and A. Alexander, 'Our Parliamentary Ombudsman. Part I: Integration and Metamorphosis', *Public Administration*, 1972, pp. 313–31.

R. Gregory and A. Alexander, 'Our Parliamentary Ombudsman. Part II: Development and the Problem of Identity', *Public Administration*, 1973, pp. 41–59.

R. Gregory and P. Hutchesson, *The Parliamentary Ombudsman. A Study in the Control of Administrative Action* (Allen and Unwin, 1975).

Inns of Court Conservative and Unionist Society, *Let Right Be Done* (Conservative Political Centre, 1966).

Justice, *The Citizen and his Council. Ombudsmen for Local Government?* (Stevens, 1969).

R. Klein, *Complaints Against Doctors* (Charles Knight, 1973).

G. Marshall, 'Maladministration', *Public Law*, 1973, pp. 32–44.

J. D. B. Mitchell, 'Administrative Law and Parliamentary Control', *Political Quarterly*, 1967, pp. 360–74.

B. Robb, *Sans Everything* (Nelson, 1967).

D. C. Rowat, *The Ombudsman Plan* (McClelland and Stewart, 1973).

F. Stacey, *The British Ombudsman* (Clarendon Press, 1971).

F. Stacey, *A New Bill of Rights for Britain* (David and Charles, 1973).

H. Street, *Justice in the Welfare State* (Stevens, 1968).

K. C. Wheare, *Maladministration and its Remedies* (Stevens, 1973).
R. E. Wraith and P. G. Hutchesson, *Administrative Tribunals* (Allen and Unwin, 1973).

Cmnd. 4059, The Law Commission, Administrative Law (H.M.S.O., 1971).
Cmnd. 4557, Report of the Farleigh Hospital Committee of Inquiry.
Department of Health and Social Security: The Welsh Office, Report of the Committee on Hospital Complaints Procedure (H.M.S.O., 1973).
H.C. 47 of 1967–68, Second Report of the Parliamentary Commissioner for Administration (Aircraft Noise).
H.C. 54 of 1967–68, Third Report of the Parliamentary Commissioner for Administration (Sachsenhausen).
H.C. 316 of 1968–69, Third Report of the Parliamentary Commissioner for Administration (Duccio Painting).
H.C. 587 of 1970–71, Second Report of the Parliamentary Commissioner for Administration (Capt. R. C. Horsley's complaint).
H.C. 304 of 1971–72, Third Report of the Parliamentary Commissioner for Administration (Census-form case).
H.C. 116 of 1971–72, Second Report of the Parliamentary Commissioner for Administration: Annual Report for 1971.
H.C. 72 of 1972–73, Second Report of the Parliamentary Commissioner for Administration: Annual Report for 1972.
H.C. 106 of 1973–74, Second Report of the Parliamentary Commissioner for Administration: Annual Report for 1973.
H.C. 127 of 1969–70, Second Report from the Select Committee on the Parliamentary Commissioner for Administration.
H.C. 215 of 1971–72, First Report from the Select Committee on the Parliamentary Commissioner for Administration.
H.C. 334 of 1971–72, Second Report from the Select Committee on the Parliamentary Commissioner for Administration.
H.C. 161 of Session 1974, First Report of the Health Service Commissioner. Annual Report for 1973–74.
Parliamentary Commissioner Act, 1967.
Tribunals and Inquiries Act, 1971.
National Health Service Reorganization Act, 1973.
Local Government Act, 1974.

INDEX